Mystic Fiasco

MYSTIC FIASCO

How The Indians Won
The Pequot War

By

DAVID R. WAGNER & JACK DEMPSEY

Mystic Fiasco

Mystic Fiasco: How the Indians Won The Pequot War.
c 2004 by David R. Wagner and Jack Dempsey.
All Rights Reserved.
All Illustrations (unless otherwise noted)
by David R. Wagner c   2000.

For Information Contact:
David R. Wagner
302 Kemp Road, Hampton CT 06274

Dr. Jack Dempsey
45 Broadway, Stoneham MA 02180 USA
781-438-3042   jd37@mindspring.com

Digital Scanning, Inc.
344 Gannett Road, Scituate MA 02066
888-349-4433/781-545-2100
www.digitalscanning.com

ISBN 1582187754 Paperback   1582187762 Hardcover

Explore these worlds further at
http://ancientgreece-earlyamerica.com

Special Thanks
to Little Owl/Ruth Duncan
for permission to include (Coda) her poem
'We Do Not Know How'
(only a poet has words to close this book);
to publisher Brian Shillue of DSI;
and to David Ostrowski and Karle Schlieff
for looking and reading as if they aren't our friends.

Illustration 'The Figure of the Indian Fort or Palizado In New England' from
John Underhill's *Newes from America* used with permission from Chapin Library,
Williams College, Williamstown MA: All Rights Reserved.

MYSTIC FIASCO
How The Indians Won
The Pequot War

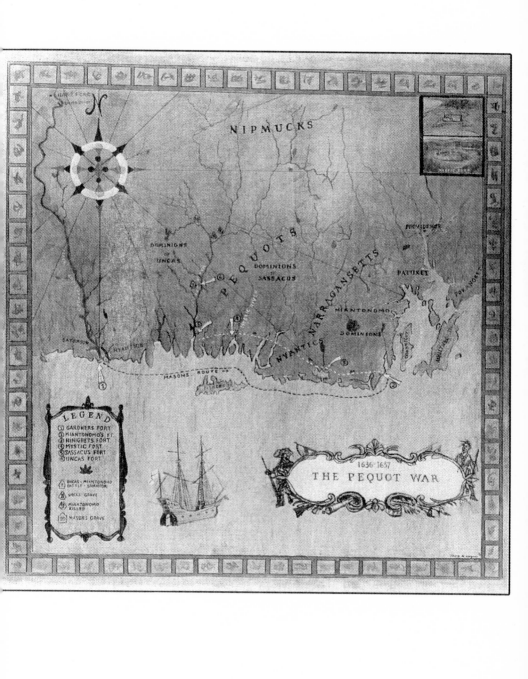

THE PEQUOT WAR
1636-1637

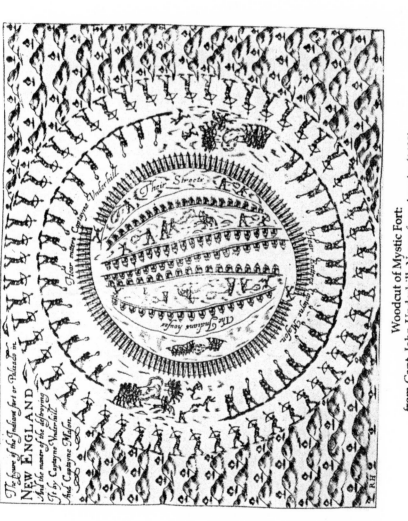

Woodcut of Mystic Fort:
from Capt. John Underhill, *Newes from America* (1638)
(used with permission)

MYSTIC VILLAGE and FORT
on the west bank of the Mystic River in Connecticutt
as it probably looked in May 1637
(seen from the east, with the Pequot/Thames River in the distance)

The Pequot fort at Mystic as it my have appeared in May of 1637 prior to Mason's assault on the 26th.
The English engraving shows 98 dwellings, double the number the reported two acres could support.

Native America New England c. 1600.

Because the Europeans lack American experience, they need to ask whether these are Pequots, Mohegans or another people of the region; and they do have many differences, often related to their particular part of the New England landscape.

*Dedicated
to the future legislators
who will have the courage
to return the original name*

PEQUOT

*to the present Thames River
of Connecticut*

The Authors

DAVID R. WAGNER began his painting and archaeological work in his youth in eastern Connecticut, walking the lands of Jewett City and Griswold in search of arrowheads and natural history. He took his Master's Degree in History from Eastern Connecticut State University in 1972, has studied Geology at The South Dakota School of Mines, and attended Black Hills Teachers' College. A self-taught painter, Wagner mentions Jan Vermeer and Norman Rockwell as two influences: his early works ranged from the prehistoric natural world to portraits, and today his paintings and murals appear in European and American galleries and showplaces. Wagner has painted over 100 scenes from The Pequot War, and scores more portraits and 'historical reconstructions' based on his archaeology and other research. The major collection of his Native paintings is today part of the Mohegan Reservation Cultural Center at Uncasville, Connecticut.

JACK DEMPSEY grew up in North Shore Boston, Massachusetts. He began his career as a writer/editor in New York City and lived two years in The Greek Islands completing *Ariadne's Brother: A Novel on the Fall of Bronze Age Crete* (Athens: Kalendis 1996: Greek translation 1998). He took his Ph.D. from Brown University in Early and Native American Literatures (1998), also producing *NANI: A Native New England Story* (distributed by Shenandoah Films/Arcata CA, and by V-Tape/ Toronto). Works include *New English Canaan by Thomas Morton of 'Merrymount': Text, Notes, Biography & Criticism* (2000), a screenplay on Morton's life, and *Good News from New England and Other Writings on the Killings at Weymouth Colony* (2001). He has taught at Brown, Wheaton and Bentley Colleges (MA), and produces public events and multimedia programs. His recent collaborative work with many artists and historians is online at *http://ancientgreece-earlyamerica.com*.

5

[*October 1636*] The governor of Plimoth [William Bradford]
wrote to the deputy [-governor of Boston, John Winthrop Sr.] that
we had occasioned a war, etc., by provoking the Pequots. The deputy
took it ill (as there was reason), and returned answer accordingly; and
made it appear, **1.** That there was as much done as could be expected,
considering they fled from us, and we could not follow them in our
armor, neither had any to guide us in their country.
    2. We went not to make war upon them, but to do justice, etc. And
having killed thirteen of them for four or five of ours whom they had
murdered, and destroyed sixty wigwams, etc., we were not much
behind with them.
              ---'Deputy' Governor John Winthrop Sr., *Journal* (DYW 105)

    I still remember a speech of [Reverend] Hooker at our going aboard;
That they should be bread for us. And thus when The Lord...turned
the wheel upon their enemies, we were like men in a dream; then was
our mouth filled with laughter, and our tongues with singing....
              ---Captain John Mason, *A Brief History of the Pequot War* (45)

    The Narragansett Indians...when they saw [the Missituc Pequots]
dancing in the flames, called them by a word in their own language
signifying, 'O Brave Pequots!'; which they used familiarly among themselves in their own prayers, in songs of triumph after their victories.
              ---William Bradford, *Of Plimoth Plantation* (FBH2:252)

    Have you fought enough?
              ---Pequot braves outside of Saybrook Fort on the
Connecticut River, Spring 1637 (qtd. in Gardener *Relation* 132)

MYSTIC FIASCO
How The Indians Won
The Pequot War

Sassacus, Great Sachem of the Pequots.

INTRODUCTION

Dawn, May 26, 1637: Surprise and catastrophe at Mystic.

For whom? This is a journey to the answer that no one expected.

According to accepted historical tradition, on that morning a force of English soldiers and Native American allies completed a long "undetected" march into Pequot Connecticut, and surrounded a palisaded village above the "great tidal river" at *Missituc* or Mystic. There, with surprise complete, they attacked and wiped out 300 to 700 Pequot men, women and children, incinerating most by trapping them inside Mystic Fort; and thus New England's colonists broke the back of Pequot dominion on the land.

In fact, Mystic was an English fiasco. The Pequots knew their landscape and their enemy. Helped by many of those same Native allies, the Pequots evacuated Mystic Village and used it as a decoy in a strategy of their own. The Pequots lured the English colonies' inexperienced fighting-men to Mystic Fort, fought a holding-action there while their families escaped; and then they counter-attacked with a force that drove the English into the Atlantic Ocean. If there is a victory to be claimed at Mystic, it belongs to the Pequots, Mohegans, Narragansetts, their allies and even their "traditional enemies." And their victory changes The Pequot War. That is what the evidence---examined rather than accepted---reveals. This book is a journey you can take step by step beyond reasonable doubt.

Imagine a history of any battle and war whose author had never walked the landscape to compare written records with physical facts. Without many kinds of reference to the land---to its hills, forests and bodies of water, its main and minor routes of human travel---we could scarcely form a realistic idea of a conflict's incidents, dynamics and actual outcomes. What did each group of combatants have to physically accomplish in order to win? What happened as each side's units maneuvered according to plans and their enemy's responses? What parts did the land itself play, what were its advantages and obstacles as each side's leaders made life-and-death decisions?

Incredibly, the land has never been asked to speak to the records of The Pequot War. That is what is missing from traditions about this fundamental American-frontier conflict, and it produces significant changes in understanding. Let this journey show you what the land reveals: layer upon layer of almost comically second-hand assumptions and beliefs that stand in wholesale defiance of physical fact, critical question and common sense. When you experience the differences between *a)* what participants claimed and historians ratified, and *b)* what was actually there and humanly possible, you reach starkly different conclusions about The Pequot War; and about many later wars conducted according to its apparently-successful methods.

This journey confronts the moment when northern-colony Englishmen first tried to impose their Old World practices of "total war"---*aka* "sheer wantonness"---on an American situation. Though historians have believed they were appallingly successful, it failed. The Pequots and their allies had a very adequate response that was neither wanton like their attackers' war, nor the "flight" of a broken people---and it worked. This journey necessarily, then, reveals troubling patterns in American histories---the books that guide the schools that teach Americans how to conceive and behave in the midst of "others."

Lack of reliable intelligence and allies, lack of "local experience" through genuine bonds; inability to identify, locate or "properly" assault targets; incompetence of pursuit, inability even to stop creating more of the foe; wishful overestimates of enemies neutralized. Above all, the refusal to adapt poorly-hatched plans in the face of experiences turning toward disaster---these are patterns foreshadowed by "The Pilgrims" of Plimoth, more remarkable in records of The Pequot War, and with us still. They persist in direct proportion to the inadmissible colonizing violence that overtook Native America and still seems, short-term, to work: the many-leveled, many-formed violence that subjects people(s), takes their labor, land and wealth, and keeps them quiet about it. This was eventually called Manifest Destiny: it produced "the lessons of Vietnam," and still persists.

The continuities are real. "Settlers" and "settlements" have been crying since the colonies for sharper definitions that could and still can save lives: on the Connecticut or in Gaza, they by no means arrive in "empty" lands. "Savages" and "terrorists" function alike across this same historical time: the words (try to) erase all other points of view, and the ability to imagine how one's own behavior might be part of a problem. No unilateral model of the world can hope for peace on the frontier. The book these English captains chose as their guide to America has had centuries, before and since The Pequot War, to prove otherwise.

How did this journey's discoveries come about? We the authors are historians who work closely with Native American peoples and academic experts, and we take them and this endeavor seriously. The last thing we want to suggest is that the Pequots and other Native New Englanders did not suffer much as England's Massachusetts Bay and Connecticut colonies intended in 1637. Indeed, until members of the Mashantucket Pequots invited painter David Wagner in the late 1990s to create a series of works about The Pequot War, we too had accepted the "traditional facts" about the massacre at Mystic (for example, Dempsey *Morton* 282).

But the more Wagner looked into those events as a painter, archaeologist and historian, studying every physical, landscape and narrative detail, the less certain he became about accepted understandings. When Wagner returned to Mashantucket with his findings about a year later, his discoveries met with silence. It seemed a testament to the powers of tradition-hallowed history that the "victims" themselves---whose true sufferings only began with the War and "Treaty"---could not accept the land-based, multi-dimensional proofs of their achievements at Mystic.

Wagner continued to investigate the records and the land. He created over 100 paintings that brought all the evidences together, shared them with colleagues for critique, did more research and experiment, and built the series into a complete, coherent and uniquely common-sensical idea of what actually happened on and after that May day at Mystic. By 1997 Wagner had also written out his documented argument, and finally he and Jack Dempsey worked together to produce what you have here. *Mystic Fiasco* shows you why no thinking person can accept the traditional story of The Pequot War, and makes it as easy as possible for you *to go in every way to see for yourself*. That, again, is what tradition has not done, and why these discoveries seem at first hard to believe.

We take you step by step through the same journey and "enterprise" experienced by the leading English captains, John Mason and John Underhill (the only eyewitness-chroniclers of this battle), from their gathering at Saybrook Fort on the Connecticut River to that dreadful morning at Mystic Village. Along the way, we present both accepted facts and new discoveries that emerge:

What archaeological evidence exists for a "massacre" at Mystic? What did Captains Mason and Underhill learn and not learn from the land they traversed enroute to battle? What can the actual site of Mystic, and other evidence from the physical and bodily realms, contribute to the textual records by the captains and the letters of their countrymen? Where did the Pequots come from, and can this tell us where they "went"?

What did these Englishmen know about their proclaimed enemy, about the Pequots' location(s), social and intertribal ways, their habits of behavior and response in peace and war---and what do we know today? How do "the hard numbers" support or subvert the traditional story? What crucial problems could not be wished away as the English chose a target, brought themselves there ideally "undetected," and tried to manage it all by reliance on a Native American guide with a mind of his own? If we grow more seasoned to 1630s New England along the way, how will those answers affect our concept of this "massacre" itself? What does Mystic's *aftermath* reveal of what happened there?

We try to include everything critical readers need to evaluate these events for themselves. We hope the Annotated Chronology helps you to the sources that do exist. But we repeat that this work is not in any way an exoneration of the colonists who tried with all their power to conquer and exterminate the Pequot people. Rather, we hope this inspires a fresh look at many assumptions about Native Americans and their colonizers, for the ones that underwrite "Mystic Massacre" have served few people well these 385 years.

Buried beneath the assumptions born of educational dogma are a great deal of Native American "observativeness" and a daring, creative use of it under fire. New documented measures of Pequot, Mohegan, Narragansett, Niantic, Nipmuc, Mohawk, and other peoples' subtlety, foresight, flexibility, cooperation, and cross-cultural understanding in such a merciless predicament. You will see more than Captains Mason and Underhill saw, more than historians after them wanted you to see: the canniness of Native courage, their openness and so their ability to learn fast; their deft

12

strikes launched with just the right force for their honorable ends; and their many acts of no less than humor and love amid the horrendous invasion of their homelands.

We trace a journey in time and space because it was, and show you with the documents how we construct each person and episode. We tell the story in present tense because our goal is clarity that assists your critique. You see events unfold as they did for those who lived them: one day and instant to the next, with no less or more of a grand historical mission on their minds than you might have in trying to fight and survive a hand-to-hand war.

The Puritans of Massachusetts Bay Colony (Boston 1630), of Connecticut's "river towns" like Hartford, and The Pilgrims of Plimoth were by no means the first English people in New England. But, very much because of their driving reasons for being here---their Christian evangelism and its need for land and sustaining profit---the English Puritans of this story were, in Mason's phrase, still "altogether ignorant of the country" when The Pequot War broke open at Mystic. The Puritans had explicitly distinguished their colonies from their rivals' and transatlantic predecessors' by their refusal to learn "unChristian practices" from "the wilderness" and its Native peoples. As you'll see, their refusals became the formula for Mystic Fiasco.

The Puritans' first American years were preoccupied with survival. They remained generically unwilling to bend their Biblical social code to the demands of the multicultural place where they lived. This doomed them to costly mistakes, and blinded them to consequences near and far which refused, even so, to go away. Few Puritans spoke any Eastern Algonquian because few tried. When hostilities worsened, they shot long-courted Native allies who lacked "some mark to distinguish them from the Pequots" (DYW 123). None of them, from their governors to their captains and

13

planters-turned-soldiers, knew "where their forts were...nor the way that led to them" (Mason 45). "We could not find them" (Underhill 54). How, then, did America lose what actually happened at Mystic from that day forward?

Listen for a clue in the words of Mohegan Sachem Uncas, the supposed "Indian traitor" in this story whose counsel and guidance enabled English victory. (Even to Jennings Uncas seemed a "groveling" collaborator: to Drinnon an "Uncle Tomahawk.") By the time of this pledge from Uncas (1638), the Mystic Massacre is, we're told, a fact believed by all sides. Uncas has come to Boston and speaks to the faces of John Winthrop and others who have just done all in their power to annihilate his Pequot relatives. As Uncas speaks, Pequot warriors wanted dead or alive by the English stand unrecognized in plain sight at his sides. And with this act, hundreds more Pequot people will survive and, one day, reclaim their forbidden name:

> "This heart" (laying his hand upon his breast) "is
> not mine but yours: I have no men: they are all yours.
> Command me in any difficult thing: I will do it. I will
> not believe any Indian's words against the English. If
> any man shall kill an Englishman, I will put him to death,
> were he never so dear to me." So the governor gave [Un-
> cas] a fair red coat, and defrayed his and his men's diet,
> and gave them corn to relieve them homeward and a
> letter of protection to all men, etc., and he departed
> very joyful. (Winthrop *Journal*, ed. Hosmer 1: 271)

There is little doubt of Uncas' and others' self-serving machinations in this story. If our journey succeeds, there will be new doubt too of such a speech. In its own time, it soon made Governor Winthrop "feel a bit foolish." It was no more sincere than it had to be: a masterpiece of Indian Blarney that helped to defend Native lives and cultures.

We hope you discover many people like this---subtle observers making the most of what their enemies want very much to hear.

Thompson, Connecticut   *Stoneham, Massachusetts*
Spring 2003

Story Note: For facts/citations on all participants in The Pequot War (before May 1637) see the Annotated Chronology. **Textual Note:** Page-numbers, unless otherwise shown, refer to the chronicles by Mason (**M11-46**), Underhill (**U47-86**), Gardener (**G121-149**), and Vincent (**V93-111**) in Orr's *History*. Having compared Orr's edition with library-collection originals, we have confidence in its accuracy but modernize original spellings. As we change quotations from past to present tense (for ex., *say* for *said*, *bring* for *brought*, *goes* for *went*), we make no change when it might distort original language any more than that. And we document each quotation so you can see that this story takes but one liberty---to arrange them, like these events, as clearly as possible in time-order for fresh examination.

Note To The First Edition (2004)

In Italian, a *fiasco* or ordinary bottle resulted from a glassblower's "ignominious failure" to make elegant ware: such a piece was marketed instead for "common" consumption (OED and colleague Karle Schlieff). *Fiasco*: a high design botched in execution but made serviceable. Because this is a study of historical events, of the production of history, and of history's relevance to our real lives from Mystic to The Middle East, we include this book's own encounters with possible publishers, from tribal presses to academic and self-styled "popular" ones; and regretfully surmise that "even" today's professional (meaning, paid) historians and other guardians of tradition must still, one way or another, find colonial fantasies serviceable. We certainly invite other explanations for the (shall we say) unprofessional behavior encountered as we presented these discoveries with all possible sunshine.

The products of the American "history industry" become the substance of children's schools, shape civic life and international behavior: the state of one's knowledge matters. Yet the Chronology's last pages here show you frontier New England in the minds of Pentagon officials. Somewhere in-between are historians, schools and teachers whose relationships to power, class and empire remain unexamined; whose sleep breeds nightmares in the refusal to look, think and change. War after American war, "the same mistakes" are obvious, needless and murderous, yet the flame's funded keepers tiptoe with little to say.

The Pequot War's flat-wrong histories hard-wired America to make untenable assumptions about violence, war and victory. When you see how incompetent these conquerors were and how many Native people did survive their intent, you read American War differently; and with the land's help, discover the same tactical incompetence, historians' apologies and secret survivals from Connecticut to California. Untried "facts" obscure the only possible "victory," that of a "guerrilla" like Uncas: one with "no great glory---except the end result" (a military officer qtd. in Chronology). Uncas' great victory was over himself: keeping his mouth shut to protect all those he saved with camouflage. Now, if it *is* "safe" for the land and documents to speak, why do tenured professionals, publishers and even tribal elders behave as though afraid?

Is it better to maintain schoolboy decorum and pass on murderous models of the world, or to discover *more* rigorous ways to laugh at their undoing? Better to mime a token colonizer's guilt, or to begin living the demonstrable knowledge that violence was not necessary to everybody's living well here? Is it better to profit by worship of violence and play-sad over "tragic necessity," or to reject both (using the light of day) as master-illusions that still make the colony *seem* to work? If there is power in being a victim, what powers does a human hero have?

We met one "seeker" who did look afresh at The Pequot War and its implications: Dartmouth's Colin Calloway wrote that "we need to look again at this," but added doubts that anybody would (end of messages). Smith College's Neal Salisbury never acknowledged his copy, nor the producers of two recent films on "Mystic." Editors at Vintage in New York "lost" another. University Press of New England's reviewers vetted these pages, "sat on" them for 8 months (in their editor's words), and then refused to make a single remark. (For nonwriters, the norm is that a book goes out to "experts" whose evaluative pages aid decisions.) Silence from readers among the Mohegans (whose ancestors helped this victory), and from Pequots, and archaeologist McBride.

Academic presses rejected this as "popularization," for it tells a clear story, includes humor, and you don't need a professor. They couldn't be sure this most comprehensive and detailed study of its subject was "serious"? "Popular" presses were troubled by footnotes (are you?), and by the demand that people actually read. They themselves "have no time" to read any more than most journo-critics, who present tidy "market reviews": not criticism but publisher-pumped PR. These, and 22 "literary agents" in quest of formulae, are the "belongers": those with more to short-term gain by turning away, than by embracing a discovery that happened to rock decrepit and dangerous boats. Should we have known? Dempsey's "startling" (MLA) edition of Morton's *Canaan* met the same: "This is important, needs to be done properly, and that makes it difficult for us." No reviews unless there are other reviews. Wagner's huge collection of paintings, purchased years ago by the Mohegans, sit somewhere all but unseen.

Belongers dread that You the reader are there: people whom these two public-speakers meet every day, people awake on their land, engaged with its documents, unpredictable in the books they buy (unless you ask them); people with historical and spiritual eyes who hope that a rigorous past can help a visionary future. Do we shed blood for freedom so that history can be something "serviceable"?

Are you a thinker who *looks* first, an artist, scholar? We include all this that you be *not* discouraged. Your audience is around you, in the devil's country between "free market" formulae and academic self-imposed irrelevance. Your community wants and needs your best, and may you be lucky as we were to find a maverick-scholar-publisher like Brian Shillue. They're out there; but first make a way to deliver your work yourself, and keep the rewards of your service. The colonies, still, are not interested.

ILLUSTRATIONS

MYSTIC
FIASCO

Capt. John Mason

Capt. John Underhill

Leift. Lion Gardener

As Uncas looks on, Captain Mason receives
his commission from Connecticutt Colony.

UNCAS

1

With Friends and Plans Like These

May 1, 1637: "Connecticut's Birthday." Four years of tension, failed diplomacy and violent vengeance-raids have harried to "New England's" southwest frontiers. The English colonists of The Long Water Land and their allies of coastal Massachusetts declare open war, this day, upon the Pequot Nation.

Reverend Thomas Hooker and the leaders of Hartford Colony commission one Captain John Mason and 70-odd planters to take this fight to the enemy. They are all green to American war, civilians not soldiers, though they have been drilling as a "trainband" through the latest year of hostilities. Mason's Hartford commission crowds his men into ready boats, they settle in among 20 more from Massachusetts Bay with Captain John Underhill; and they glide down-river past struggling, war-wounded Wethersfield to another new English post, called Saybrook Fort. From there, they'll find a way to launch this war, and win it.

They ride a beautiful river, one of the grandest in New England, and view a rich green country. In May the Connecticut runs high along its last banks into the sea, cold and strong with the melt of unknown mountains. The river is an ancient easy road leading north into this America. Northward, the Mohawk and Iroquois--- strong nations led, they say, by women---control the choice trade, the prized fat pelts of beaver and otter, marten and sable that grow where it's cold year-round. There are still fat beaver hereabouts, but they're harder to come by every year without allies from those hinterlands. The river carries American furs out to the sea and the world of money, and sends back coveted wampum white and black; English blankets, tools of steel and pig-iron, and sometimes (men being men), guns.

The main rule is simple: work hard, play the game discreetly among these "Indians" (all so alike, all so fractious), and the choice furs can be yours. In this world there is nothing more profitable: no activity more likely, for the deft and dauntless quick-learning man, to fetch the gold that makes colonists' dreams come true.

Anybody can learn the river. The real trick to success is to play these illiterate Native Americans until they're under your thumb. The rub is, though, that these cousins are all in together. Connecticut already is a world of dizzying Algonquian dialects and secret signs, a world of feuds, leagues and intermarriages old as Europe. Even the most liberal English colonists feel themselves outside the real workings of the country---and generations more "Indians" still make the map-makers crazy as they move and migrate up and down this river and back again.

The country shines, grand and mysterious in May morning sun. Hawks and seagulls swoop as the river pours peacefully into Atlantic marsh-land not far from Saybrook Fort. But no Maypole celebrates this Spring. That is not why the English are here.

Tall, portly Captain John Mason is *matchit hoggery*, plenty-angry enough as he stamps impatiently about the fort this morning. He's already lost "five or six days" (G136) trying to launch this attack. Mason's and Underhill's men have swept down here to the river's mouth---running aground just a few times on its shoals---and here they run straight into Leiftenant Lion Gardener, the war-seasoned

Master Of Works who built this fort for Lords Say and Brook. Of course there's competition among the English colonies from Plimoth to Boston, from Hartford to Saybrook. But this Gardener seems uninterested in politics: what he does question is everything about Mason's commission for war: his "fitness," his allies and even his plan of attack.[1]

Mason calls this delay being "windbound" (M21), but he cannot smile for puns this morning. He's had enough talk. He can't see what's wrong with his 70-odd Connecticut men, all "completely armed" with leather "corselets, muskets, bandoliers, rests, and swords" (U62). They look as hard as the 20 with Captain Underhill, here "at the charge" of Gardener's masters (G135); and some of those have experience chasing if not fighting Native Americans. Gardener's own professionals have skirmished all winter around this fort. To Mason, his total of 90 men look ready to "much daunt" anybody---even Dutch from New Amsterdam who defy Saybrook Fort and slip up-river, in pursuit of those north-country furs.

Mason, in his late 30s (WCL1: 173) has been here since 1633, one of many English who broke with Massachusetts Bay for the "elbow room" of Connecticut. How Mason gained this command is not clear, for though later writers deem him and Captain Underhill

---

[1] Gardener describes his company of engineers and soldiers who built this fort in 1633-34 as not the "expected" 300 (G136, 122) but "twenty-four in all, men, women, and boys and girls." By contract they are here to build and defend the fort, not wage war. Until this May 1637, men affiliated with Boston's Mass. Bay Colony, including Underhill, have brought Gardener only temporary manpower. Mason's Connecticut leaders have "mocked" his appeals for action until last month's Pequot attack on Wethersfield (below). Now they mean to move.

Gardener's forays around the fort involve 6-8 men at a time. If only 1/6 of his 24 "in all" are married men (4 plus 4 wives?), and 1/6 are children (4?), Gardener has 16 *fighting-men* to hold the fort. Thus we estimate 5 men in the "handful" he soon sends with the captains, including Saybrook's "Dr." Pell.

"famous warriors of those times" (DeForest 115), neither officer has experience of war. Perhaps this country's constant need to improvise has made their collective motto "Not To Worry." The men have drilled month by month with guidance only from New England's reigning experts, Captain Myles Standish of Plimoth and Salem's Captain John Endecott (Hirsch 1188).

Mason and his superiors expect good results through imitating the bluster, killings and maraudings led by those "first-generation" planters against New England's Natives (Dempsey ed., *Morton* and *Good News*). The only colonist so far to question Standish and Endecott as teachers, Thomas Morton of the infamous plantation "Merrymount," is banished. All else these green planters have from which to learn war in The New World is a chapter or two of Hakluyt's *Voyages*, a rumpled copy of Captain John Smith's fabulous conquests, and maybe William Wood's *New England's Prospect* of 1634---based on "little time" spent with Native people. "Clearly it was limited," says editor Vaughan (7). Wood did learn enough to warn his fellows about matchlock firearms: here, they are "more credit [for show-effect] than service." Nevertheless, according to most research on these colonists as military men, these mostly-Puritan English in the hands of Standish and Endecott "take pride in traditional [Old World] drill, seemingly oblivious to the demands of combat in the wilderness" (Hirsch 1196).

Today Captain Mason intends to have it out with Christopher Gardener, that condescending veteran of combat here and in Europe. Mason's worry and hurry are twofold. From intelligence shared by Boston's governor John Winthrop, Mason knows that some of the enemy Pequots' "women of esteem and children are gone to Long Island with a strong guard" already. As Mason feels the enemy slipping away, he also has the Pequots' outright challenge in his ears: "They profess that [at Pequot River], you shall find them; and as they were there born and bred, there their bones shall be buried and rot, in despite of the English" (WPF3: 420).

It is the saltiest war-challenge any of them record. And, "If The Lord be on our side, their brags will soon fall," Mason replies, words of comfort from Plimoth's Edward Winslow (cited above). But Mason's men here, as well as their frightened farming families back up-river, do not share the Pequots' curious confidence: "The Pequots follow their fishing and planting as if they have no enemies" (Williams qtd. in Thomas 137).[2]

Mason starts to hunt around Saybrook Fort to get Gardener to a conference again. Least of all does he want English argument in front of the 60-80 Mohegan braves who are also here (their number-estimates vary through Orr's *History*), watching the planters clean their guns. *Wolf People* they call themselves! Mason has signed them on as guides and allies for the attack. But his men, Underhill's and Gardener's too have bad stomachs just looking at them. Nobody in his right English mind fully trusts a Mohegan or any other "Indian." They are a world unto themselves, and it's unsettling---

---

[2] More on colonists' "training days" and Pequot doings at the same time: Chronology, V101, Jennings 202; WCL1: 178, WPF3: 441. "Captain Standish was of a low stature," Prince relates (1736: in Orr 4), "but of such a daring and active Genius that even before the arrival of Mass. Bay Colony, he spread a terror over all the tribes of Indians round about him....Captain Mason was...never the less full of martial bravery and vigor....He soon became the equal dread of...even more numerous nations." Peter Thomas explains Pequot life since March: "large spawning runs of alewives, shad and salmon commence": Native families "gather by...the large falls along the Connecticut," and "for a month or so" consume and process these for store. "By late April and throughout May," they plant corn and other crops, fish, and hunt "migrating waterfowl and a few mammals." Not till summer do "communities center...in the hamlets [and villages like Mystic] surrounded by family planting fields" (137).

their secret conversations, those grisly Mohegan war songs, their confident painted bodies, ugly clubs of burl and stone, their spears and quivers of sharp-tipped arrows. They share too many grins and chortles that the English do not understand.[3]

Captain Underhill sees more delay afoot too, and crisply commences new drill within Saybrook Fort's stout palisade. Like everybody else, Underhill knows the help these English need against the Pequots in a vast "wilderness." The captains have sworn to keep both eyes open, for these Mohegan allies are out to play the English in turn against the Pequots, for reasons of their own in an old intertribal family feud. "They use us as their stalking-horse" (WPF2: 442).

Where *is* Gardener? Running a patrol around again outside the fort with a few seasoned skirmishers, harrying back the Pequot braves who have surrounded this place for months now? The unproven Mason cannot get the voices of Hartford's leaders out of his mind. "Though we feel neither the time nor our strength fit for such a service," says Reverend Hooker, "yet the Indians here our friends [around Hartford] are so importunate with us to make war presently that, unless we attempt something, we deliver our persons into contempt of base fear and cowardice; and cause them to turn enemies against us" (WPF3:407-8). Mason's company they send into action "against our minds, and constrained by necessity."

Indeed, "The eyes of all the Indians in the country are upon the English, to see what they will do," warns the chaplain of Salem John Higginson (WPF3: 404). And yet Mason must grant something

---

[3] Frazier (2) says the related names "Mohican" and "Mohegan" signify "great waters or sea that are constantly in motion, either flowing or ebbing." The Speck/Dynely *Glossary of the Mohegan-Pequot Language* translates "Mohegan" as "Wolf People" (*Mohiksinug*). Bruce Grant's *American Indian Concise Encyclopedia* (1994: 209) accepts the latter.

to this cautious Gardener. They tacitly agree with Wood's *Prospect* about guns: they know, as Higginson says it, that a "common conceit" about guns is "in truth a dangerous error"---namely, "that Indians are afraid" of firearms, that with matchlocks "ten English will make one hundred Indians flee." The "malice" of these Natives is "not to be questioned," Higginson warns; but it's sure they have "experience in warlike affairs, being men of war from their youth." This gives them "advantages against us in agility and arms" (405).

Does Uncas, sharing a meal with his braves, notice these worries in Mason's face? Suddenly the Sachem rises, and lets everybody round the fort see him buck Mason up, his "intimate acquaintance" and "great friend" (M7, 25).

But Mason can't eat. His responsibilities rest upon too much uncertain ground. For Mason knows that Uncas has his own game to play against the Pequots and their Great Sachem Sassacus. Uncas shrugs, smiles from behind his thinking eyes and rejoins his braves.

Five days stuck quarreling here at Saybrook. Face it---Nobody knows exactly how to "avenge ourselves" on the Pequots, for the "innocent" colonists killed in their part of the violence running years now (M23, U57). The English know what they've been told to do. Mason's commission from Hartford (in Orr xv) allows his forces to attack "from the west" the Pequots' 77-year-old "greatest and bloodiest Sachem," Sassacus, at his chief fort, Weinshauks on that "Pequot River" (M26). There the main force of Pequot braves await battle, as their challenge says, "in despite of the English."

Yet Saybrook's Leiftenant Gardener has laid open the English captains' worries, and all Mason can hear is Reverend Hooker's zeal (WPF3:408): "I hope you see a necessity to hasten execution, and not do this work of The Lord's revenge slackly."[4]

At last Mason's men fetch Gardener in to council and, hopefully, action. But Gardener fears not to smile at Captain Mason's green hurry. Where have Hartford's and these other English been all this bloody winter-past, through Saybrook's siege? It is years already since the erstwhile cause of this war, the killing of interloping traders Captains Stone and Norton just up-river. All this, wonders Gardener, for a Virginian stealing our beaver-trade? (G123, 139). Nobody liked those "immoral" men in Boston.

Just last July off Block Island, though, there was another trader named John Oldham killed, for some reason, by "Indians." Whoever committed that crime (and it's not known for sure), it gave the English colonies fresh cause to press the Pequots for concessions in their growing power-struggle. Boston's governor John Winthrop took up his treaties with the Pequots' "traditional enemies," the Narragansetts, through their Sachem Miantonomo; and *he* dutifully reported swift and "good success" sending his braves to avenge Mr. Oldham at Block Island (WCL1: 79). To these colonists, however, there is something unsatisfactory about

---

[4] Given Hooker's urgings, Mass. Bay Boston is trying to send 40 men under Captain Daniel Patrick. But they are "delayed," and (Ch. 2) send word asking Mason to wait for them. Mason agrees only to meet Patrick later on the Pequot River (Ch. 4). On the competition over Pequot country between Connecticut's river-towns under Ludlow and Hooker and Winthrop's Boston, see Jennings Chs. 12-13. Gardener has told Winthrop (March 1637, WPF3: 382), "Stir up our friends in the bay out of their dead sleep of security...your condition may be as ours is unless some speedy course be taken, *which must not be done by a few but by a great company.* For all the Indians have their eyes fixed upon us. And this year they will all join with us against the Pequots....It is to be feared that the next year they will be against us" [emphasis added].

"independent Indian justice." No Englishman witnessed this punitive violence. Governor Winthrop's Boston needed better assurance that "Indians" really got hurt there.[5]

So last August (1636), Boston despatched the stern bungling "expert" Captain Endecott, in command of Underhill and 100 men, to unfurl their colors on the open or "champion fields" of Block Island and demonstrate justice. The "Indians" there kept a well-warned distance, jeered at the English, laughed and fled with ease. Humiliated and enraged, Endecott burned everything in reach from homes to cornfields, then was humiliated and enraged by the Pequots' diplomatic run-around along the Connecticut. "Looking for Sassacus?" they asked. "Wait here, Captain, we'll fetch him for you; and if we're not back...."

Endecott burned more homes and corn, then hacked at any Native people he found along the river. This left Gardener's Saybrook Fort with angry Pequot and other "wasps" about their ears all winter. Gardener himself did manage an October parley with Pequots and local Niantics, to make them understand they had better turn over those killers of Stone, Norton and Oldham. When the English failed to understand Pequot justice—something about their own legitimate revenge for the murder of their old Sachem, Tatobem---it was a stand-off.

And what a winter followed! At least three of Gardener's men died in sorties around this fort: three more took a shallop up-river

---

[5] In October 1636, "Miantonomo declares that [the Narragansetts] will continue in war with the Pequots and their confederates till they are subdued....They will deliver our enemies to us, or kill them." In return Boston is "to give them notice when we go against the Pequots, and they [will] send us some guides" to that end (DYW 104-5). From the start, then, the English hope of success without Native guides is meager, "considering they flee from us, and we cannot follow them in our armor, neither have any to guide us in their country."

for supply and were never seen again (G134-5). There is even a new landmark nearby called Tilly's Folly, where one Sergeant Tilly disobeyed Gardener's orders "not to land anywhere" before the river-towns, and paid with a painful death. Gardener himself has an arrow-wound nearly healed. Saybrook Fort will likely burn this summer, or grow by English victory.[6]

Boston's and Hartford's attacks complicate everything with the Western Niantics and local "river Indians," their formerly-friendly landlords who, like Uncas, bear less than great love for the Pequots' leader Sassacus. Amid the past years' increasing distrust and violent episodes, Hartford's farmers have suddenly driven their Native neighbors off the lands remaining to them around the river-towns. These Niantics and river-peoples run straight to Sassacus; and he, not forgetting Endecott's behavior, launches a strike at Wethersfield in April. The war is on. Nine English planters die there, and two women (though Gardener hears "fourteen" in all from a Dutch boat, G133). Hartford issues its commission, and here stands Mason with the fate of the colonies on his shoulders.

Captain Underhill is absorbed with his busy-drills till he sees Gardener, the true professional, stride in at last to join Mason on

---

[6] Or at least, Gardener and history assume so. Neither compare the two estimates of war-related deaths at this point. First, from Endecott's raids in August-Sept. 1636, Winthrop estimates (Oct. 1636) killing "thirteen of them for four or five [*sic*]...of ours....[We] are not much behind with them" (DYW 105). Compare the 11-14 English killed by Pequots at Wethersfield (citations below), which is Sassacus' response in April 1637. If history today can admit that Sassacus' 26 villages *could* have inflicted much worse if intending "extermination," we can see that Mason's "hurry" also ignores viable chances for negotiation, based in nearly-equal losses ("Have you fought enough?" asked Pequot braves). Note for later chapters that Uncas' Mohegans "receive and keep" Native women and children safe during those English attacks (WCL1: 119).

the camp-stools. Underhill quits his trainband with hearty blessing from his Bible, for of all his peers he most-gushes its epigrams and sermons. And though it is time to commit themselves to action, nobody invites the Mohegans or Sachem Uncas to the parley. Maybe there is too much mistrust, fear of a security-leak between Mohegans and their hostile Pequot cousins. They are very close-by. "The enemy lying hovering about the fort continually take notice" of all traffic and "supplies that...come" (U61).

Mason invites Leiftenant Gardener to speak frankly, knowing Gardener's chief concern with "Captain Hunger" and his hope that "the Bay-men...desist from a war a year or two, till...better provided for it." "Let fortification alone awhile" (G124). Gardener begins to explain his frustrating hesitations. "Mr. Gardener it seems much discourageth common men by extolling the valor of our adversaries, preferring them before the Spaniards [as warriors]" (WPF3: 419). Underhill fumbles to help Mason and Gardener lets fly at Underhill's own mettle.

"None of our [Saybrook] men should go," Gardener tells the two captains, "unless we, bred soldiers from our youth, can see some likelihood to do better than the Bay-men" (G136). This thrusts straight at Underhill's share of the late Endecott/Block Island expedition: it brought down the "wasps" now surrounding the fort.

How then can Mason persuade Gardener to contribute his own good men to the coming action? The three leaders' postures shift and don't look good to the restless men of the fort, who curse another day lost to their crops at home. Their eyes seek out "Be Strong" signals from the lounging Mohegans; and they take cue from Uncas, and gaze back at the bearded, boiled-looking English.

One or two lift and shake a club or spear. They are here, to fight their Pequot enemies; but the English cannot feel sure of them.[7]

Gardener spells out his demands. As to Mason's "fitness," he will cooperate if Mason sends home "twenty insufficient" Hartford men, and replaces them with "twenty of the lustiest" on hand (M20, G137). Agreed.

However, Gardener insists to know how Mason "durst trust the Mohegan Indians, who have but that year come from the Pequots" (G136). Uncas is here because he wants his brother-in-law Sassacus' high office. Whether it's an ancient or a recent tribal break that has divided the followers and families of Uncas and Sassacus, it is younger by far than the ties than bind them still. Mason has to confess that Native New Englanders have "many times some of their near Relations among their greatest Foes" (M24).[8]

---

[7] Few if any of these English have been in the country more than 5 years. Gardener is the most seasoned man-at-arms. "It can hardly be said that Mason was 'trained up'" in Europe's wars under Sir Thomas Fairfax (Orr 8), not least because Gardener was (Williams in Orr 16). "There is no direct proof" of Mason's being such a "companion at arms," and the same is true of Underhill; one of whose earliest recorded actions is his attempt to arrest the heretic Roger Williams, which fails because Williams knows he is coming (Rubertone 11). Underhill and Mason, like their planter men, are learning as they go. But Gardener is full of "pretty pranks," such as laying out nail-studded boards where he sees Pequot scouts' trails, and "laughing" at the blood left behind (G149). Trained in "policy" (intelligence) as well as combat, he has deadly expertise with "sakers" or small cannon (G131, 133) and the fort's two big guns, which he loads with "cross-bar shot" (G148) to rip down cover. His skill is rare until the 1670s.

[8] Scholars still debate when the Mohegans separated as a tribe from the Pequots, but sources throughout the Chronology detail strong family ties and connections as well as quarrels among the Mohegans with Uncas, the Pequots of Grand Sachem Sassacus, Miantonomo's Narragansetts and (below) Sassious' Western Niantics and Ninigret's Eastern ones.

And what choice is there? We will trust them, Mason growls, for to a man their company is "altogether ignorant of the country" (M21). Gardener agrees that "We cannot well go without them for want of guides" (G136).

But that is the difference between experience and the captains. "I will try them," Gardener demands, "before a man of ours shall go with you, or them."

Mason makes two fists on the air. Underhill chides that they must not fail to "enterprise some stratagem upon these bloody Indians" (U67). The question of whether to really trust these "allied Indians" does "perplex the hearts of many very much, because they have had no experience of [Mohegan] fidelity" (U68).[9]

Possibly, these leaders' own ways are in their way. For "on The Lord's Day" just past, Uncas' Mohegans offered to "fall out...to see whether they can find any Pequots near the fort." "But it being The Lord's Day, order was given to the contrary" (U68). Had they foregone such observances (and they will not do so later, either), they might have some "proof" by now. Mason, exasperated, "calls for" Uncas to join them. Rarely is Uncas already part of a council.

"You say you will help," Gardener tells Uncas (G136), "but I will first see it. Therefore send you, now, twenty men" to the Bass

---

[9] "Their ignorance of Native languages, their limited contacts among more remote Native groups, and the difficulty in verifying information made the English more susceptible to false rumors than were Native allies" (Johnson 37). The English can hardly track Native Americans' shifting alliances. Just after Mystic, Long Island Sachem Waiandance tells Gardener (who believes it "true") that "the Narragansetts would let us alone till they had destroyed Uncas...and then they, with the [Mohawks and Mahicans] and the Indians beyond the Dutch, and all the northern and eastern Indians, would easily destroy us, man and mother's son" (G139-140).

At Saybrook Fort on the Connecticutt River,
Leiftenant Lion Gardener (left) demands that Uncas
prove himself loyal before he'll approve Mason's plan of attack.

River---an inlet just off the Connecticut---where "yesternight" the English spotted "six Indians in a canoe, thither."

Were they Pequots? No Englishman asks. Uncas gazes in silence upon the river.

"Fetch them now dead or alive," Gardener orders, "and then you shall go" with the English attack on the Pequots. "Else not."

So, Uncas "sends his men," "early in the morning" (G136, U68).

The captains and men must wait yet again, and study Uncas. Uncas is young, perhaps in his early 30s (for he lives another 46 years after Mystic, till 1683). A writer who never sees him describes a man "of large frame and great physical strength" (DeForest 86). Born the son of Sachem Owaneco, his mother the well-born Mukkunnup ("Genealogy"), Uncas' "royal" blood entitled him 10 years before to marry a daughter of Pequot Sachem Tatobem, the father of Sassacus. This makes him brother-in-law to the Englishmen's prime enemy (more in WCL1: 115-116n11, and Chronology).

In time, Uncas' reach for power among Connecticut tribes brings him to marry six more Native women of standing (WCL1: 202). This may be a man (in DeForest's words) "selfish, jealous and tyrannical," whose "ambition is grasping, and unrelieved by a single trait of magnanimity"---"faithful like the jackal to the lion." But there is no doubt that Uncas intends to be a long-term contender. Uncas has made at least five attempts to unseat his kinsman Sassacus, been humbled for it, exiled, forgiven again: he cannot have survived this long without friends to whom Sassacus himself must show restraint. At this point, Uncas may have "few" followers and much-reduced territory of his own. But the English are hardly aware that Uncas is rising much because Sassacus' power is crumbling.[10]

How can the English trust a man so utterly foreign, a man openly bad-mouthing the Great Sachem of his country? Uncas never lets the English forget Sassacus' and his Pequots' "evil" intentions (WPF3: 270-1). They hear from planters that Uncas even exhorts Reverend Hooker to attack his own Native kinsmen (WPF3: 407-8).

The English are no strangers to feuds and power-struggles. But Uncas' reputation makes them despise him, even as they can't deny their need for him. He is their only anchor to American realities. They cannot grasp Uncas' "resistance of a different form than [that] more easily recognized" in other Natives (Johnson 46). A gifted negotiator and strategist, Uncas has a long patience the English will reckon with.[11]

Before too long, his Mohegan braves return to Saybrook Fort with several Native American heads (G136). Underhill sees four (U68). This "mightily encourages the hearts of all" against their doubts, he says, and they all accept this "as a pledge" of the Mohegans' "further fidelity." Mason (M20) looks at the heads as "a special Providence; for before we were somewhat doubtful." The men mount the heads along the palisade of Saybrook (DYW 122).

---

[10] Salisbury (208-210) and Cave (68, 182) find the Pequots at this time fewer, weaker, and less aggressive than most have believed, given Uncas' and other "tributary" groups' recent breaks away from Sassacus, as well as Dutch and English challenges in the region.

[11] "Otherwise [they] shall but run round about a maze," remarks the seasoned exile Morton (*Canaan* 18) of the need for Native language and guides. He is in England writing and celebrating this May with a letter relating his legal victory against Puritan New England's charter to build these colonies.

Uncas' Mohegan braves return to Saybrook Fort with a number of Native American heads. Though Vincnet claims they were placed on the fort, a brave at right sees to their burial and makes an offering of tobacco.

Are they Pequot heads? Uncas never says so, and no Englishman asks. Nobody wants to admit in front of Uncas and his Mohegans that they have no idea how to identify a Pequot. "We cannot confide in [them], but look at them as uncertain" (M45). "Withall, we conceive that you [should] look at the Pequots, and all other Indians, as a common enemy," Winthrop has advised (May 20: WPF3: 417).[12]

"Though they may take occasion [to cooperate with] some one part of the English, yet if they prevail, they will surely pursue...advantage to the rooting out of the whole English nation." Indeed the colonists know that Native American ties, however fractious, run deep. And there can be no victory without clearly identifying the enemy. The English cannot tell even the Mohegans from other Native peoples: they have yellow paint on hand "for their heads," but "not enough" to go around (WCL1: 84).

---

[12] Gardener's account (G136) of this action "proving" Uncas' loyalty does not agree with Mason's (M20) or Underhill's (U67-8). Why is the scenario above based on Gardener's? First, Mason says that enroute down-river with his own men and Uncas', the latter grow "impatient of delays" as the boats run aground, and they promise to "meet us at Saybrook"; where, "Captain Underhill also coming with him [Mason? Uncas?]...informs us what was performed by Onkos and his men." Underhill describes his "coming down the river...fearing that the Indians in time of greatest trial might revolt...and join with the Pequots"; and "lying aboard...my boat" with "the hearts of all being in general much perplexed, fearing the infidelity of these Indians, *having not heard* what an exploit they had wrought" (emphasis added). Hooker does hear of "six of the Pequots [*sic*] slain by our Indians" not far from the fort (WPF3: 408); but the "pinnace" with that news throws no more light on gaps and contradictions. Drake: "It is not easy to account for Mason's want of knowledge respecting...Gardener's agency in this act of Uncas' men" (ed. Mather 122n146)---not unless Gardener tells a more accurate story than the captains do.

What, then, is a Pequot? Is it a matter of language, village-origin, dress, hairstyle, "signs or marks"? The records mention not one working criterion until Native deaths and injuries make the "Indians" demand better. This war and all its records operate instead upon a single definition, unstated because it is so embarrassing. A Pequot is any person identified as such by a Mohegan, or in fact by any other "Indian." In this war, Native judgment decides who lives and who dies by the English sword.[13]

The next Native person to die by this "definition" is one Siswas (G136, V101). As we'll see, the best evidence suggests that Siswas is

---

[13] Winthrop recounts (DYW 123) that at Mystic, "divers of the Indian friends were hurt...because they had not some mark to distinguish them from the Pequots": this he had from Roger Williams, who said (WPF3: 427) that "the cause why the English hurt so many of the [Narragansetts] was want of signs or marks." "We knew not the Indians one from another," Gardener also says (G132). He tells this to "Indians" on the river during another encounter, as they too claim that they "know not" Englishmen from Dutch. Gardener deploys his excuse because he expects "Indians" can well-believe it. Jennings: "the difference" among Native groups, to the English, is "political rather than cultural" (226). The English can tell Native peoples apart only by attitudes towards themselves. The same may hold true *vice-versa*: see which matters most.

A startling possibility stares us in the face. The Chronology abstracts documents debating how recent, large, and complete the "break" was between the Pequots and Mohegans (who even so share origins, ancestors, kinsmen, language and many things of a common life and land). *Exactly which villages* supply Uncas with these "60-80" braves with him at Saybrook? For, given mostly-small estimates *of the entire "original" Mohegan population*, 60-80 braves (the "mean" of all different numbers we find) is a large-enough part of them *all* to mean that Mason's 60-80 allies here are "very like" Uncas (brother-in-law to Sassacus). That is, *among Native peoples*, Mohegans are "different from Pequot" in everything from dialect and attitude to textiles, ceramics, hair, jewelry, symbolic tattoos and atlatl-styles; and, in ways *outside of English comprehension* from intermarriage to *ad hoc* alliance, they are all as Pequot as your Mohegan uncle.

not a Pequot; but Uncas has his purposes. This one live prisoner is not cowed by Saybrook's military might, but "braves the English, as though they dare not kill a Pequot."

Is Siswas Pequot? The English seem satisfied. "Some will have their courage to be thought invincible when all is desperate," Vincent opines (V101). But "it avails this savage nothing."

The English want to test Uncas for their cause. Uncas "proves himself" by watching as they tie one of Siswas' legs to a post, and then twenty men "with a rope tied to the other" pull the man to pieces on the spot. Underhill draws a pistol and shoots Siswas "through the head." Neither captain details this spectacle. Vincent does.[14]

---

[14] Most historians say Uncas and the Mohegans "demand" to torture Siswas (DeForest 121), making Underhill's act a "mercy." The "torture" appears in neither Mason, Underhill, nor Gardener; and Vincent, who was not there, mentions no "eating" of the prisoner. Mather (167), writing 40 years later without naming sources, says the Mohegans "roast and eat" Siswas. Vaughan cites Mather as fact (141n40); and editor Drake cites Vincent about it; but "eating" is not in any chronicle in Orr. Wallace (103): Native "torture is a ritual and follows a formal, predictable course, in which the victim and his tormentors...play traditionally respectable roles. The victim...is expected to show composure and hardihood: weaklings...unable to perform the role, who break down, weep, and cry for mercy, are sometimes dispatched in disgust....Many of the tormentors consciously are not anxious to see transports of agony and emotional collapse, but rather...to see a stouthearted man with unconquerable self-control maintaining defiance and self-respect to the bitter end, and the torture is a test of these qualities. Since the victim is in many cases eaten and has in some cases been previously adopted, he is in a very real sense being incorporated by a family and a community, and becoming part of them." If Mather is right, Siswas has in a sense been "incorporated" by the Mohegans---a gesture emblematic of this story of survival in the shadow of English invasion.

Does Gardener himself now "believe" in Uncas? Or does he dislike the credulity in these green captains, and want them all out of his fort? For Gardener fetches 15 yards of trade-cloth from his stores to reward Uncas and his braves (G136), and picks out a "handful" of his own to lend some strength (we estimate 5 men including "Dr." Pell, note above). Mason, with nothing from Uncas about the killing of his catch, claps on his sallet-helmet and sounds a long-desired *Make Ready!*

But Underhill is still troubled. To him with his penchant for sermonizing (U52-3, 68-9, 72-77), things call for mystical remedy: a prayer "from the heart" of their company chaplain "Master Stone," for whose Old World home the Hartford colony is named (Drake/Mather 157n182). Stone obliges (U69):

> O Lord God, if it be thy blessed will, vouchsafe
> so much favor to thy poor distressed servants as to
> manifest one pledge of thy love, that may confirm
> us of the fidelity of these Indians toward us that now
> pretend friendship and service, that our hearts
> may be encouraged the more in this work of thine....

Then Underhill, "immediately myself stepping up" to Stone, tells him "that God has answered his desire." Unsure as it is when this action was launched and when those heads arrive, Underhill says he shares "news" of their delivery and points to them piked on the fort. The English "rejoice" and are "thankful to God," "replenished ...exceedingly." The men clasp more-confident hands all around.

But it seems there is another matter---where they're going and what the target is.

Captain Mason knows that his commission from Hartford "limits" his English and Mohegans "to land our men in Pequot River: we had also the same Order by a Letter of Instruction sent

The Pequot River looking south from Pequot Hill in Groton, CT:
Sassacus' fort Weinshauks stood atop this long steep hill.
This is where the Pequots challenge Mason/Underhill and company
to meet them in battle.
No Pequot remains have survived The American Revolution's
and today's Fort Griswold there.

us" (M22). Now it is Mason who "apprehends" an "exceeding great hazard" in doing so. He has reasons; and he has "also some other [reasons]" which he "forbears to trouble you with."

First of Mason's recorded reservations is that "The Pequots our enemies keep a continual guard upon the river night and day" (M21). If the English try to land on the Pequot River's west bank as instructed by their ministers and magistrates, and attack Sassacus' warriors at their strongest point, Weinshauks, they will find themselves eagerly expected. They will face "numbers that far exceed ours," bearing at least "sixteen guns" besides. That is where "they expect...us," Underhill confirms (U77).[15]

Well then, is there no more strategic landing-place for their only commissioned action? They have no horses or heavy guns to offload. A landing means easing their small boats (a shallop, a "pink" and a pinnace) into the shallows and perhaps casting down a two-plank gangway. They don't need a port.

Yet Mason says there is "no other place to go on shore" that is "nearer [to the enemy] than Narragansett," except "in that Pequot River" (M21). The claim is simply preposterous for this mostly-gentle coastline of 30-odd miles. More strange, just there at Pequot River Mason's company plan to come down to the shore after their attack (U84), there to rendezvous with their own boats and 40 fresh men under Mass. Bay Colony's Captain Patrick.

---

[15] Sassacus derives his Great Sachem's powers from the braves of 26 villages (for ex. DYW 126) spread across at least 30 square miles of territories unknown to the English; not to mention "tributaries" from Quinnipiac to the Nipmuc and Narragansett frontiers. The intelligence about guns in Pequot hands is from two English girls of Wethersfield recovered from the Pequots by Dutch traders who happen by Saybrook just before these events (M21, U70-2, G132-3).

Underhill (U83-4) calls Pequot River "the place appointed." They seem to be counting on a rout of the Pequot forces and on great freedom of movement through this campaign. It seems that they know and don't yet know their plan.

The English have secret help that none explain: it's Roger Williams, the fiery minister cast out of Boston for his conscientious heresies. Though the Narragansetts allow Williams a homestead in their midst, he has already risked his life (he says) to "break and hinder" a threatening new alliance between them and their "traditional enemies," the Pequots (WCL2: 609-10). Williams has "shipped" himself "all alone in a poor canoe...through a stormy wind" to from his Providence to Narragansett; and for "three days and nights" labored against Sassacus' "bloody Pequot ambassadors" to prevent a pan-Indian alliance (Ch. 6).[16]

The wisdom of Sassacus' appeal was that Narragansett help to the English would make themselves the next target. Somehow, Williams succeeded, and "broke to pieces" the "negotiation and design." At least, the English think so. The captains will find out.

Williams, relatively intimate with his landlords, also confirms Pequot activities just now: "scarce of provision" at this time of year, they "are in some numbers come down to the seaside...to take sturgeon and other fish, as also to make new fields of corn in case the English should destroy their fields at home" (WPF3: 411).

Below is Roger Williams' crucial yet unspoken help to Mason and Underhill: a map he has sketched for John Winthrop (WCL1: 74; rpt. FBH2: 250). Equally important with it comes a suggested

---

[16] Drake/Mather (168n200): "The jealousies between the heads of the different colonies came near [to] destroying them all; and the man whom History may decide saved them all was the founder of that colony hated by them all."

plan of attack, "straight" from Sachem Miantonomo---one of the leading local experts in New World warfare.

This is how Williams' map looks in the hands of Mason and Underhill. It offers no scale but incorrectly suggests that these rivers and places are evenly-spaced along the coast. The dotted lines are rivers that empty (southward) into the Atlantic Ocean "at left." The Mason/Underhill force will sail east from Saybrook ("above" the top line) to Narragansett ("below" the bottom line), and then march back west overland to their target.

***

River Qunnihticut [Connecticut]

----

*a fort of the [West] Nayantaquit men, confederate with the Pequots

Mohiganic River [the Pequot River, later the Thames]

----

*Weinshauks, where Sassacus the chief Sachem is

//////// Ohomowauke, the swamp, 3 or 4 miles from

*Mystic, where is Mamoho, another chief [Pequot] Sachem

[Mystic or Missituc] River

*Nayantaquit [E. Niantic], where is Wepiteammock and our friends

***

Like Mason with this in our hands, we gain little idea of actual distances, conditions, trails, or especially the *scale* of what this company aims to do in an inhabited and "hostile" country never seen before. It leaves out the Pawcatuck River frontier (between E. Niantic and Pequot Mystic), a place of no small fear for their allies. But we do see two Pequot strong-points: Sassacus' village

Weinshauks, and Mystic. Since the murder of Sachem Tatobem (Chronology), Mystic's Sachem is a man called Mamoho.

We don't know how this suggested plan for attack moves from its recipient Governor Winthrop to the Saybrook captains. The obvious answers, intercolonial sharing of intelligence and plans, may develop problems as this journey unfolds and the captains reveal their opinion of both information and orders. Here is what Roger Williams, more seasoned than either Mason or Underhill, tells them to do (WCL1: 72-3):

> ...To do execution to purpose on the Pequots will require...a riding by it [the unspecified target]...a falling off and a retreat, as if you were departed, and a falling on again within three or four days, when they are returned again to their houses securely from their flight.
>
> If any [English] pinnaces come in ken, they presently prepare for flight, women and old men and children, to a swamp some 3 or 4 miles on the back of them; a marvelous great and secure swamp...called Ohomowauke...Owl's Nest; or Cuppacommock...a refuge or hiding place....
>
> The assault would be in the night, when they are commonly more secure and at home; by which advantage the English, being armed [wearing body-armor] may enter the houses and do what execution they please.
>
> Before the assault be given, an ambush [must] be laid behind them, between them and the swamp, to prevent their flight.
>
> ...It would be pleasing to all natives that women and children be spared, etc.

Four things are essential to English victory. First they must show themselves (to the enemy unquestionably watching) as they leave the Weinshauks region with its waiting braves, and Mystic country too. Second, they must return and attack the still-unnamed target at night---though the given plan itself does not specify whether to make this surprise-return *by land or by sea*; and this will have crucial consequences. Third, the English soldiers are told that their weapons and body-armor will make the saving difference in hand-to-hand fighting. Fourth but not least, the English must set an ambush "behind" the unnamed target before they attack. This is a mobile enemy.[17]

Of the two possible targets in this intelligence, Mystic is the first enroute; the one described as a place of women, old men and children; and has the "marvelous great and secure" refuge of nearby swamp. This is just the first leak from between documentary lines that Mason and Underhill know, already at Saybrook, that they are not going to obey their commission, and know which fort their target is---not Weinshauks with its blood-defiant fighting men, but Mystic.

The more the captains abandon Miantonomo's plan, the more they will fail in their purposes.

Before we set sail, consider the "forts" on both sides of this war. "There is a general lack of archaeological evidence concerning the existence of [Native] fortified villages in the 16th and early 17th centuries in New England," writes Peter Thomas (136). Comparisons with peoples of the Hudson River watershed suggest that

---

[17] We encourage you to remember Miantonomo's instructions as carefully as our captains should. Miantonomo is a winner in the Native American world of war, and "they pass not a week without some skirmishes, though hitherto with little loss on either side" (WCL1: 72). And yet, be doubly careful with this intelligence, because Miantonomo gives it all to Williams while "keeping his barbarous court at my [Providence] house....He takes some pleasure to visit me." We will find Miantonomo no man to miss such attitudes, least of all from an exiled squatter on his lands.

"internecine warfare was a factor of life [there] by A.D. 1300," although "its causes are open to debate." Thomas notes that this "doesn't speak for New England"; and that "Mohawk raids occur in eastern Massachusetts" by the 1620s, "and perhaps before."

As other experts from Bragdon (51) to Salwen (167) and Bradley agree, Native New England's forts emerge on the land from a norm of ancient hunting-camps and "open" villages during the same generations that begin steady trade with transatlantic Europeans. Blankets and clothes, "bright objects," strong tools, exotic goods have practical and symbolic (social status) value in the fur-trade. But over time, New England's Native "royal" blood-lines begin to displace its more egalitarian social norms. Some of the powerful clans of families perhaps begin to reach for too much.

Some Sachems begin to offend against well-documented mores opposed to personal hoards of food or wealth (Simmons "Shamanism"). Instead of redistributing wealth in food and the fine goods got with it, the Sachems keep more to their own uses, buy more "false influence" through the control of novel goods. People being people, corruption arouses resentment, and violence.

Sassacus' Weinshauks and Mamoho's Mystic are the biggest palisaded villages in the region just now (Ch. 3). We've seen that resentment is a problem to Sassacus' dominion. What, then, is a Native fort for?

In Native New England warfare, with its familiar rules against killing anybody but enemy braves, a fort is where you keep women and children and those valuable stores from being "adopted" by your enemy's tribe. The braves fight it out to "little harm" outside. If you need a fort at all, it's because your Native enemies know where you hide in your territory's swamps. A fort, if your enemy has time, numbers and will, can trap you. A swamp is better than a fort because it's full of further options.

Most scholars, Hirsch for example, do not ask the English reasons for building forts in New England. Hirsch provides a useful summary of tradition (1188) that begins in all of 1620. "William Bradford fretted that his Pilgrim community" at Plimoth was "in continual danger of 'the savage people.' Puritan leaders at Massachusetts Bay soon echoed his fears. New England, then, promised to be a spiritual haven, not a terrestrial one. To survive and prosper in a hostile wilderness, the 'City Upon A Hill' had to be fortified with ugly parapets and ramparts."

Had to be? In an historically-accurate context that needs to begin at least 100 years before 1620, this fatalism falls apart almost as fast as traditional ideas of Myles Standish, John Endecott, and Underhill as "training experts" at "Indian war." Until the decade just before The Pilgrims' arrival, most contacts across the Atlantic were multilingual, multisided affairs of trade and other relations that often resulted in "revels," cohabitations and children, in camps where peoples richly mixed it up. (These activities persisted into "Pilgrim times" at Morton's unfortified "Merrymount," the liveliest and first rival destroyed by Boston in 1630.) Of the earliest English forts here---at Sagadahoc in Maine and on Cuttyhunk Island---the former was starved out by once-helpful but insulted Abenakis, and the latter built before it was known to be unnecessary.

Even though The Pilgrims arrived at the end of a New England decade strained by epidemics and increased transatlantic violence, they began hopefully as traders and diplomats: it was the building of their fort and palisade that most helped their relations with Native Americans to fail. Once tangled in their own mistakes, they jumped to the point of "preemptively" murdering kinsmen of the people who saved their lives. Trade died. Fortification served worse than no purpose: it starved Plimoth of the personal relations that, here, had long policed the problems of frontier exchange.

If people are people, injustice and arrogance make ugly those cities on their hills. Hirsch attempts a multicultural analysis but keeps it under control. He does mention greed, domination preferred over equality, and needless terror grown in isolation.

What we learn is that here the use of a fort in war is one option. Your enemy may not know every "hide" you have in your swamps. To the English, war is different. They have "visions of genteel combat" and "rules and customs governing every detail of the practice." Their "experts" bestow "a military system rooted in European tradition" (Hirsch 1209, 1188). To them, a fort is like a city: it's where you stay, mass resources, and fight it out against massed Turks. Outside your city or fort (ideally the same), Europe's horses will run you down, for one problem. It's still very Homeric.

Now we can see as Saybrook does. Gardener the Master Of Works" within European traditions, as well as the less-experienced captains, are looking for a European target. A city, that is, or a citadel, a fortified concentration crowded with the enemy, which (like a city of The Hundred or Thirty Years War, and other laboratories of "modern total war") can perhaps be surprised, surrounded, besieged, penetrated, fought over, captured, "depopulated" and destroyed as a token of utter conquest.[18]

---

[18] Cave 154: Underhill judges "Indian warriors" by "European standards" and so does not "comprehend" them. If so, neither captain can comprehend this war. Underhill has one known experience before this, on Block Island (U51): "they break up into small bodies [of braves]," he discovers, "so that we are forced to neglect our usual way, and to subdivide our divisions to answer theirs." Why does he not speak up at Saybrook? If this is learned only later at Mystic, then the Saybrook war-council arrives at little on which to risk so many lives. If the English ignore such "complications" or prefer their own ways, that has consequences. See Dyer, Leach and Malone on both sides' war traditions.

The English are on the wrong continent for the fight they want. At least until "Philip's War" in the 1670s, open march to a stationary "siege" is more than rare in Native New Englanders' tactical repertoire. To the last moments of the "massacre" at Weymouth in 1623, Plimoth's Captain Standish and men find they cannot "get many of them together at once": they need pretense of a feast to trap their targets in a block-house (Dempsey *News* lxvii-lxxi). Only then can they lay hands upon warriors who use the forests and the landscape's secrets to maximum advantage; who prefer to fight and take cover not in village-forts, but in swamps.

Whether they know it or not, the captains face another crucial problem of intelligence. Williams adds in another missive (*Correspondence* 1: 78-9) the precise plan Miantonomo had in mind; that they move their forces including his own Narragansett braves *by boat* to Pequot country and, as part of a sudden attack, "lay ambush" between those two chief Pequot forts. In classic Native "roving battle" fashion, the English can then "intercept" the main force of Pequot braves. As the captains are about to discover, a sudden approach by sea might make all the difference; but this is not what they decide to do.

Gardener "dislikes" the prospect of a large-scale running fight (he tells why in Ch. 4); and Mason and Underhill will show themselves also disinclined to such "open field" combat.

"At last," Gardener says, "we old soldiers agree...about the way and act" (G136). Sensible men, they want to know the enemy and the target before they embark. But we are sensible too. Unless we know of Roger Williams and his services, we cannot leave Saybrook's war-council knowing either. Williams' crucial help seems not to be in play. Instead, Mason and Underhill describe a pilgrim's progress complete with tactical guidance from The Lord.

Historian Vaughan catches "striking resemblance" between the Native and English plans, but moves on (374n45).

If this plan of attack comes instead from Uncas, why does Mason his "great friend" not acknowledge it, along with Uncas' other supposedly-vital assistances? It is not possible that Uncas himself, born to the country of Weinshauks, believes that "By Narragansett we should come upon [the Pequots'] backs," as Mason hopes. In New England, Native forts and their inhabitants do not face only one direction, like a city with a curtain-wall. "Possibly we might surprise them unawares," says Mason, apparently never consulting his chief Mohegan guide. "At worst we should be on firm land as well as they" (M21).[19]

We do not learn from either captain of their coming council with Miantonomo himself as to "what way they should go to work" (V102). Instead, Mason and Underhill write so that we believe they simply embark and learn from the hand of God. That only upon their crossing the Pawcatuck River into Pequot territory (below) do their guides inform them that "the enemy has two forts" ahead at Mystic and Weinshauks, "almost impregnable." At this, the English supposedly grow "not at all discouraged, but rather animated...so much that we were resolved to assault both their forts at once" (M26). The very idea will prove a fantasy.

---

[19] The next chapters add, to this growing tangle of unlikelihoods, the captains' belief that their plan, "crossing their expectation, breeds in [the Pequots] a security....[They] know nothing of our coming" (U77-8). Mason's/Underhill's concealment of the Williams/Miantonomo plan resembles the English colonies' power-struggles, which we are warned not to underestimate (Vaughan 376n62). Mason (Connecticut) and Underhill (Saybrook Company) want to give Mass. Bay---even through outcast Williams---as little credit as possible for their "victory"; much less to Miantonomo.

What, then, is decided at Saybrook among the "old soldiers"? We have another hint dropped by Mason amid his description of the Mystic "massacre": "We had formerly concluded to destroy them by the sword and save the plunder" (M28). But that is all their narrative reveals about a plan. Destroy them where? How?

If these men are intent on victory, as cautious as their concerns reveal, and this dubious of their Mohegan allies and other guides (below), how can they head off into this enormous country with such friends and plans? Their intent to accomplish a genocidal massacre is not, here, the point. (It animates Jennings and Cave, 218-221 and 209n47). At Saybrook, Mason and Underhill begin to whistle in the dark and sow the wind. They'll show us this.

And here, Lieftenant Gardener declines the whole "enterprise." Later he sees himself a "splinter" to his fellows---Is he chafing to get rid of them as loose cannons, like unhelpful Endecott? His refusal is significant and silent as can be between the captains' lines. Mather simply makes it up that Gardener "readily accepts" the plan (122). Trained by mercenary service in Holland (G122), seasoned by hand-to-hand fighting here, Gardener is no coward. He knows that war is best won far from home. Nor is he a fool. He doubts that Mason's company can do what it wants to do, and he's not going. He contributes a likely 4 of Saybrook's soldiers, adds his later-unwilling "chirurgeon" Mr. Pell; but Gardener holds to his commission. He will not go.[20]

---

[20] Months ago (G133) Gardener has "sent up letters to Connecticut, what I heard, and what I thought, and how to prevent [the Pequots'] threatened danger; and received back again rather a scoff than any thanks for my care and pains." Before long his chirurgeon Pell responds with prudent hold on their contracts: "only... drawing, ordering, and making of a city, towns or forts of defense" (G122).

The captains don't seem to feel they can turn to Uncas or his braves with crucial questions. The result is more disadvantage. In some way they know it, too; for suddenly, Mason (M22) and Underhill seek out more mystic confirmation:

> But Captain Mason apprehending an exceeding
> great hazard in so doing [as their commission orders]...
> [he] does earnestly desire Mr. Stone that he would com-
> mend our condition to The Lord, that night, to direct how
> and in what manner we should demean ourselves in that
> respect [*i.e.,* how to attack the Pequots]....In the morning
> very early Mr. Stone comes [back] ashore...and tells
> [Mason] he...is fully satisfied to sail for Narragansett. Our
> council is then called, and the several reasons alledged. In
> fine we all agree with one accord to sail for Narragansett....

Mason and Underhill pack their three boats with 95 Englishmen and 60-80 Mohegan braves. Jennings alone finds it ludicrous that men of war "even then" would stake their lives on so thin a battle-plan because of a minister's prayer. Cave disagrees and sees "nothing exceptional" in a minister's being asked to pray and "bless" such a plan (210n47). He may be right. To support his point, Cave notes Stone's previous prayer to God for Mohegan loyalty.

Does "God" know Uncas and these Mohegan braves? Does The Bible? Right-as-rain Master Stone? Private prayer certifies nothing about Mohegans who certainly can (in Stone's words) "pretend loyalty." How does one willfully ethnocentric tactical move turn another one into strategy worth your life? What lessons will war-leaders take from this? This is indeed Puritan military history, and mystic foundation for more.[21]

---

[21] As noted (see O'Brien/Jennings 23, 58, 79), Mystic's Algonquian name is *Missituc* for its "great tidal river." The OED defines a "mystic" as one who sees

The captains turn from Gardener and launch themselves, mostly ignorant of the country, with allies uncertain, a target and enemy they can't identify. Their fitness is doubted by the leaders who hurried them to action, doubted and refused by the country's one seasoned captain. They need indeed what standing tradition calls "a generous assist from fortune" (Vaughan 88). "The settlers' evolutions, however impractical, must have made for a brilliant spectacle" (Hirsch 1190).

Their holds this empty, buoyed with hope, the hallowed English set bold sail.

---

the world as "spiritually allegorical or symbolical"; who "maintains the validity and supreme importance of mystical theology...who believes in the possibility of the spiritual apprehension of truths...inaccessible to the understanding."
Jennings was first to scrutinize. A note to Mason (M22) suggests the calibre of previous interest: "Mr. J.H. Bromley, in his *Oration on John Mason*, suggests that 'Mason, though a profoundly religious man, had the worldly wisdom to give Mr. Stone such knowledge of the facts as to be able to lay them intelligently before The Lord.'" This almost equals Underhill, who says "God was pleased, out of his love, to carry things in such a sweet, moderate way as all turned to his glory, and his people's good" (U69). Both captains' editor Orr remarks that "the impatience of Mason...had it not resulted favorably, would seem little short of foolhardy. But...the success of the expedition...made him without question the hero of the war and placed him on the roll of New England's great men" (xix). Perhaps Mass. Bay's Rev. Higginson can help explain the captains' thinking. "We have great ordnance," he writes in 1630. "But...our greatest comfort is we have plenty of preaching, and diligent catechizing, with strict and careful exercise, and good and commendable orders to bring our people into a Christian conversation with whom we have to deal withall....If God be with us, who can be against us?" (rpt. Force ed., *Tracts* 3: 14). Yet, 40 years later even "Christianized Indians" vehement in their new faith will be "dismissed as hypocrites" (Slotkin *Judgment* 367n16).

MASON DISOBEYS HIS COMMISSION BYPASSING THE PEQUOT RIVER "OUR COMMISSION LIMITING US TO LAND OUR MEN IN PEQUOT RIVER; WE HAD ALSO THE SAME ORDER BY LETTER OF INSTRUCTION SENT US TO SAYBROOK."

MASON, FRIDAY MAY 19, 1637

2

Getting There Is Half (Somebody's) Fun

"**O**n Friday morning we set sail for Narragansett Bay," Captain Mason notes (M23). The voyage will take all day and night, plus the next day till "evening." Their shallop, pinnace and pink steer inside the serpentine shores of Fisher's Island and fly their best canvas, with flags and ensigns bright in May sunshine. At twilight, the English may even light lamps and sing their Old Testament psalms as they sail the darkening coast of Connecticut. They mean, at this point, to be observed.

Captain Underhill is confident they are "deluding the Pequots thereby" (U77). Their enemy expects to meet them in battle on the Pequot River, near Sassacus' fort and chief village Weinshauks. But neither captain tells how he knows this. Why don't Mason and Underhill---the only two eyewitness chroniclers of Mystic---share the oath from Pequot braves to leave their bones defiant on the battlefield? In Native New England, "emphaticall speech" to enemies before combat is old tradition (Bragdon). Direct challenge from a "heathen" Great Sachem like Sassacus would add color and credibility to the captains' chronicles (it sold books for John Smith). It would also oblige them in the reader's eyes to manage a meeting with Sassacus' hundreds of braves.

Why then do we know only from *Plimoth's* Edward Winslow of Sassacus' words, which produce the English plan of attack? Perhaps it's Uncas who confides what Sassacus, in *his* military tradition, will expect. After all, Sassacus knows a state of war exists, and Uncas knows his Pequot wife's brother. Because the captains are writing military history---how to prevail against an enemy in this time and place---they could teach their readers at least how they manage or "tame" a serviceable ally like Uncas. Clear complete presentation of a situation, the reasons for strategies and tactics are the life-and-death value of military education.

It is not clear how formal the captains' training as soldiers. Both use The Bible's Old Testament (if not Thucydides or Caesar) as authority for the morality, tactical wisdom, and political sense of the actions performed toward their Mystic end. Unfortunately for them, The Bible is one more "European" source that knows nothing about America. Its signifiers, shaped millennia ago by peoples half a world away, have no "natural" American referents. Whatever The Bible can offer to their actions and story, it must be imposed, for nothing between its covers has anything to do with this place. Indeed The Bible is "deranged" by its driving code of "separation" from the contexts, cultures and histories of its own origins in Canaan (Herzog). It is not designed to produce accurate ideas of "cultural others," and victories are rare without sharp intelligence.

Deeds performed "according to" The Bible can make part of the American world seem like a Bible-scenario come true, as long as the people in action believe a Biblical understanding of America. But outside such a circle of believers, the world is the world. It is not necessarily "hostile wilderness." America in fact may be a place of many circles, in which the majority do not forbid, demonize, or exterminate others in order to feel confirmed in their identities.

If Mason and Underhill follow The Bible, they will not find their way in America. More, if historians after them (like Hirsch above) follow the same lines and limits in their analysis of these events, they will not understand what happened. For 17th-century New England does not work according to wishes. "Beliefs" do not "reform" all other realities. A culture's people have the right to limit themselves, but to limit others is to invite disappointment. A monological approach to a complicated, multicultural place becomes derangement (Ch. 4). We must not approach this world with only the captains' assumptions. We watch them follow their secret map but it is not the territory. The Pequots are not Philistines or Canaanites.[22]

The most successful English-colonial war leader, Captain Benjamin Church of 1675's "Philip's War," has no military schooling (except every day from Native Americans), and no religious agenda. The main accomplishment of his narrative is what it teaches his readers of tactics wise and foolish. As Slotkin details (*Regeneration Through Violence*), it is no accident that Church's adoption of "Indian" war-tactics becomes the frontier-English standard, his book the most "cockalorum" sensible of its genre.

---

[22] Mather (in Slotkin ed. *Judgment*, 188): "Remember the errand that our Fathers came into this Wilderness for, and pursue that Interest. In general, it was on the account of Religion....It was with respect to some worldly accomodation that other Plantations were erected, but Religion and not the World was that which our Fathers came here for...so they might worship God according to his Will... according to the pattern shewed in the Mount. Pure Worship and Ordinances without the mixture of human Inventions....We are the children of the good old Nonconformists....Rulers should be men that fear God, and they that choose them...and Laws in the Commonwealth should be regulated by the Word of God, that the Lord Jesus may reign there...."

Church brings "victory" because he has come to better terms with American realities by observation and open-minded experiment.

Captain Mason half-honors the standards for worthwhile histories of war: he does list "reasons" for this long-way-around approach to an unspecified battle-location. He does not list the reasons that may "trouble" us (M22). Perhaps Mason cannot seem to offer himself as an example that includes questionable decisions to learn from, as well as wisdom. But neither captain intimates the source of their battle-plan's first assumption, though it generates their very idea of this surprise against Sassacus' "expectation," the attack on his Pequot people "from the rear."

Whether the Pequots have a "rear" does not seem to trouble anybody, though it too is a problem that will not die of neglect.

To port as they sail their crowded vessels, the Englishmen and Mohegans with Uncas watch thirty miles of May-green forested hills, "champion lands" and swamps of the Pequot country pass their view. The season's enormous rosebay-rhododendrons dot the land with islands of sweet white blossoms. River by river-mouth, they are crossing inhabited, named frontiers: first beyond the Connecticut's tidewaters, then the river of the Western Niantics, then the Pequot River itself, where Weinshauks awaits them. In time they cross the Mystic, where they may know of the "lesser" Pequot Sachem Mamoho, now in power at its hilltop village and fort. "The hill is commanding and beautiful though not steep": "Sassacus has this fort in the eastern part of his dominions to look after the Narragansetts" (W. Williams in Orr 118).[23]

---

[23] Of Mystic, Prince writes (Introduction to Gardener 118) that "The whole of the shore of Mystic River, which is about six or seven miles from what is called head of Mystic, to its mouth, and particularly the west side, is rough, rugged, and rocky, but particularly pleasant, and filled [in Prince's day] with dwellings wherever they can be placed." Since the later dwellings belonged "chiefly [to]

The captains gaze on the land, and see how little Williams' map really tells. *Look after* is an apt phrase for the complexities of Native-frontier relationships. Mystic Fort is a Pequot listening-post and base for scouts against raiding-parties of Eastern Niantics and/or Narragansetts, and the launch-point of Pequot retaliations. More commonly, because feud itself is the exception to many kinds of social and cultural intercourse, Mystic Village and Fort are also a thoroughly-connected source and destination of intertribal trade, political diplomacy and personal travel. It is a given of these cultures that bonds among peoples require regular maintenance. In short, this region is anything but what James Axtell ironically called "darkest Connecticut."

As we'll see, once the Englishmen's Native guides cross the Pawcatuck River with the force heading "back" west, they are sure to the point of terror that they are in Pequot territory. So, as Mason's and Underhill's vessels now slide eastward beyond the Pawcatuck and into Niantic/Narragansett country, with its Great Swamp wrapped in green old-growth forest, they have been counting on much more than "the least notice" in "so populous a country" (M45). Their plan depends upon it.

"I still remember a speech of [Reverend] Hooker at our going aboard" back at Hartford, Mason recalls (M45): "that they should be bread for us." "Then was our mouth filled with laughter, and

---

sailors and seamen," it is likely that Native Americans knew it too as a place to land boats. "There is a pretty meeting-house among the rocks." Prince adds that "the river is at the bottom of the [Mystic Fort] hill, less than half a mile [from the hill's foot]...and [the fort is] perhaps three miles from...where the small streams that form the river meet the tidewater....Porter's Rocks, where Captain Mason lodged [the night before the Mystic attack, below], are...perhaps two miles above [north of] the site of the fort."

our tongues with singing." However high the English spirits on-ship, these mostly-untried soldiers must be taking the measure of Sassacus as they behold the two days' sailing-expanse of Pequot lands and his "dominion."[24]

No minor player, even if 77 years old, can hold 26 villages tributary to his influence (McBride 103, for ex.), and to his own dispensations of justice. Native people as far as Wethersfield still turn to Sassacus in appeal, and he responds in force. His powers of war still have a terrifying reputation. Most people believe that Pequot braves make war as "savagely" as their north-country relatives and still-active allies, the "Man Eater" Mohicans and Mohawks (Chronology; Frazier 4-5; Williams in WPF3: 446).

But this dominion is coming apart not only under the stress of English and Dutch challenge. Sassacus is beleaguered, as Uncas' Mohegans have (it seems) withdrawn their allegiance. At least one other sagamore, Western Niantic Sassious, already (July 1636) feels free or frightened enough to "give" his loyalty to Saybrook.[25]

---

[24] DeForest suggests "very sparse" populations (59) after noting better data that "Nowhere was the aboriginal population so dense as along the seashore" and "the courses of the rivers" (47). The norm between both enemies and relatives is to keep informed of each other's affairs. When an English boy is lost in the forest near Plimoth (see Dempsey *News* n31), he is quickly found by Native men near Manomet (FBH1: 124), taken to Nauset on lower Cape Cod (Mourt 69), and reported at Massasoit at Sowams. Epidemics c. 1616-18 also traveled thus.

[25] When the shooting starts, though, Sassious' Western Niantics return to the Pequot fold. This is also why the "Indians" killed by Uncas in Ch. 1 are actually Sassious' men, not Sassacus'. The Niantics' behavior, a 1636 promise of loyalty broken by this story's time, is why Gardener calls only the dismembered prisoner Siswas "a traitor" (G136). Sassacus' Pequots had never promised Gardener anything. "Sassious...is chief actor of treachery and villainy against us" (WPF3: 381-2).

Faced with this situation, Sassacus has taken skilled diplomatic steps toward Mass. Bay Boston and his long-traditional enemy Narragansetts.[26] But maybe all these respond most now to the scent of blood. Sassacus' "master-stroke" treaty with Boston crumbles too, in two tense years of conflict over the meaning of its terms ("we could not make them understand," WJH1: 199, DeForest 104; and neither can the Pequots "make" Boston). The Narragansetts, meanwhile, are cool toward Sassacus' overtures of new alliance, wary of their own safety within such reach of the English. The truth behind Sassacus' appeal---that the Narragansetts will be next if they cooperate---is too much to be believed (G6; FBH2: 247), and Williams' speeches tip the balance. In time, Miantonomo will see that Sassacus was right and make the same appeal for help from other tribes (Ch. 5).

Aware of the territories passing by, and knowing that the enemy's "numbers far exceed...ours" (M21), the English sail on. The land's enormity, its unknown rivers and hidden valleys, its sheer populated space shows these three little boats what they have set out to do. Misquamicut's dead-end spits of white sand reach out ahead after Fisher's Island: the tidal countries of Weekapaug, Quinochontaug, Matanuck slide by, places named because people(s) spend time there. The farther east they voyage along the coast, the more they feel themselves among more-trustworthy Native friends, and victory seems a palpable possibility.

Mason feels the weight across his shoulders. "The serious and speedy prosecution of this war [may] be the greatest business New

---

[26] Jennings 199-201: "The [1634] treaty was a master stroke of Pequot diplomacy, recognizing the realities of power, retreating from untenable positions, and removing foreseeable causes of war. Ironically, however, its very existence... accelerated a [colonial] competition...in which neither colony could succeed without first reducing the Pequots to overt subjection."

England has; for it cannot be conceived that building, planting, fishing, trading, colleges, etc.---or in a word, the good of either Church or Commonwealth can flourish and go forward, without a timely removing and preventing the wars that now begin" (WPF3: 406). This is on top of the colonies' "civil (nay, worse, and religious) dissensions, abounding at home." Soon, Anne Hutchinson will be Roger Williams' neighbor in exile. Everybody is counting on these three boats: first the "Indians," then the heretics.

"And thus," Mason sings, "when The Lord turns the captivity of his people, and turns the Wheel upon their enemies, we are like men in a dream....The Lord doth great things for us among the Heathen, whereof we are glad. Praise ye The Lord!" (M45).[27]

---

[27] Mason and his editors make almost subliminal moves to reinforce his credibility: this note presents the first of them (M22-3). Mason takes pains to remind us that his departure from instructions is not "to encourage any soldiers to act beyond their commission, for in so doing they run a double hazard." To this he appends no *self*-critique, but a tale of an apocryphal "great commander in Belgia...Grubbendunk"; who "going beyond his commission lost his life." With "all" this, Mason concludes for us that "the more an enterprise is dissembled and kept secret, the more [difficult] to put in execution." Then he blurs the question with a "proverb" that contradicts his tale but supports his action; that "The farthest way about is sometimes the nearest way home." "For it is not possible for the wisest and ablest Senator to foresee all accidents and occurrents that fall out in...pursuit of a war." Clearly, the "accidents" that decide this plan of attack are the ones (given in no account) that Mason calls "troubling" and leaves out. Why? He knows he has concealed the fundamentals of a military history: what the target is and why. What to do? Mason shrugs off "analysis" and presses on with action, smoothing over the clumsy disjunctures above with mystic rhetoric. It is the emblematic gesture in all these texts. "What shall I say? God led his people through many difficulties and turnings; yet by more than an ordinary hand of Providence he brought them to Canaan at last." Next sentence: "On Friday morning we set sail...." So much for Mason's "plain, honest, blunt, unaffected, forthright, rough, simple, modest, frank" style (Prince in Orr xx).

By Saturday the English vessels are past the Eastern Niantic country of Sachem Ninigret (below). After 20 more miles, they round the southwestern cape of Narragansett Bay and heave anchor offshore from the village of Miantonomo. They do not, however, land that evening, though they believe "Love" exists "betwixt" their peoples (M23). The Narragansetts "well know...that the Pequots and themselves are enemies."

Instead, the English spend the night and the whole next day floating offshore, because it is "the Sabbath." Then, on Monday, the wind "blows so hard...that we cannot go on shore, as also on Tuesday until sunset." Their struggling boats are watched the whole time from the Narragansetts' chief palisaded village, as well as from its typical surround of fishing-spots, work-sites, lodges and *wetus* (family dwellings). Offshore in one place for nearly three days, bristling with weapons and perhaps even loud with song and prayer, the English can have no idea whether anybody is sent, or quietly departs, from Narragansett with news of ships and soldiers on the prowl.

There is enough time, between the Narragansetts' first sight of these ships and their landing, for a trusty runner *to go and ask Sassacus himself* what to do about these aggressive outsiders with their already-dangerous reputation. Roger Williams has to work against something between these Native peoples and his word is nothing final. The captains on ship don't seem to know enough to address the matter. Historians do, and don't.[28]

---

[28] The old and then-emergent traditions of military history-writing help us to understand both these Puritan planters in their own time and the critics after them. J. R. Hale (4) relates that "War has become more truly an international form of culture than...even in the age of chivalry." "Writers on military affairs and most educated soldiers share a common respect for the military prowess and skill of [pre-Christian] antiquity, and nearly all subscribe to a common ideal, that

Lt. Gardner's chirurgeon Mr. Pell declines to continue
on Mason's and Underhill's overland march into Pequot territory.

Minantonimo

But Gardener's chirurgeon Mr. Pell does. Here, he too declines the budding plan and refuses to leave the queasy safety of a boat for marching all those miles of inhabited forest. Mason's sole phrase about this is sly: Pell is "ordered to stay" at Narragansett (M31), though why an army should leave its one medic far behind is unexplained. Underhill (U82) is more open, angry that Pell is not on hand to care for men "maimed" at Mystic. Still, he tucks Pell's refusal into his pages *after* the attack, while Narragansett is the only point at which Pell could have made this unpopular decision. He is not "accustomed to war, [and] durst not hazard himself where we venture...our lives, but, like a fresh water soldier, keeps aboard."

Not to worry. At sunset on Tuesday, Mason lands first (M23) and marches up to Miantonomo's "chief residence" to explain all this. (For the dimensions and likely location of this very large village see WCL1: 181n1). Mindful of Miantonomo's stature, experience, and power in numbers of braves, Mason requests "only...free passage through his country." Uncas is not much-liked here (WCL1: 121n11). He has sheltered with these cousins in his struggles against Sassacus. In time, Uncas and Miantonomo will become mortal foes.

---

of the learned soldier to whom the pen is almost as manageable as the sword." What such men write is "not confined within the bounds of communities, but...always look[s] outward and [has] special reference to foreigners....*This involves above all the study of oneself*" (emphasis added). "Ethnology now appears beside history as a moral guide" (5): men are learning (again) to judge themselves by their relations with others. And "the sum of all this," Hale adds, is "of the greatest importance for the future: thinking comparatively rather than by analogy" (for example, realizing that Pequots are not "Canaanites"), and observing "in a secular rather than a theological sense"; learning "how to live and think from the world, rather than from The Bible" (6). To regressively ignore this has consequences for both the captains and historical accuracy.

Miantonomo, in his late 30s/early 40s now (Robinson 18, Rubertone 158), is a complex man and, like Uncas, a diplomat and tactician experienced with colonists from Plimoth and Mass. Bay Boston, Connecticut, and the "Rogues' Island" Providence of Williams. Williams' cabin stands on Narragansett ground because of Miantonomo's own need for "insiders" to the plans of the English all around his country. As Williams lets him down, he'll try again with new entangled exiles like Samuel Gorton.

Robinson (15) reviews the records on Mianotonomo, who shares a "joint sachemship" with his older uncle Canonicus, not mentioned in these histories. They describe a man "who could not be trusted" according to Plimoth's Bradford; but also "'a very stern man, and of great stature, of a cruel nature, causing all his... attendants to tremble at his speech.'" "Taken together, these records describe [Miantonomo as] an articulate, intelligent leader considered charismatic by friends and treacherous by enemies....a man who toiled to make comprehensible a world...increasingly complex and uncertain" (17). Indeed. Miantonomo's people suffer "less" than others in the first wave of European diseases (1616-1618); but just this year, the Narragansetts are losing no less than 700 people to a second (WJH1: 147).

Mason's and Underhill's now-94 men come ashore at Tuesday twilight and, with them, Uncas and his 60-80 braves, all of them clearly on an errand of war. Of the four Pequot War chronicles in Orr, only Mason's is eyewitness to what happens from this village onward to Mystic. Underhill says only that "We land our men...and march overland" (U77).

"[Miantonomo] does accept of our coming," Mason reports (M24), "and does also approve of our design; only he thinks our numbers are too weak to deal with the enemy, who are (as he says) very great captains, and men skillful in war."

"He thought our numbers were too weak to deal with the enemy, who were very great captains and men skilled in war. Thus he (Miantomomo) spake somewhat slighting of us."

MASON: TUESDAY MAY 23, 1637

At Narragansett, Sachem Miantonomo (center) learns from Uncas what this company of Englishmen plan to try.

Mason does not linger over this important advice from a Native insider---who, "feud" or not, has almost unquestionably *seen the Pequot forts* ahead. "Thus [Miantonomo] speaks somewhat slighting of us," Mason growls, feeling the Pequots' "exceeding" numbers. Then even Mason cuts to the march begun next morning (M24).

We can learn more about this stay at Narragansett, however, from Philip Vincent.[29] He (V102) reports that indeed, Mason and/or Underhill feel the need for "the advice of the sagamore... what way they should go to work, and how they should fall upon the Pequots." It is the same crucial question the English can't answer at Saybrook.[30]

Miantonomo's answer to the eager but unsure captains is, we suggest, much more than meets the eye. "[His] judgment in all

---

[29] The "orthodox" Reverend Philip Vincent purportedly creates his *True Relation* of the war from both "official" sources (Ch. 4, end) and from conversations with participants at Mystic less exalted than Mason/Underhill (Prince in Orr 90; Cave 211n58). Does that make Vincent's pages more or less reliable as fact? In the end they can be only as reliable as Gardener's: neither of them were there at Mystic. But Vincent clearly has more of a theological/political point of view than Gardener. Vincent (101) matches Gardener's Saybrook scenario adopted here, though Vincent is published and gone for Germany years before Gardener's 1660 writing is available. Vincent's and Underhill's versions are public in speech and print by 1638 (Ch. 4); but only Mason's (treated below) and Underhill's greatly confuse the whole attack's progress begun at Saybrook.

[30] Perhaps Vincent senses the same problem of military history noted above, with which Mason cannot deal. Vincent also may not share the Connecticut aversion to giving any credit to Mass. Bay for the map and attack-plan via Roger Williams. Vincent either invented this question posed to the Sachem in order to address the writing-problem; or he recorded some witness' report of the talk to do likewise. Either way, unlike the other three chronicles, Vincent does point to Miantonomo, upon whose plan Mason and Underhill freely improvise.

things agrees with the English, as though they have consulted together" (V102). Vincent's words suggest that Mason and Underhill *tell* Miantonomo a plan rather than ask for one: to attack "a" palisaded Pequot village full of people.

Their courage under constant tests, the captains cling to an uncertainty. At least "their" plan seems by now their own, "unchanged" as they received it somehow from Williams. But it *has* been changed, by Williams or somebody, after he listened to Miantonomo months ago. The captains accept and plan an overland march, not a sudden seaborne assault; and a siege for trapping and "destroying" many, not an "open field" ambush with its floating porous flanks and fluid interplay. Their plan is now a lamed version of Miantonomo's, the man and expert before their eyes. Does Mason ask, listen? When council adjourns, the Saybrook plan is still the captains' way to victory against so many.

The charismatic Miantonomo makes the captains feel they are completing each other's preformed thoughts. Vincent's language suggests seduction. Miantonomo is no passive, childish, or cowed individual, he knows Mystic and Weinshauks, and he has Pequot cousins. We cannot dismiss his further "irritation" (Cave 145) at Boston's official "No" to his own offer---a *seaborne* ambush against the Pequots (WCL1: 78). Unlike Winthrop after Block Island, these captains seem to trust Miantonomo to really hurt somebody. This Sachem recognizes his own strategy in what the captains propose.

Miantonomo realizes that the English captains, with their preconceptions about a stationary target and a Pequot rear, are taking up exactly the wrong aspects of his own idea. Now, to their faces, he nods and agrees and smiles. Mason and Underhill are delighted. It is not the first or last time an "Indian" pulls this off in "Christian conversation."

Miantonomo, being asked, criticizes only the English lack of numbers (and he proves right). Yet, if he does give the captains' plan wholesale blessing, and sends them confidently after such objectives, he is pointing them directly *away* from the traditions and norms of Native New England war. He approves a design that leads away from where his too-familiar Pequot enemies really will be; away from how he knows they will most likely handle their options---especially with warning of an enemy who does not know their swamps of refuge. Underhill on Block Island noticed how Native people "disappear," "as if they know we are coming" (U51).

Miantonomo has seen them coming. Mason's and Underhill's English company, hoping, singing and praying offshore for mystic miracles, get what they bargain for at Narragansett.[31]

---

[31] Actually things are even worse. By May 8, Williams gave Miantonomo and the Eastern Niantics "notice...of your intentions and preparations" against "the common enemy." Miantonomo's uncle Canonicus was there, "very sour" and threatened to kill even Williams for "sending plague" amongst them (WPF 3: 412). Then, nine days before Mystic (May 17), Winthrop recorded that "Having received intelligence from Miantonomo that the Pequots send their women and children to an island [likely Block or Long Island] for their safety, we presently send away forty men by land to the Narragansetts...there to take in [*sic*] Miantonomo; and he offered to send 16 men with ours; and so, in the night, to set upon [an un-named Pequot target]." The 40 men are Boston's Captain Patrick's, and at Narragansett they take over Mason's boats to later meet---and they believe, "rescue"---Mason and Underhill (Ch. 4). The point is that all this information is flowing *through* Miantonomo's village. "A number of squaws of the Narragansetts are known to keep up intercourse with the Pequots" (DeForest 126). Just as Mason's forces press on, a "runner" of Patrick's catches up to them ("we were informed," M33; WPF3: 421; Jennings 220; Vaughan 374 n45). He asks Mason to wait for the 40 Boston men: they seem to mistrust Mason's plan, for they meet him later with "rumors of a great disaster" (Vaughan 147). Mason, out to win for Connecticut and anxious about "spies," won't wait: "if anything," he takes "quicker action" (Jennings 220). As they forego these added numbers, they

In the morning (Wednesday), the English decide to leave about 15 men with Pell and their boats, reducing their combat-numbers to about 79. They and the Mohegans begin marching westward, back toward the frontier of Pequot territory. Mason must be glad for Uncas now, for in this country of woods, swampy thickets and dead-end peninsulas, if you don't have a trail you have a problem. The men's bandoliers, hung with wooden powder-and-bullet "cartridges," clack and rattle like wind-chimes as they march.

If we follow the captains' accounts of departure, they receive no promised guides or "auxiliaries" from Miantonomo's village. They set out with Uncas' braves across 20 miles of this country "to a place called Niantic," where "another of those Narragansett sachems" lives "in a fort."

His name is Ninigret, "flesh and blood" to Miantonomo through marriage, as usual, to his sister (WCL1: 205n10; WJH2: 99; Drake 67-69). Ninigret, also related to the "hostile" Western Niantics

---

diminish the chance of success. The captains order Patrick to sail their boats down Narragansett Bay at "about midnight, as we are to fall upon the fort [which?] in the morning; so that they might meet us...in the afternoon" (M83).

None of this signifies much control. Each English faction pursues a vague plan created, according to Mason, at Saybrook: in fact it comes from a Pequot kinsman. Since Saybrook Mason has said he won't go near Weinshauks where the Pequot braves are (or were, last week); and yet that place, Pequot (not Mystic) River, is where he tells Patrick to meet him. Compare the "Indian" and English command of intelligence and then review Vaughan's assertion (*Frontier* 135) that there is "no Indian side" to this story, because Mohegan and other Natives are "helping" the English. Are they? Why are he and Cave so sure? Underhill (U67) says that when the Mohegans "earnestly" ask to join, "at least to be under their conduct, that they might revenge themselves" on the Pequots, the Mohegans get only "liberty to follow the [English] company, but not to join in confederation with them." Native men keep promising to be faithful but they never are trusted. So the captains show and tell us.

NINIGRET'S FORT STOOD ON THE EDGE OF PEQUOT TERRITORY, IN PRESENT CHARLESTOWN R.I. MANY OF HIS FOLLOWERS WERE KIN TO THE PEQUOTS, AND FRIENDLY TO SASSACUS. MASON AWARE OF THIS POSTED A GUARD ONLY AFTER HE ARRIVED, AND REMOVED IT AS HE LEFT, ALLOWING NINIGRET TIME BEFORE AND AFTER TO SEND RUNNERS TO WARN SASSACUS.

"WE BEHOLDING THEIR CARRIAGE AND THE FALSEHOOD OF INDIANS, AND FEARING LEAST THEY MIGHT DISCOVER US TO THE ENEMY, ESPECIALLY THEY HAVING MANY TIMES SOME OF THEIR RELATION AMONG THEIR GREATEST FOES, WE CAUSED A STRONG GUARD TO BE SET ABOUT THEIR FORT, GIVING NO CHARGE THAT NO INDIAN SHOULD BE SUFFERED TO PASS IN OR OUT."   MASON: WED, MAY 24, 1637

Captains Mason and Underhill arrive at East Niantic
Sachem Ninigret's village on their march west to Pequot territory.

(DeForest 60), will prove as subtle and "undependable" as any dependably-Native man of the period (Chronology). Has some kind of news already passed through here ahead of the English force? It seems so. Mason's first remark is that "They carry very proudly towards us." Niantic knows something. Its people do not risk "permitting any [English] to come into their fort" (M24).

It's an insulting welcome, in its own world and Europe's too, that the English do not miss. What they do miss, or boldly ignore, is that their response to this cold reception is comically behind the most likely fact---that Miantonomo and Ninigret are keeping even hostile" neighbors informed of everything, before the English can lay eyes on the chance for "treachery." These chronicles are no Puritan allegory of "where we went wrong and how you can do better." The captains seem to expect us to be subject to their own limitations; to wage wars of our own as they wage theirs.

> We beholding their carriage and the falsehood
> of Indians [*sic*], and fearing lest they might discover
> us to the enemy, especially they having many times
> some of their near relations among their greatest foes...
> therefore cause a strong guard to be set about their
> fort, giving charge that no Indian should be suffered to
> pass in or out. We also inform the Indians that none
> of them should stir out of the fort, upon peril of their
> lives. So, as they will not suffer any of us to come into
> their fort, so we will not suffer any of them to go out....
> There we quarter that night, the Indians not offering to
> stir out all the while. (M24)

It's a miracle. Mason's and Underhill's English (and historians after them) assume that nobody Native sees perhaps 80 planter-soldiers march 20 miles into Niantic territory; that Niantic's whole population is inside the palisade and that nobody leaves at their approach, or before they surround it; that the Niantics, like children bowing to obvious righteousness and power, do just as they're told after English departure; and that there is no faster trail to Pequot country than the one the captains discover, a mile at a time, through Uncas.

According to the captains, these Eastern Niantics (like the Narragansetts) offer no assistance to the inadequate force. (Soon they will offer battle to protect "good Pequots" who try to resettle at Pawcatuck, just ahead.) Only "in the morning" do "several" of Miantonomo's men catch up to the column, smiling and "come to assist us in our expedition" (M24). At this, "diverse Indians of that place [East Niantic]" desire to "engage also." And suddenly, these new friends are loud with loyalty-oaths, signs and ceremonies that swear to their aggressive cooperation ahead. One of the captains readily "swears them after his manner upon their knees" (V102). As Mason recalls the moment, the Narragansetts and Niantics "suddenly gather...together into a ring, one by one," and make "solemn protestations how gallantly they will demean themselves, and how many men they will kill" (M25).[32]

For most of them within a few miles of the Pequots' Pawcatuck frontier, the promises prove but a good way to show these English

---

[32] Vincent (V102) does say that Miantonomo "sets forth two or three hundred" braves from there at least to East Niantic, where "two hundred more" [of which tribe?] join up. But as noted, Vincent was not along. Mason does not say that more Narragansetts join them at Niantic "in the morning," but that their arrival emboldens Niantics to join. Vaughan (143; a "specialist," lii) simply poses his assumption, supported nowhere except in a 10-month-old letter, that Miantonomo straightaway "agrees to a request for guides." The authors' photo includes a Rhode Island historical marker to this "unwavering" Native help.

the territorial door. What fighting they do will be seen very inaccurately by the captains as "pastime" (U82).

These 80 Englishmen and their matching number of Mohegans with Uncas are now marching westward not far from the coast of southern New England. It sounds rather simple, but even today with every traveler's resource, the captains' route and destination(s) are not easy to find. The land is thickly wooded, flat between its low hills, streams cut and turn among many small ponds, and all this offers almost no reference-points except sun and, when you can glimpse it, ocean. Off the paths, the land is sheer green tangle, for this region's peoples practice less semi-annual burning of the underbrush: their main food-sources don't require as much as their neighbors'.

Neither captain suggests that they can find their way without help: quite the opposite, and their peers from Winthrop to Mr. Pell know it too. We today also must hunt for it. Neither captain says outright that here or later they acquire more Native guides. What help they might get besides Uncas' amounts only to hopeful names in the letters of Winthrop and Williams, plus one name (and no deeds with it) from Mason below. First in their minds might be the name of the Eastern Niantic "friend" on Williams' sketch-map--- that of Wepiteammock, the Niantics' "number two" Sachem under Ninigret. He is nowhere but on Williams' map till later in the war. This man is called "hostile to Pequots" yet is married to one of their women (WCL1: 120n6; 1: 77n17). Also out of sight is the "number three" Eastern Niantic Sachem Wequashcook (a different fellow than Wequash below). Maybe Wequashcook is not quite old enough to help.[33]

---

[33] Wequashcook is soon Sachem of territories just ahead of the captains, "between Weekapaug Brook and the Pawtucket River." Though Mason later calls

Nor can the captains find a man of record named Soso or Sassawaw. They mention only "one Wequash," as Mason paints him (M27), standing next to Uncas at a critical moment below. Like Soso, Wequash is born a Pequot, "defected" to the Narragansetts and living with them "three or four years." (Cave sees another "unsuccessful contender" against Sassacus, 66.) Wequash, like his people on both sides, "knows every pass and passage" of the country. Before this action by Mason and Underhill, Wequash had been Miantonomo's guide of choice for his own attack on the Pequots. After the action at Mystic, he is suspected of hiding Pequot runaways (WPF3: 450). With such a future inside him, Wequash like the other guides performs no noteworthy Mystic service.[34]

---

him "a sachem as great as any Narragansett," he ranks third under his Eastern Niantic uncle Ninigret and father Wepiteammock (Mason's 1649 letter to The United Colonies qtd. in WCL1:120n6).

[34] Soso is a Pequot, whose story reminds us first of old complicated daily relationships, whose violent exceptions stand out to us as history. Soso also points the fluid nature of Native alliances and loyalties. As Williams says (WPF3: 445), Soso is early-on a sagamore of a Pequot village just ahead on the west bank of the Pawcatuck River, "near Weekapaug" (Salisbury 210). Alienated, like others, from Pequot Sassacus, Soso takes up life among the Narragansetts, and during a feud episode, pretends to renew his Pequot loyalty long enough to turn on a Pequot "captain" and kill him. (Stealth and "roving" action are key to this combat.) The deed makes Soso a "general" and "special darling" of Miantonomo's. But if Soso does march with Mason and other guides Wequash and Uncas, it cannot be easily. By July, Wequash will kill Soso in an unexplained ongoing feud. Soso offers no recorded service as a guide.

A distant fourth helper might be Cutshamekin, brother of Mass. Bay's Chikatawbak. He did guide Endecott's force against Block Island and the coast. Cutshamekin, though, kills "a Pequot" in their territory. Mather (156n29) makes the "radical oversimplification" (ed. Drake) that this causes The Pequot War, which

Wequash

This help, lukewarm if any, leaves Mason's enterprise at the mercy of Uncas.

Not to worry. On "Thursday about eight o'clock in the morning" the English force feels its momentum building. They strike out westward again from Niantic, flanked now by "five hundred" Mohegan, Narragansett and Eastern Niantic warriors (Mason's count M25). The sun shines, and they seem to be *doing* it, finding trails and eager helpers. Unfortunately, the size of their force is a growing liability with each step toward Pequot country. The enemy has no "rear." No matter what these chronicles of real events assume, a Pequot "rear" is a thought only, an assumption inside English heads. According to Native reports, the Pequots are evacuating noncombatants; and they keep as "continual" a watch on the Pawcatuck as on the Pequot River (M21).

Somebody in the vanguard must be guiding the English over tough trail. With less than twelve miles' march some of Mason's men begin to "faint" and "want... provisions" because of "the heat." Perhaps they are overburdened somehow. They carry guns and swords, food and liquid. Each man---Thomas Rumble, Arthur Branch, John Humfrey, Thomas Stanton and more---carries at least a required pound of powder (in Orr x), 20 bullets, and 4 pounds of smaller shot for survival on birds (not to stop an angry man). Somebody carries a keg of gunpowder, another man a drum they can't use in their stealth: both they will leave at their launch-point

---

Vaughan and Hirsch (1203) ratify. Cutshamekin's absence from the Mystic "enterprise" likely means he fears the Pequot kinsmen of his victim. Later, amid the Pequots' apparent rout, he does guide the chase; but his English "readily yield" to his wish to go home, "for the heathen shall not say our dependence is on them" (Stoughton's words, below). *So we look up to God. Cutshamekin will not so much as leave an interpreter"* (WPF3: 444, our emphasis).

ahead, Porter's Rocks, and they'll wish they had the drum as they run out of powder (Ch. 4).

How hot is it? Most "natives" know that oppressive heat is rare to New English May. In this same spell of weather, the morning of Mystic's attack turns so "sharp" that men perhaps-wounded will faint then too. In fact, "body armor" is coming back in use. The days of knights ended when bullets began to pierce their clanking costumes. But breastplates, gorgets, and other steel-pieces are coveted items against the New World's arrows and spears. These mostly-green Englishmen, then, must be very heavily wrapped in thick "buff coats" of leather, some with metal plate sewn in: they are hot to wear in sunshine and cold without it. They carry the weight of their faith in Roger Williams' comforting promise that, in close-quarters fighting (inside a Native lodge, for example), "armored" men can do as they intend and not get hurt. The men wearing the heaviest stuff must be those who know that Williams has never seen combat.

Worden Pond, Pasquiset Pond, Schoolhouse Pond flash bright beyond the trail's two walls of trees, their canopies loud with bluejays and cardinals. This is no afternoon's ramble to the English but a mile-upon-mile march through environments wholly new, and that is no relaxing thing enroute to battle. Uncas and other "Indian" leaders most likely steer north around the swamps of Watchaug Pond; lead across the Wood River, and follow curves of streams southeastward among the low hills, back toward the sea. That at least gives the English some reference-point.

The marchers reach the great north-to-east turn in the banks of the Pawcatuck River. With May's dense foliage and undergrowth, you can see perhaps 20 yards either side of your trail: acres of tall brown cattails make threatening ambush-blinds through which arrows can dart without exposing the archer. Just south, to the

74

MASON'S ILL CONCEIVED PLAN BEGINS TO UNRAVEL DURING HIS SECOND DAYS MARCH: "NAY THOUGH WE KNEW NOT WHERE THE FORTS WERE, HOW FAR IT WAS TO THEM NOR THE WAY THAT LED TO THEM"... "BUT THROUGH THE HEAT OF WEATHER AND WANT OF PROVISIONS SOME OF OUR MEN FAINTED"

MASON THURSDAY MAY 25, 1637

Uncas suggests a brief rest
along the westward march across Connecticutt

company's left, is Misquamicut, Soso's Weekapaug village, with its ties between Pequot and Narragansett. Here, at a shallow ford, "our Indians" warn that Pequots come here to fish; so Mason "stays" his forces "some small time" to look things over (M25).

The pause is costly. The Narragansetts begin to "manifest...great fear, in so much that many of them return" to their homes. How many cannot be determined (one group of 50 leave later, Ch. 4); but these depart with some interesting farewells. They have heard the English "often" tell them "that we come on purpose and are resolved, God assisting, to see the Pequots and to fight with them before we return...though we perish" (M25). Mason says they "frequently despise...us." As "many" Narragansetts abandon the enterprise, they mock the English, saying they "themselves will perform great things," and that the English are scared ("they durst not look upon a Pequot").

Why say such things while turning for home, unless to provoke the English to an even more intense pursuit of their plan? These braves of Miantonomo's moved not a muscle at first and then "caught up" smiling, full of eager empty menace. They are actors as it helps them. Even so, not every brave can let the English and Mohegans out of their sight. They know their guests' "desire...to come upon the enemy suddenly, and undiscovered" (FBH2: 249).

It is neither facetious nor inconsistent with documents to come that, here at the Pawcatuck frontier, no few Native men are leaving for reasons that have nothing to do with history. Many must leave because they have to be home for lunch. Or to help fix up that old dugout boat; or to share a hundred other things of their world more important today. They have no reason, least of all the English plan and hope, to imagine that anything too significant is going to happen across the river except that these clanking English are going to get mauled, grow *matchit hoggery*, and then be very unpleasant company.

Mason himself is shaken---and turns to Uncas, for "what he thought the [remaining] Indians would do" when the fight begins. Uncas delivers apparently unmemorable "expressions and some other speeches of his" (M25); their gist for Mason being that "The Narragansetts would all leave us, but as for himself he would never leave us." Hand over heart, eyes to the sky, as later in Boston (Introduction).[35]

The English press on now, ford the Pawcatuck, and after three more miles of sunny afternoon come "to a field...lately planted with Indian corn." There, they hunker in another watch-post and call council, "supposing we draw near to the enemy."

Now, according to the captains, is when Uncas (or somebody "of the Indians") informs Mason and Underhill that the Pequots have "two forts" ahead, both "almost impregnable" (M26). This council may take place just north of Wequetequock, three or four miles westward after the Pawcatuck River's ford. Well, if the captains

---

[35] Vaughan's version of events forces him to make more of Wequash (144, 325) than he does of Uncas as the guide who brings the English to Mystic "undetected." This is because there is no evidence of Uncas' being helpful except Mason's rhetoric quoted above: as you'll see, the almost "deluded" English must push through Uncas' "help" to find Mystic at all. Drake too (ed. Mather 169n204) notes lack of "credit" to Wequash (since no one can "credit" Uncas) for "this most important service." "Tis true there is no fear of [the Christian] God before their eye," Williams says (WPF3: 451). "All the cords that ever bound the barbarous [Native peoples] to foreigners were made of self and covetousness." "Their treacheries exceed Macchiavelli's." "Though I would not fear a jarr with them, yet I would fend off from being foul, and deal with them wisely, as with wolves endowed with men's brains" (445). Mason and Underhill seem uninterested in estimates from planters with, at least, Williams' experience.

Captain Mason's guides at last inform him--or so we're told--
of the two "impregnable" Pequot forts that lie somewhere ahead.

don't already know this intelligence, what have they told their men enroute, men who surely need the "certainty" of a plan for the task ahead? What do they want their men, and us, to believe?

For all the mysteries at Saybrook, it's here that Vincent reports that "as they march they deliberate which fort of the Pequots they should assault" (V102). But didn't the captains tell Boston's Captain Patrick about "the fort" they had in mind back at Narragansett? If we and they understand this plan, Captain Patrick's men with the boats will be looking for them later at Pequot River. Not at Mystic.

Mason claims that "we are not at all discouraged, but rather animated" by this "Indian" report; such that "we are resolved to assault both their forts at once." With perhaps 80 green frightened men and Mohegan allies, they don't seem to understand, like Miantonomo, what is ahead. And yet in every convenient way, they do. Mason adds,

> ...understanding that one of them [Sassacus' fort at Weinshauks, Pequot River] was so remote that we could not come up with it before midnight, though we marched hard...we were much grieved, chiefly because the greatest and bloodiest Sachem there resided....We were then constrained, being exceedingly spent with our march, with extreme heat and want of necessaries, to accept of [Mystic] the nearest. (M26)

Vincent claims as well that Mason first resolves "upon the great fort" Weinshauks, and to be "there that night." But Mystic, the "necessary" target now, is not "the great fort" of the two in any chronicler's best intelligence. (Mather at least calls Mystic "the nearest," 129.) The one English certainty born of their commission is that Sassacus' warriors "wait" near the real "great fort," on the

Pequot River. A poor certainty it is, obtained days before they left even Saybrook.

If Mason and Underhill had taken Mianotomo's plan seriously, they could attack the war-strength of "both" Pequot villages, but in "open field" ambush. That prospect they do not like. The lack of a responsible plan for "so weighty an enterprise" (U78) wreaks havoc with their histories and ours. Mather comes to their rescue: "In this interim one of...Underhill's soldiers falls lame," and so is not able "to go as far" as Sassacus' fort (171). Mather's editor Drake comes to ours: "If this were true, it would be very remarkable indeed, that through the failure of a single soldier the plan of the campaign is changed."

The English "march...on in a silent manner," and things get worse as the day's sun deserts them. The farther west they venture, "the Indians that remain all fall into the rear...being possessed with great fear" (M26). Or, possessed of caution. The "Indians" at least are not sure where Sassacus' "man-eater" braves are; where in this moonlit forest they may "fall on" the noisy English, and themselves. The enemy unseen is twice as terrifying.[36]

Worse for the captains now is what the land itself tells us, but not them. Wherever they are now, coming west from Wequetequock, they have not yet reached their night-camp at Porter's Rocks. To arrive there, they must first reach the eastern shoreline of the

---

[36] "As allies the Indians were of little service in The Pequot War. Their attitude was one of uncertainty, and so impaired the confidence in them that the soldiers [later] 'had a great itch to fall foul' upon the Narragansetts" (Bradford's editors citing Williams in FBH2: 252). Mather (170) adds that when Mason and company initially decide to attack Sassacus, more Narragansetts flee homeward, "saying that *Sassacus is all one god*, and nobody can kill him." This "makes the English yet more desirous to try what power is in this imaginary god." The Narragansetts go home to report the English "cut off": hence Boston's expectation of disaster.

Mystic River's double-bayed "Head," or Inlet. Mystic Village and Fort will be across or (in their case) around that body of water. They have to follow the long curving shore of the Head's northern end to get to the Mystic Village side, and then march south along that western shore. From there it is about two miles to Mystic Fort.

They have not quite reached that east shore of Mystic Head. The highest hill they may glimpse through the darkening trees is Mystic Hill---actually, a long ridge before them with the Inlet at its feet. Today in your approach, looking ahead west toward the Mystic River, you can see this ridge from Route 1 as your horizon overlooking the town on both banks of the river. It is the first "major" hill you see on this journey.

What neither wearying captain catches, still back here in the wooded twilight, is what Uncas quietly does to their whole expedition on this last leg of the trail.

If you are a Native person with ordinary business at Mystic Fort, from this point you start to turn left (that is, south), away from the course roughly parallel to Route I-95 today, which leads into Mystic's city. Instead, you take that "side road" to your left still there (it's old Route 184), and walk a few miles down to the Mystic's eastern bank. At the riverside, you throw your burdens in a dugout boat and have your nephews paddle you across Mystic Sound, in plain sight of traffic on the Village Hill's upper trails. If your relatives like you, they come down to greet you on the west bank's beach, where they dry fish. That is the easy and so the normal way. Harmless daily traffic is itself a web of watchmen all over Mystic Hill.

In the siting of Mystic, we see that its people already understand: if you come the other way to visit, by land, you might have

Mystic "Head" or the north end of Mystic River Inlet. Mason's company
arrive here to this view, and march to the right, around the Inlet's swampy
northern shoreline. They'll come around to the opposite shore *shown here,*
and after the night at Porter's Rocks, approach Mystic Fort along that side of
the water. When they do, the first hill they see before them
is here at center-left. It is not Mystic Fort Hill.

intentions that don't bear open scrutiny. Mystic is sited to give Pequot people a good first look at any "marching" guests.[37]

That is why Miantonomo's original plan is the one that can, possibly, produce a "massacre" by working (meaning "surprising the enemy") at all. His conception works with the land as it is. It drops seaborne warriors very suddenly on the beach at the west-bank foot of Mystic Hill, the place that in fact least expects daring aggression. The Englishmen's actual last miles of march will show you the crucial differences below.

It is not possible that Uncas does not know the importance of one's approach. Indeed, neither he nor master-planner Miantonomo ever make this difference clear to any Englishman. Instead, Uncas leads on in a way that only he decides.

None of these soldiers have ever been here. To them and their captains "that side-trail to the left" is just another of many that lead to fishing-spots. The company plunges on behind Uncas in darkness, westward with purpose. No "Indian" says a word. With

---

[37] Although Native New England is generally peaceful (compared, for example, to Iroquois country), most "home sites" are "defended" this way by very old tradition. Compare the site of Wapanucket (on the north shore of Assawompsett Pond in Middleboro MA, described by Robbins 4-6): "Obviously the area possesses all of the conditions sought by aboriginals for a place of habitation. Its elevation...provided excellent drainage, the surrounding lowland and swamps offered both security from sudden attack, and cover for wildfowl and mammals. A plentiful supply of drinking water was at hand and a more easily defended position would be difficult to find. The single, narrow, dry land approach corridor [like the one along Mystic Head's shore], with its ready-made watchtower on Willis Hill, ensured easy detection of a hostile intruder. Once warned, the inhabitants...had only to defend a narrow corridor between swamps to the north and south. Except from this one direction all who would enter the area must come across open water and scale a steep bluff, or flounder through swamps and cross sizable streams."

Porter's Rocks, Groton.

North View of Pequot Hill, Groton.

From DeForest *History* (1852: 129-130).
"Pequot Hill" is the site of Sassacus' village called Weinshauks.

a turn of his feet Uncas commits the English to just the approach their enemy prefers. Unless we are better than "ignorant of the country," Uncas takes us in.

Mason and Underhill press on till about "one in the morning," and come up against the east shore of Mystic Head. They have marched a remarkable and difficult distance over days. A full moon rises over the waters before them, and there's a May night-breeze along the dark shore. Where now, Uncas?

If you follow the shoreline's path and road (as you must, there's no hope of a crossing without boats), they bring you along flat splashy swamp-ground to the Head's northern end, where the Mystic River narrows to a much smaller stream. Up that stream to your right, the Pequots have fishing-weirs and other small useful camps. In moonlit darkness the English come around the bright waters, and on the western side arrive at another "little swamp between two hills." Pleased to discover there the bastion-like heights of Porter's Rocks, they climb up into them and at last pitch "our little camp," "much wearied with hard travel [and] keeping great silence."

Their citadel stands not thirty yards within the tree-line on the shore of Mystic Head. Go there and you'll see that 40 men cannot find sleeping-space up top, so many English must lie among the feet of the Rocks, cramped close with "five hundred auxiliaries." As Mason settles down, Uncas (or somebody) reports that they are now "very near the fort" (M26).

It proves true---and yet again, "otherwise." The land shows why in the morning.

As the company "comfortably" rest beneath the night's full moon, Mason sets "guards and...sentinels" at "some distance." These guards, we're told, begin to hear "the enemy singing at the fort"; and the sounds "continue that strain" through the night,

81

"with great insulting and rejoicing." The Pequots, "as we are afterwards informed," are sure there are no English about. They supposedly believe that the sight of Saybrook ships sailing "by them some days before" are the signs of their safety now. Presumably (for the captains), these far-off songs are childishly "private" celebrations; not provocative insults to a nearby foe, that the English are "afraid of them and durst not come near."

When the captains attack tomorrow, they'll discover that these songs reaching only their "some-distance" sentinels originate at the fort "about two miles" to the south. Are their sentinels English, Native, both? How far away from this night-camp's safety will an English planter go with a Mohegan, how close to his "enemies" will a Mohegan go? As a sentinel, neither one is much use even 100 yards away along this forested shoreline. Yet, in coastal Connecticut wilds and champion country, you are not likely to hear singing more than a mile away. You might, with brave stealth and luck, glimpse the glow and spark of a bonfire if a big one is lit for some special doings inside Mystic's palisade. Who then informs Mason of the singing, and what it means? Where is Uncas?

His guiding presence is spectral. Uncas is already the most ambitious, active and versatile Native man of his recorded generation; yet the captains let a passive reader assume that just now, Uncas is lazily lounging, between master's calls, in the darkness down below Porter's Rocks. In fact, this close to Mystic there is almost no limit to what Uncas might be doing with plans of his own. Sent for, Uncas fetches up an Indian Lullaby.

On the edge of his first battle, Mason presents himself as sure he has it right from the guide who this day and more has betrayed the mission. What Mason and most historians hear in the songs is that the naive Pequots of Mystic, with the short attention-span of their race, need to relieve their terror with insults to absent Englishmen,

"The Night proved Comfortable, being clear and Moon Light: We appointed our Sentinels at some distance; who heard the Enemy Singing at the Fort, who continued that Strain until Midnight, with great Insulting and Rejoycing: as we were afterwards informed: They seeing our Pinnaces sail by them some Days before, concluded we were afraid of them and durst not come near them; the Burthen of their Song tending to that purpose."

MASON, THURSDAY MAY 25, 1637

What Mason's "sentries" may have seen (if not heard): night-view from Porter's Rocks, about two miles from Mystic Fort.

and to rejoice in their own fearful reputation; "days after" they see three passing ships, their only criterion of security. Would a young officer trying to learn from this military history wonder if perhaps the singing, and/or Uncas' report ("They think you are gone, they are boasting"), is a Native tactic?

What if the songs mean, *We are leaving this old beloved home?* What if they mean *We can't wait to bust you up?* Like the Narragansetts' tauntings at the Pawcatuck, Uncas' translation of the songs heartens the English on their course. Perhaps he gets down on one knee this time atop the Rocks, and touches Mason's hand to his brow, and promises and everything.

The lullaby works. For at this point, just where we might expect the captains to review and apply their plan, something remarkable happens. We know the English have four main tasks from Williams to accomplish. First, they have "fallen off" the Mystic area and come back, they believe, undetected. Second, they wear the recommended armor; and third, they are now in position to "assault before day" (M26-7).

Do you recall the fourth essential instruction? Neither captain does, and nobody reminds them (not even next day, below). Instead, the Englishmen fall asleep; all of them, deeply, under the trees by the moonshiny waters. We take this lapse as true from Mason and show you why by the next chapter's end. (Underhill simply cuts his chronicle straight from the march to the attack.) In any case, for the balance of the night the Mohegans and other allies see that nothing disturbs English dreams.

Later histories too let us assume that Uncas and all the other "Indians" fall asleep with them; faithful dogs to kick when master wakes up late for work. We sleep as readers in the arms of Uncas.

"In the morning," Mason and the others wake up at Porter's Rocks, and see it "very light," correctly "supposing it...day." In

"In the Morning, we awaking and seeing it very light, supposing it had been day, and so we might have lost our Opportunity, having purposed to make our Assault before Day; rowsed the Men with all expedition." MASON: FRIDAY, MAY 26, 1637

"Quartering the last night's march within two miles of the place, we set forth about one of the clock in the morning, having sufficient intelligence that they knew nothing of our coming." UNDERHILL: FRIDAY, MAY 26, 1637

The challenges of the march from Narragansett take their toll.
Mason's Englishmen fall asleep until daybreak.
Two crucial parts of the necessary plan have been overlooked.

May here, this would be around 5:30 a.m. "We [may] have lost our opportunity," Mason fears. According to expert Miantonomo, yes they have.

Not to worry. Mason casts no glance at Uncas. He rouses his 80 Englishmen "with all expedition," calls for a "brief" prayer for "ourselves and our design to God"; and then he sets his men in motion, "thinking immediately to go to the assault." Underhill: "Drawing near to the fort, we yield up ourselves to God and entreat his assistance in so weighty an enterprise" (U78). They leave their drum and keg of gunpowder here at the Rocks, two miles from battle. Maybe no man dares carry the powder into the range of sixteen Pequot guns.

"The Indians show...a path" that leads, they say, "directly" to Mystic Fort (M27). This can only mean the "path" along the west shore of Mystic Head (see photos), for the approach presents nothing so agreeable, the land at their right (as they march south) climbing more and more steeply up into rugged rocky forest, without a trail and with plenty of points for ambush. About 500 men of war (82 English including the captains, 60-80 Mohegans, "hundreds" of Narragansetts and others) fall in and move "undetected" down this open track between the water at left and the trees at right. But this trail does not "seem" to serve as promised; for the English now encounter another trick of the land in this approach built into the siting of Mystic Fort. You can experience this today.[38]

---

[38] Cave (211n55) notes Underhill's contradiction that the English "set forth [to attack] about one of the clock in the morning" (U78). "As there is no reason for Mason to fabricate a story about oversleeping, I find his account more believable." What about the claim now of "sufficient intelligence" (U78) that the Pequots "know nothing of our coming"?

As the morning of May 26th brightens, Uncas keeps helping the English force around Mystic Head's two bodies of water: the land-approach to Mystic Fort. The captains grow uneasy as waters, land, and Mystic present their features.

Again, Mystic Inlet's northern end, from here looking southwest to show Mason's line of march. He comes around the shore at background right; then along it, with higher rocky ground to the right of the road/path. The *second* half of Mystic Inlet lies far to the "left" and beyond this visible hill, which, as noted, is not the site of Mystic Fort.

Seen from the northern end of Mystic Inlet, here is Mason's line of march (at right) around this bend in the shore. The second or southern bay of Mystic Inlet opens out to the left after this bend. Then, level ground begins to climb toward another very similar hill---Mystic Fort Hill.

Mystic Fort Hill (seen from across the second bay of Mystic Inlet). Mason's company comes from the right (north) along this second bay's shore, and up the sloping hill at center. Mystic Fort is/was on the hill's northeast side; just below the slightly-lower crest of the hill to the lest of center.

As the war-host "holds on our march [for] about two miles" in the rising light of morning, a distinct hill begins to stand out in front of them at right. As they march nearer to it, the English learn that it is not, disappointingly, Mystic Fort Hill. They must want it to be, for a 500-man column feels exposed by this place, feels visible even from across the Mystic's morning-misty waters. But that is not the hill they seek. With Mason they begin "wondering that we came not to the fort, and fearing we might be deluded."

And yet neither captain blames Uncas. This is as-usual negative testimony to his and perhaps other Native leaders' delicate skill in walking a line through the unpredictable English demands, their contempt, and the Native men's own intentions. Uncas keeps to their good side in the midst of armed impatient foreigners bent, "God assisting," on hurting somebody "Indian."

The English follow this narrow corridor of approach with a mile of water on their left. Ahead they find young corn, squash-plants and bean-hills in small clearings as they travel nearer to Mystic. A well-worn path begins to take shape underfoot. A sign of Pequot people! Is that a good thing now in the bright May morning sun? They march Uncas' garden-path. He brings their column around that first disappointing hill, around the bend that has blocked their southward view; and now they behold the "second" or southerly inlet of Mystic Head, nearer the Sound and sea. They stop short.

As you can see today, this whole place before them looks almost exactly like the inlet and surroundings just marched through. Did they make a circle? Have they been here already? They see yet another field of "corn newly planted at the foot of a great hill, supposing the fort was not far off" (M27).

That's Mystic Fort Hill alright. The sun shines down on the land and broad blue bay. But it's leafy May, and they can't see the target for the trees. Are those morning mists or the smokes of campfires floating up yonder below the ridge? The captains are now near the end of patience with Uncas and their guides. They "make a stand," and order "some of the Indians to come up."

"Up" into cleared farming-grounds. Up into the last subtly-guided approach to the Mystic they cannot see. The hill seems, from Mason's position, to have a long crest and a saddle-bow near its middle: that's where Mystic Fort is, on this northeastern face of the great ridge. Up there among old-growth trees, it half-hides within the sag of the saddle-bow's optical illusion. Up there in fact, the ground levels off underfoot in broad spaces, and fresh streams run behind it into the Sound: a good living-place.

Again the captains' call seems to say that neither Uncas nor even "one Wequash" are by their sides. So it is, for "at length" the busy Uncas and Wequash appear. Where have they been? No question, no answer.

Where is the fort? demand the captains (M27). "On top of that hill," they are told. "Then we demand, Where are the rest of the Indians?" They are "behind, exceedingly afraid"---terrified, that is, that here on Mystic's waterside doorstep their own tradition of ambush (rather than siege) is about to spring. Again, see the photos of Mystic: facing the high rocky ground to their right, this column has nothing but water at its back. If the Pequots really mean to teach their guests a bloody lesson, this is the place to "fall on" them, downhill in numbers of at least 3 or 4 to 1. But consistent with what is to come, nothing happens here.

The Narragansett and other Native men are also terrified because they know, after all, that the English have wholly neglected Miantonomo's and Williams' fourth crucial point: to *first lay that ambush* "behind" the Pequots, to "intercept" their warriors and prevent their people's escape. Why didn't the captains have Uncas remind them? Because they wouldn't tell him the Williams plan?

86

Where is his helpful initiative? The least we can say now is that the English really have no idea where the "common enemy" is, nor his strength. In war, this is supremely dangerous.

Mystic, like any major village, has lodges and campsites outside its palisade and around its corn. It's bright May morning, and here come five hundred men unheard, unseen. Not one Mystic grandmother, if there at all, gets up early to fish although she had a night of raucous music. Not one child, if there, is out for mischief before she wakes. Not a glimpse of the hundreds from a corn-tower built for scaring birds, not a clacking-sound off them, not one person atop Mystic Fort's wooden watch-platforms.[39]

If even Mason's "Indians" have seen not one Pequot, nor report being seen so close to a "great fort," the sign is a bad one. Native war is where the people are not. If the people are nowhere, hundreds of angry Pequot warriors are virtually everywhere. Suddenly, the English discover what it is to have no rear.

They have had enough help. "Tell the rest of [your] fellows," Mason sneers to Uncas, "that they should by no means fly, but stand at what distance they please...and see whether English men...fight or not."

The assault begins. What do the English discover at Mystic as they rush "silently" along the water, pass the cornfields and lodges,

---

[39] It is difficult to find records of these frame-towers. Traditions of Native farming include their use by children scaring crows. New England villages reveal layers of common sense (always near water, for ex.), and blocking your view of the land-approach with a palisade does not fit it. Mather fills more than one gap: "In the night the English came upon them [at Mystic]. [The Pequots] were fallen into a deep sleep, by reason of their long dancing the night before. And their sentinel was gone out of his place to light a pipe of tobacco, just as the English surprised them. And when our soldiers gave fire, there was not one that missed" (168).

then break into two files (U78) and charge up this gentle hill? What happens when they actually find Mystic up there and, guns and swords ready, deploy around it in an Old World "ring battalia"?

Is anybody there?

3
'It Is Naught': Going In

Mystic, at last! The 80 Englishmen under Captains Mason and Underhill charge their long-sought target, dogged and frustrated by cautious, duplicitous Native allies. Improvising on a Native-born plan already heedlessly changed, they fail to strike their target in the night, and forget to set up that crucial ambush. If they do march from Porter's Rocks after first light, then march two stealthy miles and stop twice to council, by now it must be 8 of the clock this May morning. Thousands of birds tune up as broad daylight brightens the Missituc "great tidal river" and green shores.

Up and then along the flanks of this sloping wooded hill the English charge. Above in the trees they can see floating palls of smoke from campfires inside Mystic Fort; but not a living soul. Where are those hundreds of Pequot braves, those "wasps" harrassing Saybrook, who swore to leave their spiteful bones to rot in defiance of the English? They'll be wild to find their Weinshauks battle-invitation snubbed for this action at Mystic.

Mason, Underhill and all their green planters-turned-soldiers have proven their temerity coming this far, but they can only be plenty-mad to get away with this harrowing plan. Swords drawn, their muskets primed and fuse-matches struck alight, the armored English trundle up through the trees, form two files and rush to surround the Mystic palisade. They neither follow nor wait for their "hundreds" of Narragansett and Mohegan allies (U78), but deploy them in "auxiliary" roles behind themselves as they encircle "impregnable" Mystic Fort.

Sun sharpens the crests of their sallet-helmets, and brightens the twenty yards of grass around the palisade with its handful of emptied lodges. No question somebody's in there: night's campfires flavor the air of this the Pequots' last lazy morning. The captains mean business with their colonies and careers at stake. Mason and Underhill wave the useless Uncas, his Mohegans and the remaining Narragansetts all but aside, into a second circle that turns disgusted English backs to them. "The Heathen shall not say our dependence is on them." Each gunner punches his gun-rest into the earth and sets his muzzle in the swiveling crotch. *Ready-a-volley!* The moment of truth, boys.

They and we arrive before a structure that contains a community. How big is Mystic Fort? The palisade is hundreds of stout trees set upright into a tight circle, or oval, around the "chief residences." It is two massive interlocking crescents of tree-trunks 8-12 feet tall, whose overlaps form two narrow entranceways. With its typical surround of *wetus* and work-sites, Mystic to these Englishmen must be a shocking sight. Planted atop the "commanding and beautiful" hill, it is by all accounts (like sister-village Weinshauks) larger than most other communities then in Native New England (McBride 98).

Vincent (though never there) estimates Mystic Village as "at least two acres of ground" (in 1638: V105). Prince says "well nigh an acre" (1735: in Orr 78n). Orr agrees on "two acres" (1897: xvii), and archaeologist McBride cites Vincent in his report of a Spring 1987 survey that "located" Mystic Fort atop this hill (1990: 98).

So, with 44,000 square feet to an acre, Mason's men behold a village containing perhaps 88,000 square feet. A square that size would have four sides each 300 feet long. Mystic Fort is a round or

"We called up our forces with all expedition, gave fire upon them through the Pallizado; the Indians in a dead indeed their last sleep".

MASON : FRIDAY, MAY 26 1637

Is this how the first volley was fired in the attack on Mystic Fort?

ovoid structure that just fits inside a modern football-field (300 feet from one "long end" to the other). In width it equals almost two such fields (twice 160 feet). Some of that total acreage is "lost" to the outside because of Mystic's curving palisade. But no one doubts this is an enormous and intentionally-daunting fortress. Mystic was "by no means an unprotected village" (Cave 209n47).

No historian doubts its magnitude. Yet, as we go in with these English captains, we must first be aware of how little physical trace of Mystic and this battle has survived. Historian Williams in 1832 reported "no remains" on the site (in Orr 118), though its then-owner said that "within his recollection...some few Indian arrow-heads and spears [were] found on the ground, and also some bullets." What, then, do historians such as Cave mean by "excavations" that support the traditional view of events at Mystic, citing McBride and "The University of Connecticut"? The fort's site atop Mystic Hill today has been a much-paved-over suburban neighborhood for generations. Pequot ceramics found in the area have been verified as such (McBride 99). But beyond surface-finds of arrowheads and pottery, there is little or nothing to guide us. Visitors today at the exemplary Mashantucket Pequot Museum find its Mystic display a handful of oxidized musket-balls and a glass-covered model of the fort on its hill. We do not expect today's Pequots to display "remains" for the sake of "proof"; but there is no known physical evidence to solidly support the Mason/ Underhill chronicles.[40]

---

[40] McBride 98: "The evidence consists of eyewitness accounts of the battle and oral tradition, including accounts of farmers picking up Indian and colonial artifacts from plowed fields in the area. In 1875, Horace Clift, a local resident, reported that his father had told him about a circular embankment extending several rods across a field on the summit of Pequot [Mystic Fort] Hill, where charred wood, corroded bullets, and Indian relics were found whenever any

Both of these captains' "eyewitness accounts," as well as Native oral traditions, can establish only what the people who write and speak them either claim to have witnessed, or what they were told and believe. We have reasons to read Mason and Underhill with trepidation. And while we could hardly have more confidence in Native oral traditions, it is also true that Native people, like any others, can be misinformed. Their witnesses can be traumatized. They too can see or not see a tradition grow as it ages; can be affected, over time, by the relentless production of histories by and in favor of the so-called dominant society.

Few peoples demonstrate a better grasp of their traditions over many centuries. One strength of that is the ability to recognize and go beyond what Native writer Gerald Vizenor calls "terminal creeds"---ways of understanding that become dead because they do not evolve with new information and perspectives. We repeat: as historians we have no doubt whatsoever of Native Americans' achievements of memory down generations long before May 1637. At the same time, nothing human is perfect, without influences, or unchanging. Nothing comes intact through language or history.

There is no doubt that more Native Americans than Englishmen were killed at Mystic. It happened because the English forced it to. It was not a *battle* such as Mason would have got at Weinshauks. Mystic was an assault, an attempted massacre against a target identified as the weaker of two. There is nothing in this to redeem in any way the English intentions or behavior.

The question is, How many Native people really died that day at Mystic? And what does the quest for that answer reveal toward a

---

plowing was done." But these finds match numerous Connecticut sites with no history of a "massacre." The "Clift Report" is in Carol Kimball, "Placing the John Mason Monument on Pequot Hill," *New London Day*, Nov. 13, 1986.

92

reconception of the entire Pequot War? For these reasons we hope that readers, unlike Mason and Underhill, have patience as we bring this situation before them.

We return to what the English behold that morning: a palisaded fort as lengthy as a modern football field and twice that in width. Inside these walls, DeForest and Orr estimate 70 "wigwams" (133 and xvii respectively; but remember that both claim Vincent was there, and he wasn't). McBride feels that while an "average" village might have 30 *wetus*, Mystic may have had 60 to 70 inside (101, 98).

In New England archaeology today, the usual estimate of how many persons shared home-dwellings can vary. Some reports suggest 5 persons per household (based on "low" birth-rates and the practicalities of small groups). Others prefer a range from 7 (for small homes) to perhaps 15 persons (Salisbury 26 says 7.5, with two families sharing a lodge). Given those homes' average sizes,[41] and counting up the 98 lodges in "Underhill's" sketch of Mystic Fort, we realize that its idea of Mystic's population is extreme for the actual site. Seven hundred or more "souls" with living-equipment and their Sachem's stores too would find the real Mystic unpleasantly crowded.[42]

More empirically, we know that in villages near the windy seacoasts, it's important that each home's cook-fire be well-spaced;

---

[41] Hauptmann (37) gives average dimensions for three typical kinds of homes: 9 by 14 feet, 10 by 16 feet, and 12 by 17 feet; respectively totaling 126, 160, and 204 square feet each.

[42] 700 persons (or 98 lodges x 7 people, rounded off) meets Mason's estimate of 600-700 Natives killed at Mystic (M31), if not Underhill's guess of "about 400" (U81). We can reach their mean of 500 persons with 98 lodges x 5 persons each; but again we ask patience, for what the numbers really tell cannot be known without all the evidence.

for (as Mason and Underhill happily discover), the homes' sun-dried mat coverings of "rush" catch fire easily from wind-borne sparks. We suggest that the 47 homes (plus one larger "official" or "ceremonial" lodge) in David Wagner's illustration show a more realistic idea of Mystic Fort's interior. McBride's "60 or 70" simply will not fit between typical home-dimensions, Mystic's likely size, and Native people's practical needs in such a place.

Even so, grant McBride's minimum of 60 homes inside the fort. We gain an estimate of 420 to 630 people living there. And yet, their family-groups' total domestic home-space still adds up to less than 8,000 square feet, or at most, 15 to 20 percent of the likely total space inside the Mystic palisade.

Now, grant the tradition more by imagining all kinds of tools and gear, drying-racks, woodpiles, and other things of village life, even tangling "arbors" (V105) among the homes: structures, objects and embellishments of any kind that might get in people's way and inhibit movement. For this is a key condition of the traditional Mystic Massacre---people trapped in their own crowded confines.

Allow for more of these unhelpful obstacles: grant them and the lodges a full third of Mystic's possible 88,000 square feet. Any Native people supposedly trapped inside the palisade (whether 400 or 600) still have more than an acre to maneuver. At the same time in this traditional scenario, if numbers of people jam together the battling Native and English bodies, the more useless the Englishmen's slow-loading guns. Toe to toe in a broad-daylight melee where there is no safe rear, a practiced war-club gains effect. It's that against a gun's stock or rest.

With these realities in mind, and no more physical evidence than described, we cannot accept the chief underpinnings of a Mystic Massacre. Others are also troubling. Recall for example Mather's claim (final note last chapter) that when the English open fire all at once, "there is not one that misses." Mather's sentence leaves out the impact of bullets in Native bodies, but he clearly implies it, unless he means that nobody missed the broad side of the fort.

New England braves do leave loopholes in a palisade, to shoot arrows through when their best option lies inside. Such a hole might be a foot tall and 8 inches wide. Mason's 80 men "give fire upon them through the palisado" (M27). His partner (U78) calls the first shot "remarkable...as we could not but admire at the providence of God in it, that soldiers so unexpert...should give so complete a volley, as though the finger of God had touched both match and flint." To both captains it seems the Pequot response is to turn over in bed, and stay there. Next we know the English are charging the entrances.

If this volley does begin the whole attack, what really happens? Do the English hit Pequots in bed inside their lodges by firing through loopholes from 20 feet outside the palisade? Does each one charge up silently, find a hole, thrust in a gun, and at the same instant shoot with all others through the nonexistent windows of each lodge? Not a good tactic: a boy inside can grab your gun-barrel and requite you a very sharp spear, about neck-high. What really happens?

When the fight starts inside the Mystic Fort we know today, does a Pequot warrior have to stay standing so close to a flaming lodge that his bowstring can catch fire (U80), and leave him (as hoped) defenseless? Underhill says this happened to "many." In fact, it is the granddaddy of the stuff of Fenimore Cooper, and of Mark Twain's "savaging" of Cooper.[43]

---

[43] As the English attack begins, the only response is one barking dog and one Indian shout (a Pequot's or "ally's"?) of "Englishmen!" See "The Literary Offenses of Fenimore Cooper" (reprinted in many collections), one of the fun-

With such room inside Mystic for maneuver, let alone places to hide till escape can be tried, are Pequot men, women and children really going to "run...into the very flames" (M29)? Will they stay, like fey martyrs of Europe, cowed in the infernoes of their lodges ("crept under their beds," M28) until burned to death in passive "helplessness," rather than take a fighting chance outside? In the captains' scenario, it's kill or be killed and your neighbors too. Surely one would strike a memorable blow. If there.[44]

Passsive Native Americans, white made right by might: a Mason-Underhill fantasy in the shadows of Sassacus and Uncas. Settling for it is history in the captains' shadow.

Not least as we try to go inside Mystic with some grip on realities, what about the "man-eating" Pequot braves? With their old and young families under sudden direct threat of death, will Pequot warriors be "unwilling to come out" (U80) and, instead of facing the enemy, simply lie down and burn with the people they live to defend? Mason's own first experience of combat is in "a wigwam," just as Roger Williams promised. There Mason is "beset with many Indians"---of unspecified age and gender, in such close quarters that his gun and sword are little use. "They," his first long-

---

niest cures for the frontier-romance (and Cooper one creator of "savage" Uncas). Twain, like D.H. Lawrence, simply applies physical common sense to see whether real people can do things Cooper describes. Twain: "He saw nearly all things as through a glass eye, darkly. Of course a man who cannot see the commonest little everyday matters accurately is working at a disadvantage when he is constructing a 'situation.'" "We cannot too much admire this miracle." "Almost always in error about his Indians." "A literary *delirium tremens*."

[44] Mather adds swoon: "Some of the old men taking hold of others that were willing to run away [say], 'As we have lived together, so let us die together.'" His Pequots join hands and sing like The Bible's Daniel and fellows in the fiery oven.

anticipated foes (does he kill them?), are simply "many," and they cannot "prevail." That's all Mason says about them. Then he claims to see "many Indians in the lane or street; [and] he making towards them, they flee" (M28). It is broad daylight. Are they braves, toddlers, old ladies? A gang of bold teenagers mooning the commander? We have records of that welcome, and provocation seems the Pequot order of the day.

These are a few of the unprobed vagueries, assumptions and details crucial to a massive English victory. If any of them should be dismissed, on which others can we rely? Before we trace exactly how the English get into Mystic Fort after their first shot, and what happens in there, consider how fragile is another crucial part of a massacre reported as massive (M31; U81; G137; V104).[45]

Observe the Mohegan and Narragansett allies during the Englishmen's approach and assault. Neither of the two captains there describes anything in "our Indians" but contemptible reluctance. As Cave notes (211n69), "not all" of them desert or hang back in fear of Pequot counterattack or passive inaction. Of the Mystic Pequots who supposedly come out to surrender "in troops...twenty and thirty at a time," "those that scaped us fell into the hands of the Indians...in the rear" (U81). They're doing something back there, those allies. And the odds are that more Mystic Pequots (if there) will reach them than will be cut down on the "massacre" spot. With the size of Mystic above, we find one of 82-total Englishmen every 12-15 feet around the fort.

---

[45] We are not in quest of a number that "reduces" the "massive" aspects of this event. We are working to establish a more realistic concept of what happened at Mystic, and believe that new understanding will in turn change The Pequot War. If "only five" Pequots were killed there, we still more than agree with Native comment then that English actions at Mystic were "too furious" (U84).

As Miantonomo noted (once), their manpower is inadequate to control the place of battle. Can men so spaced, with swords and one-shot guns, cut down "twenty and thirty [people] at a time" running for their lives? If not, what most likely would happen to Pequots taken by "Indians"?

Cave calls these supposed captures "systematic" (150), but we never see the system work. With what comes down on the English in retreat from Mystic (below), the count and control of prisoners is their least worry. We hear of no prisoners' disposition at the later meeting with Patrick's boats, of no heads displayed, no women or anybody marched overland back to Saybrook. It slips the captains' writing minds? Prisoners make irrefutable trophies of victory, and we have not a footnote of these conquering men either managing or receiving "servants" as pay direct from Mystic (and there is no other loot: below). Mason (M29) says there is "sufficient living testimony to every particular" of his chronicle: if only it were that simple (Ch. 4, end).

One captain's claim of prisoners, let alone "troops" of them, means little unless the conquered power and wealth they signify is displayed, by the simple, usual, glory-spreading details of who got richer by them. For other later prisoners the English take pride in such records. From here, too, there are "supposed" to be no survivors; although Mystic's known Sachem Mamoho, his wife and children and others are known to survive, and we'll see them further on.

Can and should we assume Mystic "prisoners" anyway, killed or carefully confined? Not if we want to rid ourselves of all the assumptions we can. Otherwise, we have to keep believing in thoughtless, passive Native Americans, interrelated and yet disconnected; who try no escape; who sooner cut a cousin than resist, together (at least by neglect) these omni-invasive foreigners;

and all this in favor of foreigners who constantly let on their contempt. Vincent (V104) sees them as game-fetching dogs.

It's at least as likely that prisoners do not "troop out" because they are not inside Mystic in the first place. Look at the clues we do have about "real Native attitudes" surrounding these sparse Englishmen and their massacre. Two of the best drop in unguarded moments in reports by Roger Williams; who offers to march with later soldiers but stays at Providence on May 26 (WCL2: 612). First, Williams hints that he has given the men of Mason and Underhill---"oppressed with multitudes" at Mystic---perhaps an apology, "the best reasons I could to persuade" them of why their Native allies in the battle "all either went to Connecticut [Saybrook?] for provision, or [went] upon some second assault upon the other of the Pequot forts" (WPF3: 426). The Mohegan and Narragansett allies do neither in any other source: Williams is explaining simply why they are "not at Mystic" to palpable effect. If, however, what actually springs at Mystic is a Pequot trap, the English-allied "Indians" have hundreds of unseen, furious reasons to be inoffensive and/or gone before the counter-blow strikes their friends.

Williams also reassures "Mr. Governor" Winthrop that, in Mystic's aftermath, their Narragansett allies speak only of "content and affection towards us" (WCL1: 88; rpt. FBH2: 252). The salient evidence Williams drops is that (emphasis added) "I hear no speech *at present about inequality*" from the Narragansetts. He writes in July to report this *change*: he *has* heard complaints, from allies first enlisted as crucial helpers, and then commanded to keep back in a second "ring battalia" around Mystic (which they do). They know, before this one May morning's insults, that Mason and Underhill (if not Gardener) ridicule them and their own kind of combat as childish (U82). They are angry by then not only about the rapacity of later English captains at Narragansett (Chs. 5 and 6; WCL1: 90n5, WJH:1: 277).

Is it credible that people so regarded will eagerly share either slaughter or effective guarding of prisoners whose names, language, villages and kinsmen they know on a near-daily basis? Their common relatives fish both banks of the Pawcatuck. Not long after Mystic (as noted), Native people exactly there will harbor and defend "good Pequots."[46]

We begin to wonder at the power and serviceability of stereotypes; at the power of books and oratures too, as we see that these unlikelihoods are tip of the iceberg. With evidences that the Pequots are aware of the English approach, we want to know how likely it is that anybody is in Mystic Fort that morning, and why.

We have noted Native New England traditions and skills in using the landscape to advantage in war, especially the emergency-practice of taking refuge in swamps against too many enemies with plenty of time for a siege. Let's discover that answer, along with

---

[46] Even after Block Island Endecott noted that "Their flying to [Native 'captivity'] is no submission to us, but of purpose to avoid it....They only use the Narragansetts and others as their covering" (WPF3: 482). Think it through. If you, a Pequot, are held "in the rear" (that word again) at Mystic, this means you go to Native villages studied above. A few days' rest and some fresh adornments, cousin, and unless somebody turns you in to "Mr. Governor" and his spies (below), from now on you're Niantic. These foreigners have not one demonstrable criterion to prove you Pequot. Their gold is worth little except in their world. Now, raise your hand and repeat after Uncas: "Ungh---Heap good Injun." And don't worry, because Sachems Ninigret (WCL1: 100n3) and Wequash (WCL1: 93-94n2), plus others, will refuse to "deliver" you even if Mass. Bay demands it (WCL1: 117, 128n6, 164, 203; DYW 131). In fact, if you're truly bold for proof, come along with Uncas as he swears his loyalty to Boston (Introduction, and Chs. 5-6). Records repeat this for almost every tribe of the region.

more fact and perspective on Mystic as an English victory, through the dynamics of another great fort-centered "massacre," that of The Great Swamp Fight in "Philip's War" of 1675. Historian Jill Lapore sees it as "quite similar" to Mystic (281n73).

For almost forty years after The Pequot War, the Narragansetts try to stay clear of English fights with other Native groups. At the start of "Philip's War" between the English and the Wampanoags' "confederates," the Narragansetts pay dearly for keeping neutral while sheltering many "hostiles" from other tribes and refusing to surrender them. (By now they know what promises of "kind treatment" are worth.) Most histories now agree that arrogant English ineptitude turns the Narragansetts into "enemies." Slotkin (*Judgment* 466n42): The English "began preparations for an attack...almost immediately after [the last of several Narragansett treaties] was signed."

By midwinter 1675, the Narragansetts are in it for their survival too. No war here has been so widespread and brutal. That December, most of them decide not to follow the very old winter practice of breaking up into smaller bands and hunting-camps. (After harvest "they go 10 or 20 together, and sometimes more...wives and children also, where they build up little hunting-houses," each with a "bound" of up to four miles for trapping: Williams *Key* 1: 188.) The numbers of war-refugees with them make this impractical. Instead, the Narragansetts congregate with huge stores of corn at their palisaded village in The Great Swamp near Kingston, Rhode Island. So many are there because, that year, winter-camps cannot provide for their numbers. Right now that makes families too vulnerable. They gather in the fort to survive, out of the way, not as a plan of battle.

The English have not been learning sound New England tactics from their histories of The Pequot War. That is why they're forced

Monument on the site of
The Great Swamp Fight (in Philip's War, December 1675)
Kingston, Rhode Island

in 1675 to learn from the uniquely seasoned nonconformist Captain Benjamin Church. They locate the Narragansett fort as a still-preferred stationary target and launch a huge assault (December 19-20). The Narragansett braves fight a horrendous holding-action. By the time Church takes three wounds and his men gain any control inside the fort, he observes (besides many English killed by friendly fire) "a broad bloody track" in the snow, "where the enemy has fled with their wounded men" (413).

Church, following hard, realizes that the Narragansetts have reversed the whole battlefield, pulled "the rear" out from under him in "roving" style; for "immediately they hear...a great shout of the enemy, which seems to be behind them, or between them and the fort; and [we] discover them running from tree to tree to gain advantages of firing upon the English...in the fort." Church's presence of mind in halting the English panic and reversing *this*, he owes to his lessons in Native tactics (414).

But Church cannot turn this tide right away. "The English, in short, are discouraged, and [draw] back" (415). "By this time the English people in the fort begin to set fire to the wigwams and houses within." Why? Church the writer relishes a sudden argument against his advice that "the Army"---short on supply and far from home with many wounded---"shelter themselves in the fort" (416). He is shouted down by fellow officers, the Narragansett fort takes flame; and, through the rest of this record, Church mentions not one Native person either in the fort or captured. He likes and admires Native people. He would not overlook them burning in their lodges or let us fail to see and hear them.

In frustrated rage the English torch their hard-won empty prize. It robs them of life-saving shelter and baskets of corn big enough to stop bullets. In our histories, this blunder is glossed as an English "riot" that makes fiasco of victory. Historians accept the term "riot" but they never explain it. They assume that 1675's English are just over-full of battle-rage or, perhaps, Christian and English anti-Indian ideology.

This riot happens because The Great Swamp Fight itself forces the English to give up hunting an "Indian city" to depopulate; a misguidedness that wastes generations. At The Great Swamp, they see their planter-friends die to conquer a smoothly-evacuated fort, and in response they throw a self-destructive tantrum.[47]

Consider one other similarity between Mystic and 1675. We know of Narragansett peoples" traditions about this "massacre" at The Great Swamp. No one can attend their annual memorial ceremonies, or learn from their elders and historians, and not agree that many Native people were butchered there. At the same time, where we might expect this battle's English historians to make a great traditional riot-obscuring boast about "Indians killed or taken" there, we have virtually nothing of the kind. What we do have, and where we have it from, tells much.

---

[47] Church proves right as the mauled army marches home "the same night in the storm and cold." This "riot" creates more fiasco because the Narragansetts "fled out of their fort so hastily that they carried nothing with them...[and] if the English had kept in the fort, the Indians had certainly have been necessitated either to surrender themselves...or to have perished by hunger and...the season" (416). At Mystic, then, if more Native allies "evacuate" as the fight intensifies, is it not likely that Mason's and Underhill's also-sudden decision to burn that fort is prompted by panic rather than victory? Events to come will strongly bear this out. Other studies of out-of-print primary sources on 1675 include Leach (112-13, 123-25) and Burke (144-5). Lapore (279-281, notes 53-75) offers a good guide to English "swamp" accounts, fears and frustrations. Two complain of swamps as "so soft ground that an Englishman can neither go nor stand thereon, and yet these bloody savages will run along over it, holding their guns across their arms and, if occasion be, discharge in that posture." "They fly before us...from one swamp to another."

"Some of the [Narragansetts] that were then in the fort have since informed us that near a third of the Indians belonging to all that...country were killed by the English, and by the cold that night" (Church 416). First here, what is more universally typical than a "victor" overestimating the losses to his notoriously-numerous enemy? And what is more common than the "losers," faced with a horrendous aftermath of choices, self-protectively overestimating their own losses? We will show reasons to suppose not that Pequot or Narragansett peoples "suffered less harm," but that both these tendencies are in strong play in the construction of what happened at Mystic.[48]

Even more crucial is the second implication above. Virtually every English count of Native American "kills and captures" at Mystic, and in The Pequot War itself, comes *from Native Americans.* Mason delivers his numbers: "six or seven hundred [killed], as some themselves confessed" (and he mentions no other source, M31). Underhill: "about four hundred" killed, reported only "by themselves" (U81).

---

[48] Mather, again no eyewitness, is chief architect of the tradition. Of The Great Swamp Fight he writes (in Slotkin ed. 108): "There were hundreds of wigwams ...within the fort, which our soldiers set on fire, in which the men, women and children (no man knoweth how many hundreds of them) were burnt to death. Night coming on, a retreat was sounded." Next paragraph: "Concerning the numbers of Indians slain in this battle, we are uncertain: only some Indians... afterwards taken prisoner...confessed that the next day they found 300...fighting men dead in their fort, and...many men, women and children...burned in their wigwams; but they neither knew, nor could conjecture how many: it is supposed that not less than a thousand Indian souls perished....Ninigret, whose men buried the slain, affirmeth that they found 22 Indian captains among the dead bodies." The reader is equipped for critique.

That is it. What else can or will any of these English do but depend on Native intelligence? By the Mystic captains' accounts, they are busy retreating from the fort (below) to rendezvous with their boats. The angry wounded English of 1675 march away "that night." In both cases, no English participant and nobody else mentions any later return to evaluate the ashes. If bodies are left lying at Mystic, Native people tend to them.[49]

Will Pequots captured in this war, faced with slavery or death, refuse the life-preserving wiggle-room of chained "security" they can gain by saying what the English want to hear? Compared with execution or foreign slavery, what is it to feign a mercy-fetching moan: "Yes, we are broken and no threat to you anymore"? Just this we hear echoed in "Mr. Governor" Winthrop's further twit to former critic William Bradford: that "...the Indians in all quarters are so terrified" that their "friends are afraid to receive" any camouflaging Pequots (DYW 127; Chronology 1637-end). How comforting to hear, how difficult to prove---"each and every one of them in all quarters" lives in fear of outnumbered English. Winthrop christens his supposed-Pequot "servant" *Reprieve*: the youth's captivity suggests a different inner man than Winthrop and Williams see (Ch. 6).

Mason, Underhill, their soldiers, Gardener waiting back at Saybrook, Vincent, and historians after---never having sought out the physical facts---will be glad to inscribe and accept each other's remarkable Mystic estimates: a circular assurance of their superiors' victory and enemies' crippled state. That is what they do.

---

[49] In the late 19th century, near the Mohegan Burial Ground in Norwich (about 30 miles from Mystic), the building of a Masonic temple caused discovery of now-unlocated "barrels full of bones" buried there. This is the only such report we know of in the area. We leave possible Mystic connections to your judgment.

But the successful, enduring Native practice of evacuation and escape into swamps cannot be forgotten at Mystic. Williams has more than company before and after he describes the Native norm by which "in half a day, yea, sometimes at few hours' warning, [a Native village-population can] be gone and the house up elsewhere" (*Key* qtd. in Rubertone 103).

The question becomes the degree to which the Mystic Pequots evacuate before the assault, and why. Recall how much time, how many possible informers, how many hints the Pequots have before the English enter their country. Miantonomo reports them slipping away in groups at these dark approaches. It grows hard to believe that the Pequots "know nothing," as Underhill says. And we realize with those Pequots that, with the English force coming overland from the east, Mystic Village lies between the attackers and Sassacus' men of war. Early-on to the captains at Mystic, those braves seem to be "six or seven miles" off to the west at Weinshauks; but they counterattack before morning ends at Mystic, below. In the meantime Uncas controls the English approach; and for that, a Pequot response is waiting.

In the battle to come, we'll find that Owl Swamp is virtually Mystic's backyard. Reports locate assumed Pequots hiding there after the "massacre." Not before? With no ambush to stop them? That is not an assumption, but another fragment of massive likelihoods smashed apart for us by the racism and violence of Puritan histories. These have done their work so that few people realize the habit English colonists themselves have, of putting their own women and children directly on the frontiers of wilderness-conquest. (What Vonnegut calls *hors de combat*.) There is no evidence that Native people do so. To the Pequots, war is where there are no old people, women and children.[50]

Neither Mason, Underhill nor their men at first see or hear anybody at Mystic, though no village of its kind will lack at least two watchtowers. This utter stillness stymies the charging captains and makes Native allies fall back "exceedingly afraid" (M27). The first real obstacles---after the hot reception of a barking dog and one Indian shout of "Englishmen!"---are Mystic Fort's two entrances. They are "blocked up with bushes about breast-high" (M27, U78-9).

When do Native villagers block entrances "breast high"? When they expect an attack like this they will not be in a fort. (Compare Massachusett tactics via Winslow *Good News* 51: their Sachem "would fain make his peace again with us, but...having forsaken his dwelling, and daily removed from place to place, expecting when we would take further vengeance on him.") They do not block entrances when adults and braves are on hand on any given night to take shifts in a tower or other position. They close entrances this way when they have deserted a fort for some reason: it keeps out animals while they're gone, or it can help to turn the place into a decoy of what a particular enemy is looking for.

Even on a normal spring morning when they are not being shot at in their beds, will all the Mystic Pequots with Sachem Mamoho sleep in after a late-night sing? Consider what Mason tells you; that at Porter's Rocks on the verge of this risky attack, he and his men fall asleep well-beyond their plan's best chance. Perhaps he assumes that drowsy, sleep-seeking readers will assume that the

---

[50] "...Native logic would say, Well, you don't bring your women where you're going to make war...." (Wampanoag historian Nanepashemet/Anthony Pollard, interview in Dempsey film *NANI*).

Pequots do so too; and, given their savage childishness, through so significant a sunrise.[51]

---

[51] Underhill (U78) says that the English march down from Porter's Rocks at 1 a.m.: they either camp again enroute to wait for his "break of day" first volley, or attack in the dead of night. Which is it? Day and night are just that to a military history. His first shot brings forth "a most doleful cry" from the Pequots inside, "fast asleep for the most part." What are "the least part" doing? Mason (M27) describes a direct charge on both entrances "at once." That is when the dog and "Indian cry" sound, and then his men fire through the palisade, "the Indians [still?] being in a dead indeed their last sleep." Yet he still "sees no Indians" (M28) when, the "bushes" cleared, he enters the fort and can find fight only in a "wigwam." Below we'll look at the Pequot side of this and learn who really starts the fight inside the fort.

On Mason's falling asleep on the edge of battle: "The rocks were our pillows, yet rest was pleasant: the night proved comfortable, being clear and moonlit" (M26). Mason's rare sleep-out seems to have seduced him into a "dead sleep" of his own. As a writer he knows how to set some matters up for his ends, for example his sympathetic "ignorance" at Saybrook and his "questioning the morality" of Mystic massacre, neatly resolved by "The Lord...filling the place with dead bodies!" (M30). His amazing doze-off at Porter's Rocks is as self-critical as he gets, and its narrative purpose is to blunt any question of the Pequots' doing likewise. Even if this were to them just another spring night and morning, their norm would be as always: keep your eyes open.

"The Battle of Mystic" begins according to Captain Mason.

4

'It Is Naught': Getting Out

The "plenty mad enough" English commence their assault on Mystic with a booming, all-together volley at its massive palisade--- an action either vainly symbolic or fearfully foolish. Firing all at once is just what they should not do, with slow-loading matchlock guns and a yet-unlocated enemy capable of lightning-charge. Forty years later, Captain Benjamin Church is still trying to keep his troops from panic-firing and being overrun. But the Pequots have a plan of their own this May morning, and it yields Mason and Underhill another mercy. Thanks to Uncas, they've already led their guests straight through Mystic's most dangerous approach.

The English fire, and Mystic Fort's response of silence draws the English in. Whatever their Native allies are doing on Mystic Hill (the captains record only hesitance and desertion), the captains each now gather half the men from their "ring battalia" and prepare to enter Mystic Fort by both its entrances. With 80 armed planters, this means that each captain has 40 men with whom to conquer half of it.

They know that the Pequots' war-strength is not *in* the fort, but roving the forests somewhere outside it and, now, alerted by their guns. To prevent being trapped themselves inside Mystic Fort, the captains need to leave some men around its outer environs.

"Hundreds" is what they know of Pequot strength: each can only take his chances and post perhaps a prudent 20. So they enter and hope "to destroy by the sword" Mystic's hundreds of people with a combined force of maybe 40 men, 20 to storm each entrance. They have perhaps 40 outside to manage the fort's circumference and entrances, "hundreds" of allies and, they say, Mystic Pequots charging out 20 and 30 at a time.

As it turns out, the average of an English every 12-15 feet around the whole claimed action is a ring of gaping holes, whose men's first task is to hold the entrances (or now, escape-ways) and wait for hundreds of Sassacus' braves. All this the dauntless captains must improvise that morning, with "so inexperienced" men.

When you go to Mystic and explore these and later historians' claims, you know why Miantonomo laughed. If present this day he might say, *Time to worry.*

There can be no denying the Englishmen's courage, whatever kind it is. But they have no experience and say start to finish that they can hardly find their way. In well over their heads now, they attack the breast-high brush in each entrance with fearful haste---a feeling that may also explain a 50 percent difference between the captains' reports of Pequots killed between them.

Gardener and Vincent estimate 300 and 300-400 (G137, V104): skeptical of Underhill's "about four hundred souls" (U81) and Mason's "six or seven hundred" (M31). Later historians, knowing what happens to casualty reports, also deem Mason's number high. His chronicle's publication-time is the least certain of the four in Orr's *History* (note below). The longer Mason waits, the higher his claim may be amid his post-war ascension to Major General, Governor, "great man" etc. Underhill, even in May 1637, is suspected an Antinomian friend of the Anne Hutchinson's Boston that so threatens Winthrop's. Demanding his (denied) reward of

Captain Mason's version of his first reception inside Mystic Fort.

land for service and eventually banished altogether, Underhill's published number may be one kind of play to the Boston gallery, a total more "conservative" than his Hartford partner's.

Trauma, confusion, self-inflation---Whatever the reasons to differ by 200-300 persons in their most important Mystic assessment, they must connect with the captains' other eyewitness-contradictions about a "massacre."[52]

"Not above five" escape them, says Underhill (U81): Mason says "about seven" (M31). They disagree about the day-or-night time of the attack, how it progresses, the winds and other aspects of the great fires they set. They do enter Mystic from opposite sides, and the Pequots' deployments within explain some of this discord. But a "Killed In Action" difference of 200-300 "souls" casts doubt upon them both.[53]

---

[52] "Worthy reader, let me entreat you to have a more charitable opinion of me... than is reported in the other book" (U79). Prince's note is sure this refers to Vincent's account. Mason, in print only well-after Underhill (note below), perhaps conforms to the assault on Underhill's "morality" and casts aspersions on his first deeds at Mystic (M30). It may result from the different strength of resistance each captain encounters inside the fort's "two acres," and from how afraid they are to be cut off from each other.

[53] The facts of Mason's public (spoken and printed) history can assist your judgments. Mason says (first page) that he is asked many times for his story before he writes it. But only echoes of it and his numbers appear, in other men's letters, for uncertain years after Underhill and Vincent reach print (1637-8). By March 1638, one Edward Howes tells Winthrop Jr. that he "read in print the relation of your fight," which might be Mason's in manuscript (WPF4: 21), but that's all he says. Mason, like Underhill, never accounts for what happens at last to their nemesis Sassacus---which is believed known to the colonies 3 months after Mystic. Though Mason does make one pious "Addition" to his pages about "special Providences" that helped all this succeed, no editor can date his work's sure-first appearance. [ctd.]

Underhill is not clear as to who first makes the fort "too hot for us" with arrows and resistance as he struggles to clear his entrance and storm in (U81). By design, Mystic's entrances force any foes to come through bunched together with backs to the wall. There is no hint that Uncas or one Mohegan goes in. Underhill can hardly have more than twenty men with him and he reports "near twenty" with almost immediate wounds: these quickly give up hunting skirmishes (that is, the enemy has pulled back among the lodges) and begin to set fires. But suddenly, these twenty find themselves facing Pequot "prime men." Though Underhill doesn't tell their numbers, he shows how he feels with a phrase (U81-2). He says these braves emerge and confront him in "the open field," *inside the*

After Mason's death (1672/3; Prince in Orr 9), Colony Secretary "Mr. John Allyn" "transcribes it with various alterations and additions, and allows it to pass for his own work" (Drake ed. Mather viii). Allyn brings this "new" manuscript, if there was ever a first, to Reverend Increase Mather; who promises not "the least alteration" (Drake 45n17, 114n128). Mather first officially publishes this putative Mason's *Brief History* as Allyn's account in his *Relation* (1677). This creates a new phase. Mather "pities" that no "memorial" is published already--- as if to clear the deck of Underhill, Vincent, and Hubbard's 1677 account of this war too. (Drake notices, 113n27: Gardener writes c.1660 but remains "in mss." till the 1800s; Orr 112.) What will be the minister's data-bank as he edits "Mason" for us? Gardener's papers? In fact he says there is a "mystery author" to help him. "I have been willing to add some particulars out of a manuscript narrative...I lately met with in Rev. Mr. [Hugh] Davenport's library." This will supplement Johnson's neo-orthodox *Wonders*, Morton's *Memorial* and Bradford's manuscript *History*. "We are quite in the dark respecting the authorship of this manuscript," Drake concludes(45n18). Mather: "The author...I know not, nor can conjecture, saving it was one who had a particular and personal acquaintance with those affairs. It doth in substance agree with...John Allyn" (159). Soon (1682) Mather will also fashion Mary Rowlandson's captivity-trials into another frontier parable of Native peoples' "causeless enmity" (Rpt. Slotkin *Judgment* 318). The most we can say about the authors of her or "Mason's" *History* is "Mather, ed."

fort. To him, *open field* is the kind of place---spacious, with room to maneuver---where Underhill sees "no advantage against them." We are left to assume many Pequots killed here without an English fatality.

Mason, charging into the other side of Mystic Village, is "very much out of breath" with his first fight in the lodge and from chasing those vague "Indians" who "flee." It seems that Underhill's is the "hot" side of the fight, because now Mason observes something significant: two soldiers "standing," incredibly, "with their swords pointed toward the ground." It is not even an alert posture: they and other Englishmen must have made a disappointing discovery. Mason too, for he has to give an outraged general order that "burning" do the "killing" (M28-9).

Why not despatch his men to help Underhill, if that end of the fight is hot? If "hundreds" of Mystic Pequots are hiding under beds inside the lodges, why not shoot and stab at them? The language about this battle from both captains is filled with harrowing violence; yet when we probe, we seem to come nearer the real reason why those fires are set so quickly.

Just as the above unfolds, Mason claims to encounter the real Pequot strength inside Mystic: "one hundred and fifty fighting men from the other fort [Weinshauks]" (M30). Underhill records these warriors not at all: DeForest finds them there without explanation (129-30), Jennings and Cave also disagree. Mason leads us to think he can now tell Pequots of Weinshauks from Mystic ones, till he yields his "Indian" report that these 150 braves have been here since "the night before," intending "to go forth against the English." Which partaker of Mystic's last music shares this? If it is true, are we still to believe that Mystic woke from a "dead sleep"?

We need not choose sides about these 150 spectral braves. They may help to enlarge Mason's kill-numbers beyond his partner's or to transform this assault into a "preemptive strike." But there is a plan and a source for a frighteningly-big contingent of braves waiting ambush of their own inside Mystic---down to the smoking campfires, from which the overmatched English will rush to set their blaze.

In so much confusion we forget Mamoho, Sachem of Mystic since the murder of Tatobem (Chronology). Mamoho is a maternal kinsman to Uncas (WCL1: 77n16).

Neither Mason nor Underhill mention Mamoho, but he is an active presence through Winthrop's and Williams' private war-letters; one of the Pequots' "biggest" men with "great troops" (WPF3: 427). Mamoho and "captains" of his own are the war-leaders of Mystic this day, not least one Monoonotuck---*aka* Momomattuck, or to the English, Momonotuck Samm. Him they call "a mighty fellow for courage," for his "desperateness" later defending Pequots in their swamp-hides (WPF3: 480; WCL1: 77; his fate Ch. 6). From those same letters (written with no effort to confirm Mason/Underhill), we know that Mamoho, Momomattuck, the Sachem's wife Wincumbone and children, plus "many" more Mystic Pequots are still on the run months after the Mystic "massacre." Where are they, then, this day?[54]

---

[54] Winthrop seems to accept "our English from Connecticut's" word (Mason's) about Mystic; for he adds (DYW 122) the uncertain 150 "fighting men" neglected by Underhill, to Mystic's "about [150 other] old men, women, and children" supposed killed. (And yet, that total of 300 is half Mason's claim on M31.) It "happened the day after our general fast," Winthrop muses. June 16 will be "a day of thanksgiving kept in all the churches for the victory obtained against the Pequots, and for other mercies" (123). Who were the "two chief sachems" killed at Mystic according only to Mr. Governor? Neither captain records them; maybe ambivalent Roger Williams, who "certifies" Mason's return to Saybrook "by letters," is helping out (somebody) again. As noted, it is in the interest of Pequot "survivors" to agree with or expand every English claim.

The Pequots have a plan and stick to it: evacuation for their families to at least Owl Swamp and Cuppacommock, The Hiding Place; and at Mystic, a decoyed ambush as a holding-action. (Later the English find Weinshauks too abandoned: WCL1: 83). The Pequots lure their enemy in, give people escape-insurance time, and the warriors of Weinshauks time to descend upon the English. The patterns and details of the captains' fight in and around Mystic, together, show us their response---to Pequot braves who shower them with missiles and emerge from hides to join and break off battle where they choose. Mason's men hunt for a fight while Underhill gets one across this enclosed double-wide football-field of space, and in broad daylight the latter misses Momo-mattuck and 150 "prime men"?

Some of these braves surely die, and when the task is finished the others melt away, or wheel about with Weinshauks' coming braves to fight again. That's how a warrior does his job here, and why some are alive after Mystic (Chs. 5-6; DYW 125; Cave 158-60). Williams alone credits the Narragansett allies "thrice" against Pequots that day: at the fort, in the counterattack and helping the English out of there (WPF3: 427). The records know this if our captains' chronicles don't, and beyond bribes and threats that mostly fail (Ch. 5), the colonies can do little about the escape of the Pequot "body."[55]

---

[55] Jennings sees few braves at Mystic because none of the Pequots' "sixteen guns" appear, while Cave sees nothing reliable in that because guns are "of somewhat limited use...in close quarters in any case" (209-10). Yet Cave takes no hint from that about Mystic and the war. The braves with guns are elsewhere such as protecting hidden noncombatants. Guns in fact reveal more Pequot observation and adaptation. However much Native peoples do fear guns at first, records show that they soon demand them for furs and goods (Dempsey, *Morton*

Typical New England "swamp" and "thicket" (this at Narragansett)
--- without its spring-through-fall greenery and leafage.

Why does no history explore Mamoho's Sachemship of Mystic and his family's and "Samm's" escape? The sanctified assumptions that underwrite an easy slaughter are untenable. The tradition proves an illusion: "as in a dream" (M45), as "outside" factors break in, we start to wake up. The Mystic Massacre seems to be made up of untried assumptions; of wishful Euro-American claims about race, culture, violence as title to land and power; about order, justice, true manhood and total victory; all of it imposed on colonials and Natives in willful defiance of the speaking land and modern science; in denial of evidence before our eyes, in degradation of Native Americans willing from the start to help accomplish something better.

Underhill says "Let the ends and aims of a man be good, and he may proceed with courage" (U77). And if not, not. It remains to see what more we can learn once the English discover who controls this place.

A common trick against imperial force is to trade space for time and then bleed (or "attrit") the invaders. Sachem Mamoho and his people are either in flight to Sassacus, to their "great and secure" swamps, or fighting to help others flee. Who is in the fort? There may be a tragically stubborn family or two inside the lodges, easy marks if caught without braves near. The most parsimonious answer is that Mamoho's "captains" lead an elite force of braves who turn their wooden decoy into a live one.

How many? The very brave are relatively few. If Mason and Underhill each command twenty "so inexperienced" soldiers, their

---

and *News*). Not to make themselves military equals---guns won't do that. Rather, the Pequots (like others) realize how much the English fear guns and use them to political advantages: at Mystic they never intend to make a stand. Jennings and Cave expect the "sixteen" to deploy as artillery or to be nowhere.

men feeling no "advantage" here may meet their Pequot match in a force that seems like "150" (about 4-to-one odds); but is more likely under 100 braves, who harrass and provoke the small English groups, then fall back and wheel among the lodges to harry others, above all dragging out the fight. Whatever you think of that estimate, see how "the numbers" resolve by the end of The Pequot War.[56]

The captains claim that they set Mystic Fort ablaze because the Pequots won't come out of their lodges to fight. No matter how vivid the details of their wished-for slaughter, virtually nothing beyond their claims supports them. The two English reported killed have likely shot each other in crossfires (M31, U80-1, V104), and the captains find most other men "doleful," uneager for any part of this "duty" (U81).

As we'll see, this war's typical difference between claimed and "verifiable" enemies-killed is substantial. If Sachem Mamoho deploys War-Leader Samm and 100 braves inside Mystic, the 40-odd English inside kill perhaps 50 braves in the first of two hours-or-so of hand-to-hand fight and maneuver. Half the English take wounds and arrows in return. The realistic numbers are no "massacre." And that attrition must be just what prompts Mason and Underhill, now, to pick up firebrands from the Pequots' decoy-campfires: they are winning control of a massive, all but empty prize. Are they seized by a riotous rage at the trick? Do they panic to realize that Mystic may trap *them*, that the fight has only begun? Mason says "command" is given to abandon the fort (M29).

---

[56] Cave (150-1) sees room for both "open field" battle and trapped, incinerated families by the score. It can hardly be both. Any Pequots inside Mystic Fort "by mistake" are perhaps like the Narragansetts, "not in the least imagining the English could [or would] destroy them" (M7).

Perhaps some of the 40 men with them are beginning to poke around, to see if they've truly been mocked. The mat-roofed lodges of Mystic kindle so quickly to flames that the English are forced back outside the palisade.[57]

Out there facing the wooded hills now, the English must shed any last sense of their advantage, and find themselves in a situation horribly consistent with Miantonomo's strategy for ambush. Now, they are in the trap between forts. Immediately from the west (or inland side) of these flat open spaces around Mystic Fort, the Pequots' gathering warriors charge "upon us with their prime men, and let fly" their weapons. Are they just arriving as claimed, or, knowing the English target for days, waiting *en masse* until the English find their backs to the burning fort? The Pequot counter-attack uses Mystic as an anvil.

Underhill's "twelve or fourteen" handiest men manage to volley, and they kill enough Pequots to break their first charge with "bullets [that] outreach their arrows" (U81). But the real battle has only begun. The brightening morning can bring only more and more warriors to sap the isolated English of strength and gunpowder. It is time to worry, and the captains know. Here are two rare long correspondences between their reports, Mason (M31) and then Underhill (U82-3):

---

[57] (U80): "The fires...meeting in the center of the fort, blazed most terribly, and burnt all in the space of half an hour." Mather here inserts "eighteen" prisoners taken (171: none accounted for). "A memorable day," he sighs. "This does not agree with the other accounts," Drake notes. Boston men have a precedent for indignant burnings of useful places: see the Dec. 1630 torch of Native-friendly Merrymount, done against Native advice and the needs of Boston's just-landed Puritans in the coldest winter of then-recent memory (Dempsey *Morton*).

Captain Mason applies Peqout camp-fire
to what his Englishmen find inside Mystic Fort.

> And thereupon grow many difficulties: our
> provision and munition near spent, we in the enemy's
> country who doth far exceed us in number, [and] much
> enraged; [and] all our Indians, except Uncas, deserting
> us. Our [ships] are at a great distance from us, and when
> they will come we are uncertain....

> We are forced to cast our eyes upon our poor maimed
> soldiers...but only constrained to look up to God, and
> entreat him for mercy towards them....Distractions multi-
> plying, strength and courage begin to fail with many. Our
> Indians that had stood close to us hitherto, are fallen into
> consultation, and are resolved for to leave us in a land we
> know not which way to get out....

Underhill's first move against the Pequot counterattack is to consign the open-field fight outside the fort to "our Indians." In action he is admitting lost advantage and for us he feigns control of it with a sudden tourist-request "that we might see the nature of the Indian war, which they grant us" (U82, "they" meaning Narragansetts and allies not in "consultation" for flight, below). Mason is already looking for Captain Patrick's boats.

It's time to worry because from here, on the forested northeast face of the hill where Mystic stands, nobody can see "the river" seawards where they hope those boats will beach. You have to walk some distance out of this "saddle" in the hill to see that, especially in leafy May. Worse, the river where Patrick plans to beach is not the one that flows down below the far southwestern side of Mystic Hill (as noted, a good 1/2-mile walk along the hill's crest). That river is about 7 miles overland west: Pequot River.

For all their other blunders, this flaw in the captains' plan tells us of nothing less than English dumbfoundment; for suddenly here as they discover themselves nearly trapped, their best hope is that

Patrick will disobey instructions. Clearly, neither colonists nor critics (below) have demanded much sense or consistency from this Mystic feat. But like the rest of the captains' problems, this will not go away, and we'll see the land force them to terms with it.

Mason records his wish but realities keep closing in: the boats and Patrick's fresh forty men (if only they had waited!) can't help them now. The distance begins to grow between the captains' experience and their "calm and collected" descriptions:

> They [Natives in general] might fight seven years
> and not kill seven men. They come not near one another,
> but shoot remote, and not point-blank as we often do [in
> Europe] with our bullets, but at rovers; and then they
> gaze up into the sky to see where the arrow falls, and
> not until it is fallen do they shoot again. This fight is
> more for pastime, than to conquer and subdue enemies
> ....(U82)

Underhill here is consistent with most observers. "Pastime" means social purposes, very little like European purpose in war. New England braves do not "shoot" all at once. They face "rovers" rather than try to break ranks of "pike pushers" (Dyer). As noted (Ch. 1), that is not to say that Native braves are no threat to men with matchlocks. Gardener in a Saybrook skirmish says that "Though we gave fire upon them, *yet they run onto the very muzzles of our pieces*...and if The Lord had not put it in my mind to make the men draw their swords they had taken us all alive" (WPF3: 381-2, emphasis added). The hoary conceit of guns as advantage is dispelled: they break, get damp, explode, are inaccurate, and reload in the time you can take six arrows.

Lion Gardener has seen more action than any man at Mystic. He has not come because he knows what his fellows are up against when New England braves intend more than pastime:

> Within a few days [after a skirmish], after I had cured myself of my [arrow] wound, I went out with eight men to get some fowl for our relief. And found...the body of one [English] man shot through, the arrow going in at the right side, the head sticking fast, half through a rib on the left side, which I took out and cleansed...and presumed to send it to [Mass. Bay], because they had said that the arrows of the Indians were of no force....(G130)

Gardener finds other men shot through the head with arrows (G129). This does not just fall out of the world on May 26th. The Narragansetts, Mohegans, Niantics and Pequots know this is not a day for their own mortal troubles. The captains have just managed to repulse a first wave of "enraged" warriors, and now they have time to "observe"---because what the Native men "grant" them is by no means what they are capable of in war.

These braves are not uncontrollably *hoggery*---with each other. You recall that they pass "scarce a week" without fighting, yet "with little loss to any" (WCL1: 72). The differences, today, lie with the English presence and purpose, to slaughter their common kinsmen.

Uncas alone seems able to imagine what English war is about. He hopes to benefit by it, but not as the English intend. If he provides good service this day, where is he either inside or outside Mystic to take charge of this Native fight and make it count? He does later use Mason's forces to rob Pawcatuck Pequots of corn. Where is he now to lay down the law of New-English war? The captains say no brave finds inspiration to kill or be killed. Native rumor of "two" felled by this action means little. Uncas, doing nothing, is up on secret everything. This is another *show*---of strength, and not the killing-kind; another part of the Pequots' holding-action. None of this occurs to Mason or Underhill. What they see is your history.[58]

Vanity refashions this remarkably canny, intertribal gesture of restraint---in context, the one genuine miracle of this book---into the "play" of hopefully-harmless, submissive children. Their lives in their hands this day, their later colonial confidence never what they long for (Chs. 5-7), the English swallow their own Mystic lie for comfort. 1675 will startle them from a dream.[59]

---

[58] At "harvest time" to come Mason assaults an East Niantic village harboring Pequots (M41-2). Its details confirm the above. Taunted as usual by Native people "running up and down jeering us," then "marching...up to their wig-wams, [the English find] the Indians...all fled, except some old people that could not." Mason and Uncas with 100 men (M40) get busy "plundering" when they "espy...about sixty Indians running toward us." First they mistake these for some of Uncas' men, but the Mohegans do not speak "one word, nor move...until the other come within...paces." Then the Mohegans "run and meet them, and fall on pell mell, striking and cutting with bows, hatchets, knives, etc., after their feeble manner. Indeed it hardly deserves the name of fighting." Failed again, Mason's men "endeavor to get between them and the woods" (having learned something the hard way?), to "prevent their flying; which they perceiving, endeavored speedily to get off [by way of] the beach." "Some of them growing very out-rageous [as prisoners] we intend to make shorter by the head"; when one Otash *aka* Yotash, a brother of Miantonomo, intercedes---as "a friend to the English." Johnson's portrait of Uncas (in Grumet) includes a similar attack with 300 braves against Pequots at Nameag, almost 10 years after Mystic. "The purpose of such a war was to make a statement: usually few people were killed....The attack was met with virtually no opposition and the Mohegans could have slaughtered many. Yet none of the accounts...mentions the killing of even one person" (40-1).

[59] "Traditional enemy" Native Americans trade, marry, "revel" and otherwise meet on regular intertribal grounds, and so are capable of restraint with a reason based in common observation (exs. Dempsey *News* lxvi-lxviii). In 1623, after a

There is another show coming for Mason, Underhill and the few uncertain allies still with them at Mystic. The enraged Pequots now begin to deliver them Sassacus' second personal greeting.

Suddenly after the quick "consultation" above, fifty more of the Narragansetts fall "off from the rest, returning home" (U83). With Weinshauks' fresh reinforcements pouring eastward now, the Pequots attack again. and a "sortie" of theirs gives the deserters immediate attention: it clears the ground of Native foes they know. And then, as in The Great Swamp Fight, the Pequots reverse the field on attackers who forgot (and lack the numbers) to deploy a force behind them. "Hundreds" of braves start to drive the English into the lower ground off Mystic Hill.

Since Saybrook the English have had scarce control of anything. They do not understand what is really happening, let alone control it. Vincent (V104) has no problem turning English panic into a moral nugget by means of Underhill's fearless sortie; because Vincent is not at Mystic, and never feels what it is to have enraged Pequot braves pressing in all around him.

Neither Mason nor Underhill forget. Their state, that sharp bright morning, is such that they make different pure guesses (M29, "we guess") as to how many braves they see, fight or kill. Neither do they remember alike when and where the brunt of Pequot force comes down or when they sight salvation in their boats.

---

year of insults, robberies and violence from colonists in Massachusetts, the peoples of Mass. Bay/Cape Cod are assumed to be hatching retaliations. It proves false; but, not long before Plimoth's needless "preemptive" massacre, another roving sea-captain tries to kidnap more Natives (Nausets), who escape. The region's tribes providing crucial food to Plimoth turn for justice not there, where they should expect it under "Thanksgiving's" treaties, but to the Council for New England, which records their complaint if not any justice.

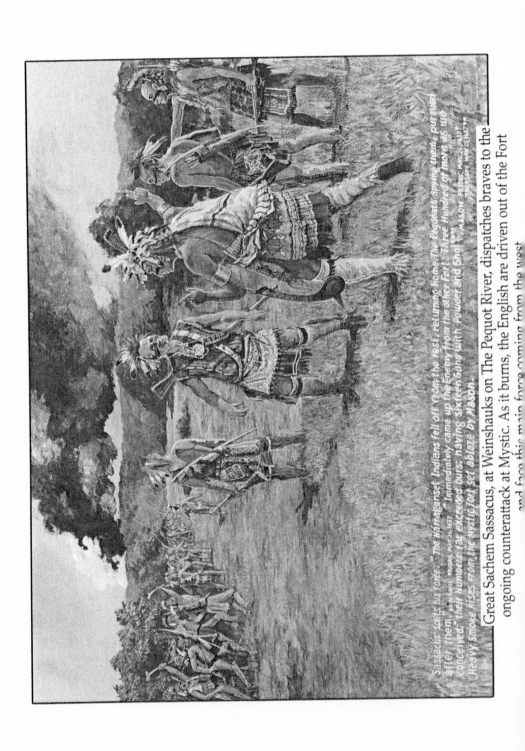

Sassacus spits his rage: "The Narragansett Indians fell off from the rest returning home. The Pequots came upon them, pursued after them _____ Immediately came up the Enemy from the other Fort. Three Hundred of [to]d, as we conceived, their Numbers far exceeded ours: having Sixteen Guns with Powder and Shot." MASON, Prince (page 437) Heavy smoke rises from the Mystic fort set ablaze by Mason.

Great Sachem Sassacus, at Weinshauks on The Pequot River, dispatches braves to the ongoing counterattack at Mystic. As it burns, the English are driven out of the Fort and face this main force coming from the west.

Beleaguered, with no chance to plunder as planned, the captains gather almost more wounded than they can carry ("Indians" carry them to free English hands, below), and they begin to relinquish the high ground to make away from burning Mystic Fort.[60]

Once they detach from there, they have no precious tactical rear. As more braves pour into the swirling fight, showing "hundreds," raining missiles and screaming ugly promises, the English panic grows. For look as the captains must at their options now. Go to Mystic, follow these actions and see what you would do.

---

[60] Underhill says that now he launches a sortie of "30 men" (Mason says it happens much later, U83/ M31), against hundreds of Pequot braves. It deflects their whole attack and clears the way for wherever it is they're going. He says he flies into a rage about the deserting Narragansetts' "cry" of "Oh help us now, or our men will all be slain" (U83). "How dare you crave aid of us, when you are leaving...us in this distressed condition, not knowing which way to march out of the country?" He says that "in the space of an hour" his dash rescues the Narragansetts and kills or wounds "above a hundred Pequots, all fighting men, that charge us both in rear and flanks." If he makes casualties of hundreds, how many does he attack out there in the woods? The sortie's odds are ten ("300 as they conceive") against one, and neither guns nor terrain are advantages. Suddenly the same odds and circumstances in Higginson's warning (Ch. 1, WPF3: 404) cast light on Underhill's claim. Mason reports Underhill's act not as a breath of life as they leave Mystic, but later as sport, as they sight their boats (below). He adds swagger to his partner's deed, deeming it "chiefly to try what temper" the Pequots have: Underhill coolly "puts them to a stand." Vincent, though he paints all Natives cowards, records from his sources that Underhill's sortie is a matter of "five muskets discharged [and] the Pequots fled" (V104). Either way, the Pequots have bettered their situation and can turn harder on the English with their "allies" gone. Two pages later Vincent recants, fetching out "news" from the Mohegans, that "about an hundred Pequots were slain or hurt" by the sortie. Which is it? When was it? Vincent publishes and then moves on to Germany to write about "sin" (Orr 91).

They have sort of a plan to march, victorious at Mystic, towards "a certain neck of land that lay by the sea-side, where we intend...to quarter that night, because we know not how to get our maimed men to Pequot River" (U83). Another "jar" between where they're going and where they think Captain Patrick will be with their boats. They must connect with Patrick as their only hope of English help; and supposedly, the lucky sighting of those vessels diverts the English force from heading for that "neck of land."

Who sights and signals to whom? If they're heading even vaguely west toward that "neck near Pequot River," how can they possibly see where Patrick will, in fact, reach shore? Do they spare even five men to scout ahead through a maelstrom of Pequots? We cannot learn from either captain. They maintain cool presentation and take us with them toward "the river" (U84). Neither man says which river they hope to reach, and with reason.[61]

We know by now that each captain's chronicle is shaped to some degree for its audience with a pleasingly-Christian "object lesson," a harrowing yet God-guided pilgrims' progress to victory through doubt, danger and the candle-power of their American war-experience. When they say they "know not" which way to turn on the land, we can rightly give some benefit of doubt: perhaps they mean they do not know how to reach "the river" *safely*. But what do we, as real world historians, gain for it? If they truly knew enough from the start to judge themselves ignorant of the country,

---

[61] Cave: "English casualties at Mystic were higher than is sometimes realized." The English begin their retreat with about 60 able-bodied men short on the only "provision" crucial to their minds here, gunpowder. More men must deal with further wounded. Cave and Hirsch (156; 1206) have it backwards that Native people do "not understand their adversary," and that this explains why the English are not massacred themselves. Watch what happens and see if you agree.

wouldn't that be a reason to plan at least one other walking-way out? Why can't they follow the Narragansetts back east into allied country? Somehow as they leave Mystic Hill, that's not a good idea: after all, they don't do it.

Should they turn, fight their way back north up that narrow approach-corridor along the Sound, and hedgehog at Porter's Rocks with their keg of gunpowder, like Romans in Germany until Patrick's assistance comes? He's looking for Pequot River. He'll be days finding them up there, miles up the double-embayment of Mystic Head.

Perhaps he'll come sooner---if the secret plan we never could nail down has specified Mystic as "the fort" after all for Captain Patrick. Perhaps. Wouldn't a soldier wish now to understand why both captains make pages of pretense about their ignorance and how they discover the target?

Blast---They'll just have to try to reach Pequot River. "A memorable day." Here at Mystic they feel so close to the Atlantic--- at least that would put something at their backs. To follow their spoken plan, they must now turn toward the Pequot attacks, "back into" the land and its daunting wooded trails. They shoot and struggle their way southwest off Mystic Hill. Up one side, in-out, and down the other.

This westward way takes them straight to Sassacus. Time to worry how many Pequots he has called to the neighborhood since last week. Do we hear Mason's soldiers now? Shouts for powder and more than birdshot. "And the captains said we'd take both forts!" "Can't you smell that Mystic water, brother, so near?" "Why are we going *this* way?" But Mason and Underhill press them all onward, refusing to change their plans in front of the company, and one of Gardener's "handful" cursing them out (blunt Thomas Stanton). "Prudent chap, old Lion!" "And his seasick doctor, too!"

Captain Mason's and Underhill's 75 Englishmen fight their way down
Mystic Fort Hill (at right), following streams and Pequot trails to the nearest water
they can reach—not "appointed" Pequot River, Mystic River.

Wherever they can see very far ahead, they see "nothing" but seven miles of march. If you travel this southwest route today along New London Road and other paths, you lose sight and even sense of where the rivers and the Atlantic have gone as landmarks. Connecticut land descends, levels and runs, slopes up small steep hills and down more, thick with trees, without "English reference."

And the time? Was it a 2-hour march from 5:30's sunrise to battle, half an hour to penetrate Mystic Fort, plus the captains' "hour" to conquer it? By 10 a.m. Mystic is in flames and the English are outside it again. They "observe" Native fighting, perhaps launch an hour's sortie to get going somewhere---and now it nears noon as they try for Pequot River. If they want to reach "safety" by marching this forced westerly way, before them wait 6 or 7 miles of heat with the sun falling into their eyes, a trail without doubt full of ambush. Should they survive sunset, they'll reach the even more imposing hill of Sassacus' angry fort, and face combat all night alone unless Patrick shows. Will *he* answer Sassacus' challenge?

No guide at their side says a word. Where is Uncas? Wequash? This place is home to every Native with them. Not one points a creditable finger toward tactics or "the way." Why should they? The captains think they're in control and each move finds them less so. If the captains still can't bear to coax, bribe, or press Native guides for the best way out, they haven't learned much coming in.

The only consistent thing in early American war-history is the incredulous frustration of the Captain Churches. We almost have to conclude that Church's brethren and their descendants study Mason and Underhill as scripture. If these chronicles are not war-histories, subject to a reasonable expectation of practical sense and usefulness, what then are they?

Experience in editing early New England writings teaches that, when a Puritan writer suddenly loses control of that famous "plain style," and cripples our understanding with suddenly antiquated syntax, etc., there is something uncomfortable at stake for them behind that "lost" clarity. As we move chronologically through Mason's and Underhill's experience, we now find an increasingly garbled account from each and between them. From here in withdrawal from Mystic Hill, Underhill recalls Pequots "playing upon our flanks" until the men see and reach their boats "at Pequot River" (U84).

Mason---as if Pequot River is at the bottom of Mystic Hill---blurrily recalls almost no delay of "rejoicing" at "sight of our sails." The other significant detail beside that good news is that, as they now move down the hill, "immediately comes up [*sic*] the enemy from the other fort": Weinshauks' "proper braves," "three hundred as we conceived" (M31-2).

In spite of his own details about this retreat, Mason surrounds them at both ends of this passage with cool collected words and images. At the latter end (just below), his men are shown enjoying the sport of shooting Pequots they can see. Here at the front, Mason places Underhill's miraculous sortie as a quaint pastime that "teaches" those hundreds "a little more manners than to disturb us" (M31-2). Indeed "Indians" cannot win. If they don't kill, they're children: if they do, "savages." They just don't understand that they shouldn't be there at all.[62]

Between these claims of calm, we see with the land's help that Mason's English must in fact quickly give up moving overland toward more disaster at Pequot River. We invite you to go and

---

[62] Cave merely restates the captains' descriptions of their retreat (154-6) without question. He seems to notice every detail of Pequot wrath yet looks for no signs of effect: the captains are in cool control. He even writes that *Mason* leads Underhill's sortie (154): the accounts in Orr disagree.

walk this entire journey, try both options (the bay-water at the foot of Mystic Hill, or the 7-mile march to Sassacus), and see which option you choose in their situation. As you and they lose the hill, even in winter with no foliage on the many present trees, you will not sight your boats in any direction.

Even to keep plunging toward Pequot they must scramble southwestward down under a hail of weapons. With all these symptoms, we come toward an idea of English rout. They do try the westward march; and when you do, you arrive after "about two miles" at today's McGuire Brook. Are its low ground and stream-bed the place where Mason "refreshes" his brow (below)? They are in fact fading "leftwards" off the westward way, slogging by harried stages in the one down-hill direction they can let themselves really take: toward the nearest Atlantic on the "back" side of Mystic Hill, where their backs can feel safer fast.

Maybe the captains keep pushing west beyond McGuire's Brook. When you do, you soon reach today's Eccleston Brook, another lovely spot for rest if you have time. From there it's still 5-6 miles to "Pequot River." But, a mile below to your left just here, these two brooks converge as they fall away and empty into Mystic Sound. Based on the captains' time-frame, landmarks, distances and story-strictures, their stop at such a brook for refreshments is just where they head for the nearest ocean. Either of these streams cuts an obvious easy path down through thorny underbrush and seems a fast way to relief, even if it leads to nothing but the sea.

Surrounded, bleeding, short on ordnance and without their drum too, Mason and Underhill come upon several "wigwams" (likely a fishing-camp near the water), "fall on" and, not surprisingly, burn them with no mention of enemies there. To them this mile-or-so detour to the "water-side" seems twice that (M33). But the "water" cannot be Pequot River. Maybe those wigwams "fall" on them, more decoys for ambush as they scramble down along the stream-beds. The braves know that Englishmen look for huddled masses.

As the captains tell it, at "their" water at last, they "sit down in quiet" with "colors flying," and all is well. The Pequots have their kinds of show. Now look between the lines of martial poise.

> Four or five of our men are so wounded that they
> must be carried with the arms of twenty more. We also
> being faint, are constrained to put four to one man...so
> that we have not above forty men free [and not above
> ten as Underhill sorties here with 'thirty']. At length we
> hire several Indians who ease us of that burden....(M32)

Suddenly we understand historian Vaughan: Mason "learned not to count on his Indian allies for much more than scouting duty, and at the same time discovered that this could be a crucial element in forest warfare" (153).

That is tradition in a nutshell. Native helpers are "there," yet really do nothing for the English except somehow turn it all to victory. Victory is impossible without their help, and they scarcely do what their captains claim. Historians have made up the differences, traditions full of "sound and fury" signifying little but their dreams.

For example, the English at this actual point can no longer see Mystic Fort, up the hill behind them through the trees. According to DeForest, though (134), as packs of Pequot braves from the whole area join this pursuit, their enraged latecomers "behold...what is done" at Mystic, "stamp" and "tear the hair from their heads." The captains have given us horrid images and touching justifications of Mystic's supposed carnage, but they cannot see any such discovery by the Pequots. One of the more lurid contributions to colonial "closure" is Henry Trumbull's of

ARRIVING AT THE BANKS OF THE PEQUOT RIVER AND THE SAFETY OF HIS SMALL FLEET, AID BY CAPT. PATRICK WITH HIS 40 FRESH TROOPS IS REFUSED: "BUT WE COULD NOT PREVAIL WITH HIM BY ANY MEANS TO PUT HIS MEN ASHORE, THAT SO WE MIGHT CARRY OUR WOUNDED MEN ABOARD, ALTHOUGH IT WAS OUR BOAT IN WHICH HE WAS. WE WERE VERY MUCH TROUBLED BUT KNEW NOT HOW TO HELP OURSELVES". —MASON: FRIDAY MAY 26, 1637

With Mason's boats, Captain Daniel Patrick is on his way to Pequot River. Luckily, he sights smoke from burning Mystic Fort on that river, and steers up Mystic Inlet. There Mason (right) and Underhill (left) encourage him to bring the boats in to shore.

End of the attack on Mystic: the mouth of Mystic River today,
at a point nearest the hill's descent from Mystic Fort. The coastline just visible
farthest out is part of Fisher's Island. Without Mystic Fort's smoke to fetch in
Captain Patrick's boats, Mason's company would not have been seen onshore.

Looking east (vs. previous south) from the same point on the Mystic River's
mouth where Mason's company reach the Atlantic. This is near the merging
mouths of the two streams that they follow down to the water; rather than
continue west, as planned after their assault, to Pequot River (and Sassacus'
fort Weinshauks). Just opposite here is "Mason's Island." Captain Patrick's
boats also may come around the isle from the left of this beach.

1836, treated later here. DeForest draws upon it (134 below) for his 1851 *History of the Indians of Connecticut*, long a standard:

> At [this] moment a large body of warriors, seem-
> ingly 300 in number, is discovered rapidly approaching
> from the west...coming to revenge the destruction of
> their kinsmen. Such, however, is the feebleness, the
> perfect imbecility of bows and arrows when opposed
> to firearms....The Pequots follow them until they come
> to the sight of the recent catastrophe, where they halt to
> gaze at the scene of destruction.
> In place of their late fortress with its 70 wigwams, bid-
> ding defiance as they thought...they behold only smok-
> ing, smouldering ruins, mingled with scorched and
> mangled corpses. There lies the aged counselor, the
> wise powwow, and the brave warrior; there lie little
> children who but the day before played in mimic war-
> fare about the hill; there lie mothers and wives, and young
> girls just entering upon womanhood: all dead by a horr-
> ible and agonizing death, and so disfigured that not even
> the eye of love can recognize them. The stoicism of the Pe-
> quot warriors gives way under so terrible a blow....

Posed as "history," this is pure creative departure from any eyewitness; yet another comforting reassurance of victory invented because not there in the "facts." "And the English, as they look back"---says DeForest, quietly closing the seam of his insertion---can see "the Pequots stamp and tear their hair in grief."

Did he walk Mystic Hill and find that this "look back" is physically impossible? He claims to write "like a witness on oath" (143), and his book's "Testimonial" from 1850's Connecticut Historical Society vouches: "...they have read the manuscript...with as much attention as time and circumstances would allow, and...have not thought it necessary to look at the authorities on which Mr. DeForest relies" (iii).[63]

The Pequots have reason for rage without any of that. They charge, says Mason (M32),

> ...come mounting down the hill upon us in a full career, as if they would run over us....Some of them being shot make the rest more wary. Yet they hold on running to and fro and shooting their arrows at random....

At random: meaning Mason sees no meaning. Either he does not know or doesn't want readers to know his situation, what the Pequots intend, or really can do. Mason's recommendation to future generals in such a plight? "There is at the foot of the hill a small brook....We rest and refresh ourselves," and watch Underhill at play (M32). Of Siswas dismembered at Saybrook we recall, "Some will have their courage thought invincible when all is desperate" (V101).

---

[63] "Time and circumstances" meaning the normal business day. As we'll see, tradition has built a genre of such fictional spectacles: history as a kind of Virtual Coliseum of American blood-sports, soon popularly known as "blood pudding" (see Reynolds' *Beneath the American Renaissance*). What is it for, what "cultural work" do these inventions accomplish for Anglo-Americans who conquer a continent by the lights of Mason and Underhill? Like a lampshade (a dead, harmless artifact) made from the skin of a once-terrifying "other," these inventions are "holy smoke"---comfort for a national psyche in love with violence, addicted to its short-term rewards and, in the long term, sick with fear of revenge and guilt for its needlessness. Indulge those voluptuous, violent, swelling phrases above, the "sad necessity" that culminates in two dead young girls about to blossom nevermore. It proved enough to make many a red-blooded man forget he caused the "tragedy." See Ch. 7.

But the roving, encircling waves of Pequot men with bows and spears, flying hatchets and clubs keep up attack, and herd the English where they want them. The ocean is where the captains' column is going with or without boats waiting offshore. We know why they bother at this point to burn "wigwams," anything "Indian." "The enemy [is] still following us in the rear, which is to windward," Mason says: we are to believe that a May-day breeze reduces bone-breaking missiles to "little purpose":

> Yet some of them lay in ambush behind rocks and trees, often shooting at us, yet through [God's, not the Pequots'] mercy touch not one of us; and as we come to any swamp or thicket, we [have to shoot] to clear the passage. Some of [the Pequots] fall with our shot, and... our Indians...then...take so much courage as to fetch their heads....Within two miles of Pequot harbor [sic]...the enemy gather together and leave us....

Across the colonial records, matchlocks, slashing-swords and halberds are less effective than arrows or spears in this environment. (See the photo of typical New England "thicket" that flanks both sides of this Pequot trail onto which the captains stumble, and see what weapon you'd prefer.) Yet according to the captains, they are not at all in retreat: they stroll down to the nearest beach passing the medicine-brandy. So in love are tradition and triumph that they march right past the question: If all is under control, why not head for Pequot River? That's what the captains claim they're doing, and it is not supported by the least investigation.

On the way both captains say that they're short of powder. Yet a "pretty courageous soldier" with a 3-foot "carbine" steps from the struggling ranks "at a venture" and draws aim on a Pequot lying flat "upon the top of a rock" (U84). With "so unexpert" ease the planter "turns him over [dead] with his heels upward"---a peculiar posture itself for a man left on his back. The "Indian allies" "greatly admire" the sport, and hundreds of Pequot braves are so "much daunted" that they dare nothing further. They watch some of the English board their boats "in quiet" and let others parade back to Saybrook, as they go freely "punishing" Western Niantic villages under Sassious, and "burning and spoiling the country."[64]

We simply have to laugh. The English achieve all this with a handful of powder at the wrong river. Before them is the Mystic River, seven miles from their "appointed" Pequot River rendezvous; but they seem to think or want us to think something else. They find themselves strung along the shore of Mystic Sound, a mile from the actual Atlantic, and in their faces now is Chuppachaug, the future Mason's Island." The very name proves (and is ignored as) the place where Mason finds the "safety" of water at his back. If they do glimpse their boats as they come down and across the hill, it's pure luck through heavy trees on lower trail.

---

[64] A "carbine" is a gun "between pistol and musket" (OED), a sawed-off blunderbuss for close range killing. Its short barrel robs it of accuracy and has no rifling that spins a bullet for better aim. With this gun and range the man is lucky to hit the rock. On weapons see Peterson and Pollard 4-45. The "burning and spoiling" causes "great want of provision" later (Mather 158) and is why Mason steals corn with Uncas at Pawcatuck. Cave "explains" the English survival (thanks to Pequot withdrawal, next) by citing later Edward Johnson, who "explains" that "The Lord" keeps the Pequots from realizing they can massacre the English on the beach. Historians see and find a way not to see. During this summer's further English attacks, Cave relates a misreading (162) that the Niantics (for ex.) believe in English "supernatural powers." But their "jeering" and insults at the "supermen" mock the fantasy. Compare other examples of Native speech taken according to English whim in Dempsey ed., *Canaan* 31n103 and *News* lxv.

Mason and Underhill not only lead their men to the wrong river: they find that they can't signal to the boats from here. From this beach (see photo), all they can see is the strait far out along Fisher's Island. What if Captain Patrick steers east of that island to make time toward the "rescue" at Pequot River, as instructed? Mason might see a sail: no one can see him without coming up into the Sound. By every physical likelihood, Patrick should miss them completely. What is the answer? And, before that in importance, why does the fighting end at just this point?

We reach strange answers with the logic of tradition. "Just as Indians reacted initially to colonial weaponry with panic," Hirsch says rightly, while going wrong, "so now [at Mystic, the Pequots] panic when confronted for the first time" with a genocidal "colonial strategy" (1203). That is to say: the Pequots supposedly behold the captains' unprecedented, total-war carnage as in DeForest's savory scene; and we the readers stand for one moment with them, and see it too, feeling "what anybody would feel" at the sight of one's butchered family. Thus, we can "understand" (that is, accept the idea) that the Pequots "flee in disarray" through the rest of this war. Here, you have seen and will see that they do no such thing.[65]

---

[65] DeForest 138: Mystic was an "expedition conducted with admirable skill and courage, and crowned with the most astonishing success." 140: "Had Mason continued to fight on as he began [at Mystic Fort], so many of his soldiers would have been killed and disabled that the rest might have been overwhelmed by the warriors from the other village, or at best, obliged to abandon their wounded and make a calamitous retreat. Had he, at this critical moment, ordered a retreat ...the Pequots would... resume the offensive, and the whole object...would have certainly been lost. He did neither....A piece of stern policy, mingled with something of revenge, from which floods of argument cannot wash out a stain of cruelty....It would not be fair, however, to try the men of a stern and iron age by the high standard...at the present day" (1852).

This "victory," believed-in but riddled with doubt (below), is the birth of the Puritan colonies' confidence in themselves as here to stay. Its bloodsoaked miracles begin and predict the imposition of a tragically-sublime Calvinist cosmos on Native America's. (Hence Connecticut's Birthday). But "colonial America" then and now is secretly most in love with the tragedy. It "owes" this love as long as it conceives itself *as* colonial, as owing its existence to violence. For violence is the only component of colonial method that can actually "work"---take away real-world wealth that belongs to other very real peoples. History's convenient, erzatz sadness over "the story of civilization" is the secret trace of real knowledge---that violence was not needed to get rich here. That is why multicultural Merrymount was burned first, and fascinates still with its success.

The Pequots, and by extension all Native Americans, lose their wars because of English war, because they don't understand the new rules their opponents bring. What are those rules? Are they the ones still alive in Early Modern Europe (noted above), a body of post-chivalry traditions working across the lines of national identity, battered as they are by The Thirty Years War? According to tradition in Hirsch's words (1204), war evolves, right here at Mystic; from the European-style "oblivious drills" of Hartford and Boston (above) to a method called "sheer wantonness." DeForest's Pequot "imbeciles" fail to understand that there are no more rules.

Following the captains' wishful books rather than their trail at Mystic, history chivvies us to a wistful false assumption. "If the Pequots had come down and massacred the captains and men on that beach, The Pequot War would have ended very differently." By this illogic, if the Pequots can just steel themselves to the necessity of sheer wantonness, they can hold onto their land and their universe by a massacre, "man and mother's son." Only something that awful, we confess, can awaken the colonies to the story's other side. The Pequots thus conceived have two "real world choices" that both come from Europe---disarray, or wanton retribution. And the "sad" part we accept is that neither will save them anyway, as what they truly are.

In their world, war is another way to make a statement to others, not a "tragic" way to find oneself a neurotic mass-murderer, with "innocent" hands full of windfall-wealth.

"We had formerly concluded to destroy them by the sword and save the plunder" (M38). Mason and Underhill, intending massacre, are sucked in, spun around and backed down onto the wrong beach at Pequot mercy, and tradition comes to their rescue. The captains conceal, confuse, bluster and browbeat, present us their model of innocent courageous public service, thrill us with their encounters with death and share their triumph against all odds. We the colonists "bond" by a terrified affirmation that "This is nature and people as they are: Thank God for the fort and a few amazing miracles." Accepting this in our terror, we consign ourselves to a colonial fort that we come to call the only "realistic" history. Violence polices the edge of our conception of the possible.

By this illogic, we grow into true Americans as education browbeats us never to consider Native imbeciles---who just weren't advanced enough to wipe out Progress while they could.[66]

The land lays bare the Mystic foundation of Indian Doom; and even this late generation's "multicultural analysis" (Vaughan for example, Hirsch, Cave) contains its true potentials in an old trap of

---

[66] According to Hale's study of war, "Both secular and clerical writers continued to stress the moral dangers that beset a man who joined an army, the temptations ....But to this was now added the fear that he would become habituated to violence. 'Can someone be even minutely sensitive about killing one person when mass murder is his profession?' asked Erasmus" (10).

new steel. Hirsch's and other studies are "aware" of the heart of Native warfare, *symbolic ascendancy* (1190), in essence "one-upping" the enemy for today. Unless the captains are covering up more killed Englishmen, this is why we find only two of them dead and many "wounded" at Mystic, for all the Pequots' numbers and assaults. Especially with small hints that the two dead English died from friendly fire, that tally is "about normal" for a Native battle. A wound from a man who can kill you is a message.

But, for the good colonial reader, the Pequots' choices remain either a fight to the death or racial/cultural extinction. There *are* other options, but tradition gives us one self-serving definition of victory. Belief in the success of wantonness comes as we learn these many ways to close our eyes.

We need to right our boat. The reason Native Americans "can't win" in American tradition seems to be that at Mystic and surely elsewhere, they actually do.

Mason's and Underhill's outnumbered English bleed with their backs to the sea. Perhaps only now in this corner do they realize the magnitude of what they were dreaming. In their rage they must wish they could burn the ocean. They're on the wrong river and near out of powder. Mamoho, "Samm" and the Pequots above them can hear this, a dying-off in the rate of gunfire, and press down for the kill if they choose. If they come, it will be with weapons and numbers to do it. This is the situation behind the captains' chronicles when yet another element gives the lie.

The boats! It's Captain Patrick! How in the world---a miracle? No: a pillar of cloud, or rather, smoke. A fiasco is burning up there behind them on the hill while the Pequots suffer Mason's men to breathe. That smoke is the only thing to catch a far-off sailor's eye this afternoon as he hurries for the right rendezvous. Lo! comes Captain Daniel Patrick with Mass. Bay's "forty able soldiers...ready

138

Captain Patrick,

to begin a second attempt" (U84). Whatever Patrick hears and sees from offshore, he yells to Mason that he's come to "rescue us, supposing we are pursued" (M33). As noted, Boston expects disaster from Mason, if Narragansetts know their war.

"Not any the least sign of such a thing," Mason shrugs.

Nor does Underhill give Patrick the time of day in his last pages. Both captains grudge Mass. Bay's delays. "Delays? Why didn't you wait?" Patrick must wonder. The captains never let us hear him, and paint Irish a coward. He can only be a coward if there is trouble on that beach, such as hundreds of Pequots driving their mauled guests into the waves. Patrick refuses to come ashore or land the boats that Mason "might carry our wounded men aboard" (M33). No "fresh" man leaps the gunwales to lead a new charge. We don't see "Dr." Pell even bring the brandy.

"We are very much troubled, but know not how to help ourselves," Mason says. "It is our own boat." As with the other riots we've seen, we need to know why Patrick acts this way---to know whether Mason's poise after Mystic is genuine.[67]

Here on the beach a comically-irrelevant argument breaks out "to a great height" between Captains Underhill and Patrick over who owns the boat or has the greatest "interest" in it (M33). And that's all we are trusted with. The real issue is what those boats will do

---

[67] Captain Church's "little company," surrounded by "multitudes" at the famous "Pease Field" fight of 1675 (Church 406-9), notice a "canoo" or boat nearby that can pluck them out. His men begin to cry out "For God's sake to take them off": Church "fiercely" tells the boat-master to come in or be gone, "or he would fire upon him." Next sentence: "Away goes the boat and leaves them still to shift for themselves." After Church leads another tactical reversal that we cannot expect from Mason/Underhill, the boat returns; by which time Church feels safe to fetch his hat and cutlass (409).

right now. Inquiry again wakes up Mason's "men in a dream." Patrick and Underhill do not resume a legal quarrel at the river. Mather gives us Patrick's "contempt or envy, without cause" (140). In fact the two men disagree on the English situation; and we note such a starkly-opposite view from this first outsider to arrive. Whatever the English options here, title to the boat is the means to claim command of all three. They need a decision fast.

"At length," Patrick relents: whether or not his men came ready to counterattack, the hundreds of Pequots who held the wooded shore let their statement stand, and fade away. Even better to maul most English and now waste Patrick's company's voyage. The boats sidle in and the parties decide who sails, who walks. And before Patrick's sail is out of sight he puts Underhill ashore again. Bad blood grows between them after the war, to end in it.[68] Mason's remaining Narragansetts also refuse here to "go home" by land until a Saybrook escort makes it safer (M35); or as Cave sees it, until Underhill makes a second voyage back for them. Here at Mystic, they can't fit into the boats full of wounded English. Do they "greatly admire" this planning too?

Mason finds himself "absolutely necessitated to march by land...with our Indians and small numbers" (M34). Now he seems

---

[68] In January 1644, Plimoth's Winslow informs Winthrop (WPF4: 427-8) of Patrick's death, at which Underhill is present. Underhill, having been "immediately attacked" by Boston's magistrates after The Pequot War for his politics (Jennings 225n64), finds his way with many English including Patrick to the next "Indian wars" waged by the Dutch. These troops too need to force Native people to be "their guides." As usual less than pleased with the result, they ask Patrick to help them to a more reliable guide; and he, supposed to "bring them to a fort," instead "leads them amiss the whole night." A very frustrated Dutchman returns to call Patrick a "traitor." Patrick spits in his face and is shot dead by him. "The delinquent" is "committed to the safe custody" of Underhill, and "escapes."

Captain Underhill lets fly at Captain Patrick for hesitation. Unless there is more than an emergency of wounded men on Mystic Inlet's beach, there is no reason for arguments.

more aware of the facts, "it being near twenty miles" to Saybrook or any other quasi-friendly place, and through "the enemy's country." Indeed, that way they still have to get past Sassacus' dreaded Weinshauks, and nobody explains why they apparently can without a second major fight: it has to do with the Pequots' post-Mystic plans (below). Patrick's judgment refuses the risk: he returns ashore "with his men" to add numbers to the marchers. "In truth," Mason's men do not "desire or delight in his company," they "plainly" say. But Patrick and his forty "will and do" march along as the boats sail for Saybrook with the "maimed" (U85).

There are no prisoners. We are to assume that allies turn them in (next chapters). There is no plunder to pay expenses of the enterprise, for the English burn and run. No one dares to mount back up to Mystic Village. Captain Patrick, with time and more daring, would have made a priceless observer. But from here on, only Pequots know how many bodies lie at Mystic.

Somehow, fact and even likelihood begin to evaporate. We close this chapter asking how so little substance could prosper as it has.

Captain Patrick's treatment and his silence begin a new order after Mystic. (Drake deems him "a good soldier," in Mather 140n167.) From here on, anybody who doubts total victory at Mystic will prove unwise. We saw Winthrop's sharp answer to questions from a peer, William Bradford. What can "lesser" men expect? A sacred willingness to believe that "we are safe, the Pequots are broken and gone," will thank the Mystic heroes wherever they go, whatever they allow to become "fact" with tight-lipped smiles. Their return with "rights of conquest" to Connecticut land, and with priceless relief and inspiration for Puritan colonists, begins to build Mystic tradition.

There simply is no one with adequate reason to tell the truth. Underhill is banished, Vincent in Germany: Gardener knows enough to withhold his remarks for three decades. And Mason? His commission for "offensive war" lays the future of New England across his novice shoulders. He must produce, one way or another. The colonists send him to deal with their terror (fear of reprisal for what they do to Pequots); and now the best thing helping Mason is the Pequots' next move: their "flight" and/or "disappearance." It proves the colonists' desired results---to them.

Mason has no reason to forfeit the immense rewards of his peers' need to live credulously. What man of the line will challenge Mason, or miss what happens to Underhill, or complicate even the praise of his planter-peers? With what reward? Scarcely half the English at Mystic actually go inside its fort and are quickly ordered out. They are the only 40 men with eyewitness-grounds for doubt of Mason's claims. A man who keeps quiet becomes the crème of his crop---even as another year fails to run down the Pequots.

A new generation of "frontier experts" and believers is born. This is not to deem the majority of colonists corrupt or consciously collusive; but they are for the most part church-fearing stay-at-homes. Mason's Mystic is (literally) heaven-sent, and vetted by the wounds and trauma they see in most of his men. Less thoughtful desire for Pequot spoil closes more eyes, ears and mouths.[69]

---

[69] Yet the men of Mystic *do* talk, and this note provides you with the best example(s) we can find. On June 7th, veteran John Humfrey writes to Winthrop (WPF3: 429-30). His letter is a young man's awkward address that struggles to say something while keeping clear of consequences. "Hitherto [by Mystic], the honor and terror of our people to all the natives is abundantly vindicated and made good," he begins. "Only to my shallowness, it seems considerable whether it were not safe[r] pausing to see what effect this will or may work....Secondly, whether [it is] not best to rest in certain victory and honor acquired, upon so small a loss [of men]." Should we not, sir, count ourselves lucky? "The loss of three men more, if we [do] not exceed [that], may not be paralleled with so many hundreds more of theirs [killed]." No other source so doubts the budding myth

Enroute back to Saybrook Fort after Mystic, Captain Patrick soon puts Captain
Underhill off his boat; then decides to march with his men and Mason's
on another overland route through Pequot territory. Underhill sails with the wounded.

The laws of Puritan church and state already punish the quotidian contacts (casual trade, cohabitation) that teach anything "real" about Native Americans. That is Boston's first court-order of political business in banishing Morton of Merrymount in 1630 and it is why the later Puritan orthodox accuse Captain Church of "lack of vision" (lack of blinding preconceptions). We know too much to imagine Uncas or any other Native questioning "massive" numbers at Mystic. Their plans (below) and their interest now lie the

---

of English lives "well spent." The governors disappoint him with a war that costs 16 English lives and scores wounded (V107). Yet Humfrey wants Winthrop to wonder "whether we must not be forced at last, and it may be in worse circumstances, to take this course [of running down all Pequots]---unless divine justice will miraculously show itself in bringing [the Pequots] all into our net, which according to reason is not likely." Humfrey proves right. The "dreadfulness" of Mason's "battalion" seems "better to measure by [Pequot] fears raised on this last [at Mystic], than to...think that our former victory [there] was not so much of valor as accident, which we ourselves do acknowledge [as God's] providence."

Whose voices are in Humfrey's ears? Is Mystic's fiasco straining at the seams among men who took wounds, but no plunder? Mason hides in the other eyewitnesses' fear of consequences. "Much more" is on Humfrey's mind but he takes back even the above: "Much more, and to as little purpose might be said. But," he closes, "if you continue your resolutions to proceed" in chasing the Pequot Nation, Humfrey has new ideas for weapons against the challenge of Native forts. "Consider...these bottles [to be] used granado-wise" like incendiary cocktails, he says, and he'll get them ready for new mass burnings. Indeed Humfrey has the surprises of Mystic on his mind. "If the fort be so *difficile* as it is reported," a startling bit of news itself, perhaps Mr. Governor will like "a petard or two to command entrance" to the next one. In bastard-Italian picked up from officers Humfrey echoes quiet talk of Mystic as "difficult." Maybe he knows that with Uncas' help, they all were all *in bocca al lupo*. "Thus laying my low thoughts and myself at your feet to be kicked out or admitted as you see good," Humfrey closes; in the shadow of Winthrop's latest "public order" that persons deemed dangerous to his state and church be banished.

opposite way. Three years later the colonies still pike the heads of "Indians" in public for any suspicion of a part in Pequot hostilities (Cave 163). Why the victorious English still feel that to be necessary is one major trace of the Mystic falsehood.[70]

"All we English would be thought and called Christians," writes Gardener (G146). Who then, as Mason commands more war, spoil and status, will question the story he tells "many times" through the years before writing it up? "What can I say?" you recall him shrugging, "God led his people...."

What Puritan has enough knowledge of the Pequots and most New England Natives---their social and political ways, their kind of war, their idea of victory---to say what the Pequots' "dis-appearance" means? Because the colonists don't know these things, they can only suspect what the Pequots *really* do after Mystic. Religious, civil education and military training leap into the breach to enforce "facts" that nobody dares to examine.

Mason's editor, Reverend Increase Mather, is qualified to represent the first "lesser" preachers who, before Mason's book, spearhead the colonial theocracy's public "thanksgivings" and imposition of "divine intervention" on behalf of Mason's Mystic. In publishing Mason's *Brief History* Mather displays the elite's assistances to "truth" in his choices of epigraphs for Mason's title-page. The first is from The Bible's 46th Psalm: "...For they got not the land in possession by their own sword, neither did their own arm save them; but Thy Right Hand, and Thine Arm...because

---

[70] Rubertone (78) for example: "For the leaders of the English colonies, The Pequot War brought the realization that they could instill fear into their enemies and conquer them at will, though even this did not give the colonists any real sense of security." Why is absolute power shot-through with anxiety? Are the Pequots "gone"?

Captain Underhill arrives back at Saybrook Fort with the Englishmen wounded
at Mystic. When Mason arrives by land, he is forced to spend the night
camped with Captain Patrick on the other side of the Connecticutt River.

Thou hadst a Favor unto them." This is not just Puritan-traditional self-abasement, but a word to the wise who see cracks in Mason's chronicle. Hence Mather's second selection (Psalm 18): "This shall be written for the generation to come; and the people...shall praise The Lord." This means You.

"I have sent you a piece of timber...unfit to join to any handsome piece of work," says Gardener of his pages that follow the others' by decades. "You [friends] must get somebody to...smooth it, lest the splinters should prick some men's fingers; for the truth must not be spoken at all times" (G121). "But I think you may let the Governor and Major Mason see it." Gardener himself has been a splinter, but by the time he lets his views circulate, the colonies are far from any need for his subtle, seasoned, hence "uninteresting" questions about the Mystic enterprise. By the time of his writing, "little" has been done "to keep the memory of such a special Providence alive," as Mason agrees (M11); and Uncas is "forgotten, and [Native New Englanders] for our sakes persecuted to this day with fire and sword" (G147).[71]

Gardener knows that "Mystic" can offer the future life-saving lessons, but that they'll be hard to face. He finds that all the colonies really want from Mystic is myth. Roger Williams, as ever the complicit heretic, chides in 1670 that

> However you satisfy yourselves with the Pequot
> Conquest...upon a due and serious consideration of
> matters in the sight of God you will find the Busi-

---

[71] Prince's note in Orr, G117: "In the mouth of Mystic River there is an island, now and always [sic] called Mason's Island...containing five or six hundred acres. This island [Gardener] took possession of by right of conquest....I believe it is the only spot in Connecticut claimed in that way." Surely Prince jests.

ness and Bottom to be, first, a depraved Appetite
after the great Vanities, Dreams and Shadows of this
vanishing Life, great portions of Land, Land in this
wilderness, as if Men were in...Great Necessity and
Danger for want of great portions of Land....This...will
destroy and Famish....(WCL2: 614)

Something seems missing amid the captured yet unmeasured plenty. "Philip's War" explodes five years after Williams' words. Few have listened to Gardener:

...And thus far of The Pequot War, which was but
a comedy in comparison [with] the tragedies which
hath been here threatened since, and may yet come, if
God do not open the eyes, ears and hearts of some that,
I think, are willfully deaf and blind, and think because
there is no change that the vision fails; and put the
evil-threatened day far off. For say they, We are now
twenty to one to what we were then, and none dare med-
dle with us. Oh! Woe be to the pride and security which
hath been the ruin of many nations, as woeful experience
has proved. (1660: G139)

From history we derive ideas of the possible. The enforced belief in "victory" against the Pequots *has created a false choice* with generations of bloody consequence: the refinement of practice based on experience, or "truth." This is what Morton predicted from the Puritans' Old Testament/"martialist" approach to America, with their laws against all uncontrolled contact between English and Native Americans. This is how our journey begins to "arrive at Mystic"---by understanding how Mason and company "got out" of what really happened there.

To find our way, we need a kind of seasoning very different from "oblivious drill"; a different kind of guard against the clamor of voices as we go.

Listen: "It's true, it's true." That is the urgent burden of the first reports of a Mystic massacre; for all New England waits for news of disaster from the Mason/ Underhill action. For Mason's return to Saybrook and Hartford, Underhill's to Boston, and the spread of their words go on precisely while other Englishmen track large "bodies of Pequots" in their moves toward the Connecticut River (and thence, to villages of shelter from Quinnipiac to the Mohawks: next chapter). Who are they? Not only Sassacus and "his," but Sachem Mamoho of Mystic and his family. Reports of their freedom trouble English victory to its core.

"I find the first news of the cutting [off, or killing] of the whole fort of the Pequots at Mystic to be certain and unquestionably true," Williams tells Winthrop (June 2: WPF3: 426). He notes that the English "were oppressed with multitudes...and...wanting powder and shot" there, and that the "Indian allies" should be forgiven their non-participations: he reports only hearsay and leaves out the fact that he saw nothing.

Plimoth too waits for word, its soldiers girded for battle if not eager to help the countrymen taking over "their" Connecticut. Hartford and Mass. Bay let their old river-rivals sit. "Underhill and Patrick are [back] at Narragansett, and have been, days," Winslow complains (FBH2: 248). "I pray you therefore let us hear." But when Plimoth hears of Mystic, it's from "Captain Standish his Indian," Hobbamock. A "loyal" Native, Hobbamock is sent for second-hand word to Nemasket, a Wampanoag village with strong Narragansett ties; and he "saith the defeat of the fort is true" (WPF3: 428). This is no less second-hand than what all the English get. There is no reason Nemasket's people should challenge it, and more than one reason not to: the same is true for the planters of Plimoth still agitating for "elbow room" of their own.

In Governor William Bradford's hands (FBH2: 250), the word becomes flesh.

> Very few escaped [Mystic]. It was conceived [*sic*] they thus destroyed about 400 at this time. It was a fearful sight to see them thus frying in the fire, and the streams of blood quenching the same, and horrible was the stink and scent thereof. But the victory seemed a sweet sacrifice, and they gave the praise thereof to God, who had wrought so wonderfully for them, thus to enclose their enemies in their hands and give them so speedy a victory over so proud and insulting an enemy.

This is comforting fiction, a holy wish for things nobody saw. Bradford knows how "wonderful" an "enclosed" group of Native people can be. Nobody investigates because this is what they want, and like a racist joke, it tells us only about the tellers.

Plimoth's other historian Edward Winslow wants more, right away. Perhaps the rank-and-file is not what it should be. "Let not this [Mystic], though true, discourage the sending of your 160 men," he urges Winthrop's Boston. Indeed Winslow wants to see Englishmen "take such revenge as may be a service to after times, for any of the barbarians to rise against us." He wants Native New England punished in advance---terrorized, in a word---and he writes this from within a colony crippled by its own needless massacre of 1623 (Dempsey, *News*). The Native heads and bloodsoaked "flag" that hung above Plimoth's church have produced their still-anxious "results"; and yet he urges that it's time not to adjust Christian-colonial methods, but intensify them.[72]

The English language, symbols, rhetoric and repression of "Mystic" make wishes come true because of the Pequots' next plans. But, because "belief in Mystic" is itself backwards in relation to what we call "the larger reality" (land and "other" peoples), these wishes come true as nightmare. Winslow's son Josiah is General of the Army at 1675's Great Swamp debacle: the fathers' sins kill Captain Davenport's son there, and maim Bradford's son with an inoperable bullet in his body (Mather 108).

Can we hear the Pequots and other Native people who were there express themselves about Mystic? Yes, and what we have is more spontaneous and direct than their enemies' words. Beyond what will prove to be more of their yes-man performances in English company, Native peoples have no fantasy or deliberate misinformation to manage. Pain is what grows "Mystic" in their later ages. In these first utterances they do not "deploy tropes." They are cries of rage, of challenge and relinquishment of home, of shock, grief and indignation. These are Narragansett men at Mystic as the English cut down every Pequot they can lay hands upon:

> Why should you be so furious?....*Matchit* [Enough!]
> *Matchit*....It is naught [evil], because it is too furious,

---

[72] More on this dynamic in Ch. 7. As New England's spiritual leaders do their jobs, English captains such as Davenport take up Pequot pursuit and new attacks. Captain Stoughton arrives at Narragansett, murders suspected male "Pequots" there and chooses out "tall" comely women for himself and fellows (next chapter); all of it blessed with Old Testament precedents. Roger Williams rushes in to tell the enraged Miantonomo how "displeased" Mr. Governor will be about such conduct; and then assures Winthrop that he knows his Governor better. "I think it is not so" (WPF3: 445).

and slays too many men....(U81, 84)

Tradition hears what it wants to hear in this, that the Pequots are badly hurt to the number of hundreds and hundreds of souls, "prime men" and families. By now we know that the loss of "only" fifty brave brothers inside the decoy of Mystic will make them cry, with a force like nothing seen or allowed at Puritan funerals.[73]

In the light of the Native American relationships seen and to come further on, we should not ignore one other report from the center of what happened. Plimoth's Bradford hears something remarkable from Narragansetts. Though never shown fighting inside Mystic's palisade, they reportedly "see" Pequot people "dancing in the flames" of their burning lodges, and say something about it. What may separate this from Bradford's inventions is the meaning that he credits to a Native translation. For as the Narragansetts witness in some way the Pequots' courage at Mystic, they begin to "chant" a "word in their own language" that signifies, "O brave Pequots!" It is a word or song that they use "familiarly among themselves in their own prayers, in songs of triumph after their victories" (FBH2: 252).

Siswas in Chapter 1 showed us the warrior's death that those fifty met inside Mystic: one with purpose never guessed. Tradition translates this into our share of Bradford's ironic delight that, as he thinks, the Narragansetts mock their falling "overlords." More likely is that, consistent with all their other provocations, those "unwavering allies" chant to hearten the execution of a brilliantly bold and working strategy. They are watching some cousins die so that most of the others will live.

---

[73] Wood (93): "Laughter in them is not common, seldom exceeding a smile"; but at "the death of friends... they lament most exceedingly."

**MAJOR JOHN MASON MONUMENT (Mystic),
GROTON, CONNECTICUT**

The Mason Monument (1939 photo from Peale 179). Supposedly erected on the site of Mystic Fort, it was taken down in the late 20th century and moved to Norwich, CT where Mason lived. A paved suburban neighborhood intersection "marks the spot" of Mystic Fort today.

" The Pequots, undefeated in battle, and surrounded by enemies decide to engage in a mass exodus from Connecticut. Consulting what course to take concluded there was no abiding any longer in their country, and so resolved to fly into several parts, the greatest body of them went towards Manhatance." Mason, July 1637

One of many Pequot options for surviving "The Pequot War".

"Feud" here is not the same as European war---and it remains to witness something crucial to our journey, how the Native New England way of war in Pequot and their kinsmen's hands can and did stand up to that supposedly all-conquering "sheer wantonness." The English victors at Mystic don't want to know how Native New England really works, and it will cripple their confidence in gauging their own war's results.

Does any Native person describe Mystic as a "massacre" beyond the terms above? There is only this sign of burgeoning hearsay, that (as Gardener tells us, G137) "three days after the [Mystic] fight came Waiandance [*aka* Wyandot], next brother to the old Sachem of Long Island...to know if we were angry with all Indians." Wyandot has "heard" about Mystic, but this proves no numbers of people killed there. Miantonomo, next, turns Mystic into a frightening inspiration of his own, but he'll have reasons that don't require gross invention.

More attacks and killings across Connecticut prove too real. The Mystic Pequots' "fate" of wholesale displacement opens a year of massacre up and down the coast. It is enough to convince those already moving of migration. They have elders with stories of that, stories of good places old and new all around the Pequot Nation.

In New England, "good Pequots" now play dead. We need to know about this diaspora, to see if its numbers can help understanding of Mystic and this war.

5

Aftermath:
'So Must We Be As One'

Wise, warned and waiting, Mamoho's Mystic Pequots make their threatened home look alive. Their night of provocative music and campfires lure eager confused Englishmen inside, away from their long-gone human targets; inside where close fighting can foil slow guns, where arrows, spears, clubs and numbers can take on panicked swords. Then, for their own reasons, the Pequots almost fulfill English nightmares. Their Mystic is a holding-action to protect Pequot families, their counterattack "a statement" that drives their guests into the wrong Atlantic. Yet, at more than one point of potential English massacre, the Pequots let them live. Virtually every aspect of Mystic proves the green English overmatched: its aftermath suggests more of the same.

Certainly Mystic scatters the Pequots. As unprecedented violence it demonstrates the English will to exterminate. But the scatter does not follow a DeForest fantasy. It is not Vaughan's or Hirsch's "disarray" (1203), but the Pequots' next coordinated move. At Mystic, the Pequots test their war against Europe's and find it too costly in their own terms, given other options. In a "loose confederacy" like theirs (note below), dispersion is not defeat but the use of a further strength in political structure. Their attachment to their land proves as flexible as it is deep and patient.

To most Europeans, diaspora is destruction. But overnight after Mystic, Great Sachem Sassacus and many Pequots hold council, blame and argue: then they agree to burn their other chief and ancient home Weinshauks. They disperse across Connecticut in bands of different size and direction. Direction it is, guided by each clan's or family's idea of where relatives can best help. It makes massive massacre impossible.[74]

What do "the numbers" in these records of struggles after Mystic reveal about it? We answer by bringing those records and numbers carefully before your eyes, and then we ask you to consider this question:

Which is more likely: that Mason's, Underhill's and traditional claims about Mystic are accurate; or, that the Pequots of Mystic find more than enough room in those records, numbers, and post-

---

[74] "Loose confederacy" describes both Native American leagues and a consensus-based organization of many European cultures older than those familiar to mainstream education. Bronze Age Crete with its "thalassocracy" was the basis of "The Greeks": the multicultural Canaanites/Philistines were displaced by Israel: Rome buried its debts to the Etruscans. All these predecessors were (and are) criticized for a "lack of national and historical consciousness," for not being "able to unify." But even into the "dawn of history," the Phoenicians (for ex.) inherited those older political ways, and they were "unified": eclectic, multiracial, far-flung trading cultures "lacking" obsessive militarism and free to decide their separate fates. Each knew the Mediterranean like no others of their time and made the most of their options. Native Americans too are faulted for seeking individual consent and tolerating refusals of war, as if victory means one thing and history is the last word. A minimal attention to archaeology today reveals mainstream education teaching an almost comic one-sidedness as "the" history of The West; an "objectivity" that would tax the Navajos with failure to develop the Buick.

Mystic options to be remembered not as victims, but (at least) as survivors?

A credible conception of Mystic requires hard numbers. Surely, the histories that generalize about Mystic and The Pequot War "do" them---but we never see it done. We always find citations of a few primary documents (below). But then, another language takes over: "A number of Pequots were killed there"; "The prisoners were divided up"; "The main body was in flight"; "women and children," "those," "some," or "a band." These are mini-generalizations, and they cannot support tradition's larger ones.

We propose more accuracy. Let us present a few points of orientation about the Pequot diaspora after Mystic. Then we'll complete our journey with the English and Native Americans who continue The Pequot War by other means. The numbers will show that, like "the Mystic Massacre" itself, the long-assumed "destruction of the Pequots" does not add up---except with the other evidence of this book.

What general conditions prevail in the months and years after Mystic? Recall that convincing, face-to-face oratory is the key to social and political power in these Native cultures. Narragansett Sachem Miantonomo delivers this speech before many different groups during his 1641 travels through Native New England (qtd. in Gardener 142):

> ...A while after this comes Miantonomo from Block Island to Mantacut [Long Island] with a troop of men ...and instead of receiving presents, which they used to do in their progress[es, or official visits], he gives them gifts, calling them brethren and friends.
>
> 'For so we are all Indians, as the English are, and say Brother to one another. So must we be as one, as the English are, and say Brother to one another. So must we be

as one, as they are; otherwise we shall all be gone
shortly. For you know our fathers had plenty of deer and
skins, our plains were full of deer, as also our woods, and
of turkeys, and our coves full of fish and fowl.
    'But these English, having gotten our land, they with
scythes cut down the grass, and with axes fell the trees:
their cows and horses eat the grass, and their hogs spoil
our clam banks, and we shall all be starved. Therefore, it is
best for you to do as we, for we are all the Sachems from
east to west, both Moquakues and Mohawks joining with
us; and we are all resolved to fall upon them all....'

Informed of speeches like these, Massachusetts and Connecticut colonies see their vision as something to worry about in the wake of their Pequot War. They know of Miantonomo's widespread relatives, his sophistication and courage, and to them this seems the politically realistic start of a "pan-Indian alliance" that might yet drive the colonies into the sea.

Miantonomo has many motives for his travels by 1641. May 1637 at Mystic opens a year of brutal bloodshed followed by threats, demands and more killings, under a one-sided retroactive "justice" (below). All this brings Miantonomo, Uncas, and the English of the colonies to The Treaty of Hartford (September 21, 1638: text in Vaughan 340). The Treaty, however, signifies not peace, but the start of another new kind of war. For years after these ceremonies, the English never shake the anxiety that despite "victory," the Pequots are still all around them.

They are. In the year of horror (1637-38) we're about to witness, the English try different ways of annihilating Pequot existence. When their own sufferings force them to it, the English shift methods from military to symbolic ones. Under Hartford's treaty, on pain of death, they force all Pequot war-survivors to henceforth play a part for them. As of Hartford, anybody identified (as usual) by Native people as "Pequot" is to be henceforth known as Mohegan, Narragansett, Niantic, or "other." Anything but Pequot.

It's a strange demand, because when it really counts, the English still cannot tell "Indians" apart. The treaty seems to work most on the English---or, not to work. It's growing easy to become deranged around here. Are they gone? Are we safe? In control? Gardener feels "infected" (G147). The English try to annihilate, then to "reform" other peoples' persistent being with a category---Non-Pequot, for beings who walk and talk pretty much as before Treaty-day. The English create and police a fiction of symbols to ease their terror of bloodthirsty Pequot being. The new rules cloud their ability to measure real success. This is a "go-away" project that, by definition, can't. Or how can the English confirm they are gone?

As post-Mystic time goes on, frustration feeds suspicion of "treachery." "The United Colonies of New England" order Miantonomo's murder as their "first official act" (Cave). But Miantonomo's purpose is not treachery.[75] He remembers and draws upon his "enemy" Sassacus' appeal to himself before Mystic, that their feuds should be second to a cooperative defense against the

---

[75] Salisbury (231-2) sees Miantonomo as "desperate" by 1641, but this does not describe what the Sachem intends. There is "No more succinct statement of the impact of English settlement on Indian survival and cultural autonomy [to be] found in the 17th-century sources....And in its depiction of a pre-English utopia within the memories of most adults, it anticipates such American Indian prophet movements as those led by Pontiac and Tecumseh, as well as The Ghost Dance. Though an anti-English uprising is part of his plan, Miantonomo's prior record and his friendship with Roger Williams suggest that any movement he leads will be less likely to result in violence than in an effective institutional counterweight to [English expansion], and in the long run, stabilization of Indian-European relations."

English definition of "the common enemy." The two Sachems' words ring across Native actions before and after Mystic. At the war's end in 1638, Miantonomo and Uncas purchase relief from most English violence through familiar means. They formally "agree" and "promise" to stop fighting each other, and to capture or kill any Pequots "guilty of killing Englishmen" in the war.

The English of Hartford and Mass. Bay believe these forced promises enough to stop their offensive war. Three years' more anxiety drives them to Miantonomo's murder. What is it they "know" in-between? That a treaty imposed by force is merely one-sided "peace," and therefore nothing that "Indians" will be bound by. Native Americans have a world, and will not be confined by needless English rules that make them feel "safe." Obvious is the treaty's demand for more killing---of Native people, with "a hand in murdering or killing" in open war. Even historians of LaFantasie's calibre adopt this one-sided term "murder" (for ex. WCL1: 166n10). Miantonomo and Uncas see it for what it is.

There is no agreement for peace where the choices are cultural extinction, slavery or death. We must not surrender our under-standing to the limited terms on Hartford parchment. Native deceptions that (for example) falsely vouch for a kinsman's non-Pequot identity, their running away or hiding themselves and others, are not automatic admissions of defeat.[76]

---

[76] Leland's imperfect collection of Algonquian traditions will survive the crude academic assault by Parkhill (1997); and tells (170, 214) of the American/Canadian Lynx, "a kind of wildcat, none being more obstinate"; admired and imitated as the "hardest-hearted, toughest and most unconquerable, being ever the first to fight and the last to give in, which even then he did not, never having done it and never intending to; whence...he was greatly admired and made much of by all the blackguardly beasts."

At Hartford, Miantonomo and Uncas---those relentless rivals who lose New England between them---smile, and agree, and promise, and mark a big special parchment surrounded with English pomp. They "sign," a ritual-act of shallow meaning to them, because it's what the English demand to stop the killings. The Sachems can see how much and how little paper means to the ink-obsessed English, and swear to help make "Pequots" disappear. Then as you'll see, they take subtle thorough care of the people this peace intends to destroy.

In the violent year after Mystic, some of the English do grow "almost averse [to] killing women and children" (WPF3: 437). As the war begins they execute as many "adult" Pequot males (of warrior or reproductive age) as they can identify or trick into surrender: by its end, they are willing to deport males into slavery or (they believe) erase their Pequot being by declaring them Mohegan or "other." But the Pequots know that the long-term price of true cooperation will still be their people's erasure. As with Mystic, we need to see this situation not with Mason's, Underhill's and tradition's monological eyes alone, but also with a fresh fundamental recognition of the intelligence, pride, imagination and courage in the Native peoples who respond to it.

This is not to idealize Native people, but to describe more fully what happened among all these parties on the land. Consider what has been missing. You, for example, are born of Italian heritage. One day, a new law proclaims that henceforth you are Irish, on pain of death. Who is affected most by this? You, or the police? Should your continued resistance count as part of the story? People are not broken or erased when they mark a paper to that effect. The Pequots hold tight to concepts of home, time, victory and proud identity that are flexible; filled with places in which to survive or even live. Places the English cannot see, conceive or acknowledge, let alone permit.

Uncas proves this after Mystic to both Native peoples and ourselves. Winthrop and Williams, the last ones in on his outrageous joke, tell how (WCL1: 166, notes 7-10).

The year after Mystic is so brutal that Boston refuses Uncas' first gesture toward convenient new relations (June 1638). The colonies well-suspect Uncas of hiding Pequot "murderers" and others. Rejected, Uncas comes back two days later with his "great speech" (here in the Introduction); and as LaFantasie puts it, Governor Winthrop is so "pleased with this *display*" (emphasis added), a display practiced on Mason and Underhill, that Mr. Governor decides "to trust Uncas and to believe his many professions of faithfulness." Winthrop decides to face his colony's need for "Indian intelligence," and Uncas makes the usual use of such need, as you'll see. The most outrageous proof of Uncas' Boston Blarney is that, as he delivers it, the "Mohegan" company of men standing beside him includes "six Pequots," and two of the "known [*sic*] murderers" or braves so badly wanted by the English.

If even one brave is recognized it will shatter Uncas' confidence-game and hopes for power of his own. But there the hunted Pequots stand at his sides as Uncas promises (that phrase again) to turn them in, "were he never so dear to me." At a stroke he "proves" himself to get what he needs from the English, and proves to his kinsmen that the English truly, still, have no way to know who is whom among "Indians." Their only criterion is political attitude. Uncas must have coached this group to smile.

"Winthrop must feel a bit foolish" (LaFantasie) when Williams fills him in two days later on Uncas' outrage. And yet, Boston's need for an Uncas turns most of Winthrop's anger instead against Miantonomo's Narragansetts (and Williams as their pawn). This helps to bring about Miantonomo's murder: again, the English do not know where their foes are. They go on living, as the colonies' "common enemy."

After Mystic the war continues in Native communities across Pequot country: the Eastern and Western Niantics, Quinnipiacs, Shinnecocks, Wangunks, Nipmucs, Mohawks and other nations play parts. There is some compliance with Hartford's demands. "Pequot" individuals are turned in or killed, their identities no more certain than those of the heads brought to Saybrook by Uncas. Each betrayal---a small proportion included below---is based on avoidance of slavery or death. Native collaborators may even use the demand for heads just to enrich themselves while settling old feud-scores of no Pequot War relevance. Once-dominant "man-eaters" leave some scores to settle. But like these English, we have no way to know the difference.[77]

Cutshamekin of the Massachusetts serves as a guide in the Pequot chase and gives up in disgust, careful to leave no interpreter

---

[77] DeForest asks (144) why the English pursue the Pequots and attack other Native groups along the way into southern-Connecticut regions where there are no English "settlers" for miles. He refers us to the Israelites' Old Testament pursuit of the Amelekites. We refer you ahead to Captain Israel Stoughton's behaviors and rewards, his New London "Possession House" and a personal harem picked from prisoners. At the same time, Pequots may well be anywhere: New England peoples have a common share of "matrilineal 'ideology' that emphasize[s] commonality, collective relationships, and lineage or clan affili-ation"; because "members of the same clan might be found living in different homelands," this the "basis of many...connections that link people across space and through time" (108). "Even when the vision of the horizon looming before them was clouded, the bonds of kinship and the sense of community were still strong enough to overcome the dissension...among different factions and individuals" (Rubertone 164).

THE DEATH OF MIANTINOMO.

Page 196 from DeForest's 1852 History

behind. Long Island's Sachem Wyandot fears a Mystic "massacre" on his own or "all Indians," as he says in rushing to terms (G137). So Wyandot does report Miantonomo's speech in 1641, with fatal effect. "Mystic" as a hollow but potent Trojan Horse gets inside Wyandot and others and convinces them of the stakes of New English war. Yet beyond Miantonomo's death, the collaborators add up to little. Native defeat does not hang on one Sachem or group, not even in the colonists' minds. Uncas and Ninigret soon have many fast dugout-boats fetching scores of Pequots from Long Island to better safety.

The great majority of Native New Englanders, however imperfectly, take in hand the ancient structure of their "pan-Indian" community. "Political leadership [is] community-based," Peter Thomas affirms in his study of "cultural change" in this time and place. On that basis, "leadership is generally a matter of group consent" (138). What characteristics would best elicit *your* consent to life-and-death decisions needful in this year after Mystic? Thomas concludes that a leader is known by generosity, the "ability to reconcile differences" and (undefined) "success in war." In times of "external threat," a leader meets "complex" problems with ingenuity and diplomacy.

"Each one of us is a sovereign being," says the Wampanoags' late Supreme Medicine Man, Slow Turtle (interview in Dempsey film, *Morton*). Each person is a leader when she/he acts like one and produces results. At the same time in this post-Hartford war, simple negligence in favor of justice can help (for example, ignoring a "Pequot" in your village). People are free to follow their judgment, which is "invariably reinforced and broadened by means of extending family relations." They have what they need to meet the day. Thomas (138):

> From the time the English arrived in The New
> World until the 20th century, colonial administrators
> as well as most subsequent writers have seen Indian
> 'tribes' in southern New England as well-defined poli-
> tical units with recognizable leaders and identifiable
> territorial boundaries (see for example Alden Vaughan
> [*Frontier* 53]). Upon reviewing specific chains of historical
> events during the 17th century, however, it becomes
> apparent that persistent tribal unity is a figment of every-
> one's imagination....The 'tribe' as such was episodic.
> Generally, what defined a...tribe was cooperation among
> communities in response to outside pressures. In retrospect,
> it is nearly impossible to define the 'tribal' affiliations of
> most of New England's Indian villages.

So does Johnson rightly notice Uncas' broad "success" after Mystic in "attracting former enemies" (35). The Pequots and Mohegans have been (human) feuding relatives for generations. Life-and-death "outside pressures" help Uncas to reconcile differences, except with Miantonomo. His point of view is a generation older than Uncas', and outdone at last by what colonial history brings to America.

Blindly, it outwits even Uncas. But the contest between him and Miantonomo is about who will lead "Indians" to a future. "The Indians struggle for larger shares of the Pequots' persons and former tributaries, [while] the English strive for wampum and the Pequots' former lands" (Jennings 227). This is another way to understand Mystic: the English achievement is that for a handful of years, "Pequots" can't live there openly.[78]

---

[78] "If we believe what we used to read, we allow the Indian strand in New England's history to be cut short...and we offend Indian people today who know that their history did not stop there," notes Calloway (*After King Philip's War* 11). "Clearly, the disappearing act...was more apparent than real." Thanks to

As our journey takes us into the details, documents and numbers we need, we can see better than those who left them. We invite you to keep tabs on these numbers as we make each event and subtotal clear, and then process them all for your consideration. Here, we discover the numbers of Pequots reported as Killed Or Enslaved; slavery a "choice" we must separate from "human" life, even given Axtell's remarks below. The next chapter discovers the numbers of Pequots reported as Escaped Or Assimilated to other Native groups; circumstances more conducive to "life" than permanent forced labor.

What happens to Sassacus himself? Though Mason and Underhill risk death to kill their capital enemy, neither tells us or seems curious to know. Underhill's story may be in print before August 1638, when Sassacus is reported dead, below. Mason wrote years after; yet the captains' best merely reports Sassacus (or somebody like him) heading west across the Connecticut River. This Sassacus---the identifiers can only be "Indian"---wins a fight there with three men from Saybrook (M35-6; U85 brands him "all for blood"). Vincent reports only his escape to the Mohawks (V107).

Several records show us (on Native reports) the "last council" of Sassacus and his "close followers." The numbers of their dispersion groups "deserting the country as never to return" (WPF3: 430-1) grow sharp in only four English sources. How many Pequots go with Sassacus after Mystic, at May's end? We hear of 80, of 40 "plus

---

Calloway (26n67) we note James Axtell's point (from his *After Columbus: Essays* 1988, 50): "Only if we persist in equating courage with mortal resistance to the forces of change can we condemn the praying Indians as cultural dropouts or moral cowards. For life is preferable to death, and those who bend are also possessed of courage, the courage to change and to live in the face of overwhelming odds as well as the contempt of their brothers who died with stiff necks."

INDIAN MEMORIAL VILLAGE,
Fort Hill, Groton, Connecticut.

From Peale 181 (c.1939)

females," of 7, and of 20: the first and last are Williams' numbers with two July weeks in-between (WPF3: 446; WPF3: 491; DYW 127; WPF3: 436). Those numbers produce an average of 39 (147/4). So in this case, being reasonably conservative, we suggest that 40 is the round number of Pequots including Sassacus. It rings well with other casual estimates of a senior Sachem's wartime company, and it puts most strength and less danger around the other Pequot bands. There is one more report treated below---from Uncas---that echoes this number, and we will enter 40 below from these documents.[79]

Sassacus' story gives a royal idea too of English command of their crusade. "Not a Pequot to be found," Williams writes six days after Mystic (WPF3: 427). Sassacus "is resolved to sell his life and so the others' as dear as they can," Stoughton reports on June 28 (WPF3: 435). Once (perhaps) sighted "foraging" for shellfish and the coast's easy food (WJH1: 226), "Sassacus" is gone in several directions: north to the Mohawk country from which the Pequots "originally" migrated (WPF3: 436/438, and Chronology); east by July 6 to Long Island where Captain Patrick takes men to "salute" him (WPF3: 441); and by July 15/17, north again "to the Mohawks they say" (Williams, WPF3: 452). Maybe "our men miss of him"

---

[79] We will keep all numbers clear before you. Be aware that in Sassacus' case, because he and most of his company are reported (by "Indians") killed, we add his 40 to both sides of our calculations. This seems more flexibly responsive to further possibilities of his fate (below) than just canceling them out. Important too is that the men who record these numbers typically count men (fighting men) and casually if at all "women and children." So, while there may be 40 "definite" braves with Sassacus, many have families/dependents with them, from 2 to 5 to 7 persons (as in Ch. 3). To keep this study conservative, we include Sassacus' dependents in the total of 40 here; and we do not "add" to any number without indications you can see.

there as the English, "fast by a hideous swamp," "divide themselves, and range up and down as the providence of God [not new tactics] guides them; for the Indians are all gone, save 3 or 4 and they know not whither to guide them, or else would not" (July 28, WPF3: 456).[80]

July and August are the hot New England months. Humidity, mosquitoes---At last a break for the hunters on August 5. Winthrop's Boston gets news that Sassacus, at 77 dragging along his people's 500 English-pound wampum-bank, is (by Native reports) betrayed by his kinsmen the Mohawks, somewhere up in that Hudson River country where he sought refuge. The Mohawks reportedly kill Sassacus, "twenty of his best" including his brother and five Pequot Sachems, and pocket the cash. Winthrop and Bradford cite "rumor" that the Mohawks do so to curry future favor with themselves (DYW 127, FBH2: 258).

Proof? "A part of [Sassacus'] skin and lock of hair" delivered, or "mixed," with those of "others," by Mohawks who hand them to Connecticut River-traders (WJH1: 227-9, 260). Nobody can admit this latest joke. Gardener alone recalls Sassacus' "head" (G138) as Boston's prize. He never saw Sassacus, and no Englishman claims to---let alone recognize his personal coiffure.

Not to worry. By August 23, Uncas and/or his "Mohegans" pass along reassurances. Captain Davenport and men travel "up to the head" of the Quinnipiac River "to cut corn or gather beans," meaning steal Native crops beyond any "Pequot" commission; and

---

[80] This includes July 6 "promises" of Long Island's Squa Sachem to give "the utmost aid" in catching Sassacus there. By this same time, suave Captain Stoughton learns to try "gifts" toward "peace" and good hunting in Native villages that let Pequot fugitives "sleep with" them. "The terror of our swords and our God's doings is upon them" (WPF3: 482).

there they find "a great company of Mohegans [?]...returned to their country, about 500 of men, women and children." That is the biggest group of "Mohegans" on record so far (compare Chronology 1614, 1636): a sudden host for "little Sachem" Uncas. These people are "somewhat fearful at first," but "after speak with us and lovingly entertain." They say "for certain that Sassacus is killed...and forty men with him, and some women" (WPF3: 490-1).

From where are they returning? If this report isn't enough, and it isn't, other "Mohegans" know what boys like. They bring Davenport (just before his scavenging-trip) the severed hands "of a great Sachem, as they say greater than Sassacus." Now, why describe a brave in a way so clearly out in front of the dogs chasing Sassacus? This "testimony" all but closes with *Best Wishes, Uncas*. Momomattuck Samm is a convenient consolation-prize, for whom we enter 1 person below.[81]

You know how this study will handle the mystery of Sassacus' and his close followers' fates. What happened is open to debate, as much as the final fate of Mystic's Sachem Mamoho and his family.[82]

---

[81] This may be the fate of Mamoho's Mystic "captain" (here spelled "Mono-whoak" and "Momoonotuk"), that "mighty fellow" dreaded in the bloody mop-up operations around Quinnipiac. "Samm" escapes Mystic like Mamoho, joins Sassacus, then leaves their group after an in-flight quarrel (490-1). Thus he survives (like 6 others, 491) until these "Mohegans" kill him. "I perceive," adds Davenport, "that the Indians would be glad to make women [noncombatants] of all the Pequots now, except the sachems and captains and murderers; but them they would kill." The hands are a blood-price paid for English killed by them. Or at least, the "Indians" would stop English worry about such "murderers."

[82] Note below the Mohawks' new, strong and threatening "interest" in New English colonies. Whatever happens to Sassacus among them, something of him is alive there for years. Also: because Mystic's Sachem Mamoho counts as an Escapee, we tell his story in the next chapter; but his wife Wincumbone (G125)

Mystic's battle occurs on May 26. By June 28, the English hear that 70-72 Pequots have surrendered themselves to Miantonomo's Narragansett village (they are never specified as prisoners brought there from Mystic: WPF3: 435; WJH1: 277; WCL1: 90n5, 3: 446). Captain Israel Stoughton takes charge. The Narragansetts know the survival-value of "attitude" and display. When Stoughton's soldiers arrive, they find the Pequots identified for them and somehow "cooped up as in a pound."

What we learn is that Stoughton has 22 of the group's 24 Pequot men (ages 22-30) killed on the spot in front of the village. The other 50 or 52 are women and "children" (numbers from Williams, WPF3: 435). Stoughton, knowing his Joshua, picks out "the fairest and largest that I saw amongst them, to whom I have given a coat...it is my desire to have her for a servant." His men step up: "a little Squa...Steward Calacot desireth," "a tall one" for Davenport marked with "three strokes upon her stomach," and Stoughton's new guide "Solomon the Indian" gets "a young little squa" too.[83]

---

and their "two or three" children (DeForest 151) are captured at Quinnipiac (WPF3: 457). Therefore we enter a subtotal of 4 (Enslaved) for her and them. Wincumbone appears again in Ch. 7.

[83] These victims "don't understand" Stoughton's policy and he doesn't understand their responses to it. "Wanting a guide" (WPF3: 481), he sends some men "towards the Narragansetts to get one." He locates "diverse people [hidden] in Pequot corn." But "they all run away," even though "we formerly expressly told them, they must not [do] that, for we should then take them for Pequots."

"At length, they tell [Stoughton] that Englishmen have some of them in prison in the Bay [colony], and they know not what is meant towards them. But we are also told by a squaw that they are mixed, Pequots and Narragansetts together." Nearby in plain sight are "signs of two rendezvous"; and "she says, one [group of 20 dugout-boats in sight] is the Pequots'."

Totals to enter below: 22 Killed and 50 Enslaved. Why the latter? Stoughton's "pinnace" sent to Mr. Governor holds "48 or 50 women and children" likely to be counted against his letter when they land. And now it's off to see "what we can do against Sassacus, and another great sagamore, Momomattuck: here is yet good rough work to be done. And how dear it will cost is unknown."

By July 5 and 6, reports count 11 Pequots killed by Narragansetts (WPF3: 443); plus one more, snatched mid-ocean from a Block Island dugout and shipped to England (WJH1: 225). By July 17, Davenport tells comrade Hugh Peter that "three leagues from Quinnipiac" he falls upon two Native people, kills them, and forces two more to guide him to Sassacus (WPF3: 452-3). When they prove "not particularly helpful" (Cave 159), Davenport beheads them too, and so bestows on a place called Menunkatuck the title "Sachem's Head"; where Uncas watches him pike them to rot. This report relates 5 more men and 2 women (Pequots?) run down through a "heavy rain," the men killed, the women "taken." We total as 20 Killed, 3 Enslaved for all entries in this paragraph.

At July's end (about the 28th), the English in Quinnipiac swamps stumble into the hiding-place of about 180 Pequots (WPF3: 453-4). First they find a sick, hungry "old man" with "a boy" hiding in thickets. The old man they kill and, likely, four other Pequot braves who come charging and "learn to repent." The boy's fate is unspecified, (next chapter). Then, in this horrific fight that goes on through the darkness between two days, "many" Pequots are deemed killed, "some" run away. We "count" neither. The English try to surround their prey. Stalemated ("Sassacus is gone"), they offer surrender-terms, and then murder 80 Pequot men who believe them. Like Stoughton, of their 180 they actually deliver "almost 100 Indian [sic] women and children" (454). "Some" are given to "river men" who've helped them, "some" are shipped to "Bermuda" slavery, "some" die on the spot. The soldiers hate these swamps as they hate Pequots. Altogether, we count from this episode 85 Killed (80 plus 4 braves and the "old man"): the fates of the boy and the "almost 100" appear next chapter.

Quinnipiac, Fairfield, Stamford---This running fight nearly gratifies the frustrated lust for a target packed with people. "Although they had marched in their arms all the day and had been in fight all the night...they professed they found themselves so fresh as they could willingly have gone to another such business" (WPF3: 458).[84]

Roger Williams, meanwhile, reports that a son of "old" Connecticut River-Sachem Sequassen has "cut off 20 Pequot women and children, in their passage [north] to the Mohawks" (July 21: WPF3:

---

[84] This is where Sachem Mamoho's wife Wincumbone and their perhaps-3 children are captured (citations above). "I have taken charge of her," says Mr. Governor, remarking her "very modest countenance and behavior," and her telling request that the English "not abuse her body, and that her children...not be taken from her." She merits such mercy because "by her mediation...the two English maids" are recovered from post-Wethersfield Pequot captivity (more on them Ch. 7). Winthrop deems the maids "spared from death." The girls report no dangers beyond what seems the older one's harrowing experience of lust for a Pequot man, only just "escaped" by ardent prayer (G125, 133; U70).

Wincumbone's requests support our reasons for not counting Slavery as Survival. She echoes Mason's "reflection" (M39) that these "servants" could not "endure that yoke; few of them continuing any considerable time with their masters" (he means they died). Now-Major Mason must have put it just as delicately over wine at the Winthrops' "thanksgiving" banquet-table. Maybe it's good Madeira they're drinking. Winthrop "confirms" or gloats to the hapless Plimoth's Bradford that this "Quinnipiac" group includes 80 men and 200 women and children (WPF3: 456). A few other courtiers follow, but we stand by our numbers above and to come.

455-6); plus "one sachem" who, years ago, sent Governor Winthrop "a present" inviting his English to "settle" that country (refused: Chronology 1631). In these records, "cut off" usually means killed; but no record says more of these Pequots as dead or delivered. Maybe Sequassen's people assimilate them: it is not Native custom here to slay them. Still, we cannot assume their heads not sent along, another goodwill-present in an unspeakable situation created by people on all sides. On what you see, we count these 21 Pequots as Killed.

These are all the "precise" numbers of Pequots killed or enslaved *after* Mystic. How many Pequots die there? Mystic is "two" events, the fight in/around the fort, and the English retreat. Though you must bear with us for all the evidence, we stand by our estimate that "only" about 50 Pequot braves perish inside Mystic Fort. There is no massacre of "civilians" because they aren't there. If any are inside, we include them in our estimate. We count 50 Pequots Killed "at" the fort: that is 10 more than Mason's "guess" for the first fight with "40 of their Stoutest" (M29).

In the second event (the Pequot counterattack/English retreat), Underhill claims to kill "or wound" 100 of at least 300 Pequot braves; in a sortie-situation whose odds, by his numbers, are 10-to-1 against him (U81). Mason's only help here is that "some" of their hot pursuit "fell" (M31). At this stage, we must not allow Hawkeye/Fenimore Cooper to help us. Nor, though, do the captains forget the ferocity of "enraged" Pequot braves turning from "pastime" to drive the wounded English down the hill, and Gardener shows them full-willing to charge men with guns and fight hand-to-hand. We come to the curious position of granting the doughty captain half his claim, 50 Pequots killed in their counterattack, in the name of parsimony. This means a total of 100 Pequots Killed (either outright, or died of wounds) at Mystic.[85]

We will present all total-numbers clearly. But to truly "reach Mystic," we need as well a precise idea of Pequots Escaped or Assimilated. May this book about impatience survive it! The people in question matter, and the history.

---

[85] Our present total of Pequots Killed or Enslaved is 346, including Mystic. Whatever you think of this figure at this point, compare it with Cave's 1996 study. Carefully examined for its use of records with anything like hard numbers, Cave's total of Pequots killed/enslaved is 72 without a Mystic "massacre." He somehow finds that "Most of the residents of Fort Mystic were burned alive" (151), and accepts Mason's "six or seven hundred" as "probably more accurate" than Underhill's "about 400." More to come on this comparison.

UNCAS MONUMENT AND ROYAL BURYING GROUND
OF THE MOHEGAN, NORWICH, CONNECTICUT.

From Peale 169 (c. 1939)

6

'O Brave Pequots!'

Just above (July 28, 1637), we see the English locate the largest known band of dispersed Pequots in Quinnipiac's summer swamps. It happens because Captain Patrick provides June 19 intelligence of "300 [Pequots] fit to fight" in that region (WPF3: 431); and because Mason acquires a new Native guide, one "Luz," renamed for "Light" (and "so faithful is he...though against his own," M37).

Quinnipiac's horrors show the Anglo-American planter-soldier doing---well, he tries. Mason fills a page with his company's already-frustrated strategy council, held there in the midst of miles of tangled summer-green swamp. As for the enemy, Native groups can make swamps a "marvelous great and secure" refuge because only they know the very few useful "passages" and trails, and the best hiding-places "off" these. An untutored Englishman not only carries too much stuff and finds his weapons (slow guns, slashing-swords, halberds) less effective than spears and arrows. The swamp treats him as it will you today, if you go and try your way through. On-trail, you can be ambushed from every side's wall of cattails mixed with 12-foot-tall other bushes. Try to charge off-trail through these, and within 10 yards the bush wrestles you to an exhausted halt, and strips you of direction. You've scarcely room to pull a knife. Mosquitoes are constant unless you know the plants to rub on, or fancy a coat of mud. Every promising grassy maze with space for the chase dead-ends in moss and thicket, deepening ooze, quaking-bogs of bottomless peat, or quicksand.

Mason writes of this swamp-council years after it happens, and he still describes it as a talk among men so irritated that they debate the ludicrous. They want to cut the swamp down, wall the Pequots in with a "pallizado," build "hedges...like those of Gotham," "force" the swamp, block its "open passages," and more (M38)---anything to keep the Pequots confined (again) for victory. These men of "Mystic Massacre" feel a twinge, grow "loth to destroy women and children" if they can manage better and turn them into docile plantation-labor. At last, Gardener's old left hand Thomas Stanton intervenes with something useful: Pequot language. Because he "speaks," he can shout his way safely toward the Pequots with promises of "parley"; and surrender is arranged. Mason is allowed into the Pequots' daunting hide and finds there "but few slain" by combat (M37, 39: including 4 braves and an old man defending that boy, last chapter). We can see Mason's reaction after a hot summer goose-chase: he and his men find it refreshing to butcher each of the 80 Pequot people just disarmed, and then ship the spoil of "almost" 100 noncombatants to Boston.

We have counted and "hold aside" the people killed---Now we're discovering/counting how many Pequots Escaped or Assimilated to "other lives" in this war. You'll find this "almost 100" from Quinnipiac in the totals below.

In the midst of "victory" again, Mason's men confess how "easily" Pequots "escape in the night." Where are the psalms, where the legendary Mystic nerve? "We keeping at a great distance, what better could be expected?" (M38).

And as this goes on all night, what about the great tradition-attested advantage of guns in these "thickets"? Maybe the Pequots *are* somehow trapped right here, but swamp is foggy and dampest near dawn. Just then, "sixty or seventy [Pequots] as we are informed" smash their way out right through the English line (M38-9). Can we take a reliable number from this action that we must not dismiss?

First above we saw Captain Patrick's original intelligence of "300" fighting-men at Quinnipiac. The Pequots are in dispersion and their women, children and elders are with them: many historians grant 2, 5, or even 7 "dependents" as uncounted with each recorded brave. With 300 braves reported here, how many Pequots out of at least 600 do you now think slip away, before the English "close" one wing of a vast swamp never seen before? Subtract the previous chapter's 85 Pequot males Killed. And, we'll be skeptical of Patrick's daunted report; to enter below only Mason's report of 60 as Escaped (besides the "almost 100" also shipped from Quinnipiac).

Patrick also reports 40 to 50 Pequots "at Long Island": Williams first-says this group includes four "Sachems" (WCL1: 117), and that they total 60.[86] Given that Uncas, when pressed, shrugs that "actually," it is 40 Pequots out there (WCL1: 184), Williams may add noncombatants to arrive at the 100 Pequots he last-claims are actually there (WPF3: 446). Having granted Underhill 50 of his claimed 100 braves killed at Mystic, we think similar proportions reasonable for Long Island; and you note below a great deal of almost-secret sea-traffic conducted there by Uncas and others. With

---

[86] Recall that Sassacus' "tributaries" include 26 Sachems. Pequot "women" say that at least 13 of them survive/elude capture (DYW 126). Most likely to be with their people, these Sachems we include within this Long Island total.

all this considered, we enter 54 Escaped/Assimilated Pequots for this Long Island group.[87]

As you recall Captain Davenport's August sighting of 500 so-called Mohegans in the last chapter (WPF3: 490-1), consider Williams' next report of September 9 (WCL1: 117). "Soldiers...relate to me that Uncas...has about 300 men with him on Pequot River... which I believe are most of them Pequots and their confederates" (he names Nipmucs and "their Inlanders"). Williams swears that "not above 40 or 50" of the 300 are "actual" Mohegans. But we recall Uncas with anywhere from 60-100 braves back at Saybrook. With the much-debated low numbers of "original Mohegans" in mind (Chronology), can we now feel our captains shudder to think that *most of their Mohegan allies were Pequots all along*?

Let us handle this carefully. Discount, then, 100 "Mohegans" from this group (we're looking for Pequots), and 50 "confederates." This makes half of our concerned 300 on Pequot River likely to be "fugitive Pequots" (150 fighting-men). And, given the evidence of

---

[87] It's a wonder that Uncas himself survives: he certainly never rests. He first tells Williams he has "but 20" Pequots in his care. The seasoned Stanton knows Uncas as "very false," for rumors say Uncas is taking 30-40 Pequots from Long Island with each dugout-boat voyage (WCL1: 184). Under pressure, Uncas "acknowledges" he has 30 Pequots at Mohegan; but he won't name names. By October Uncas is "lately at Long Island" again, takes another 40 to safety, and new Eastern Niantic ally Wequashcook takes 30 more to his villages (WCL1: 27). How many are out there, since Ch. 1's word of Pequot evacuations weeks before Mystic? Williams hears that "Uncas harbors as many as 200-300," and "large numbers...on Long Island" (WCL1: 161n6). He thinks the English "strangely bewitched" and "marvelously deluded" (that word again) by Uncas, Wequash-cook and the entire post-Mystic business (WCL1: 157). And that is the best opinion of the Williams who, in his old age, confessed himself not so "masterful" in his Native knowledge, dealings and influences (Rubertone 93-4). Across his time with them, the Narragansetts "preferred not" to answer many questions.

Uncas' busy summer and fall 1637, we will add to this 150 only an average of 2 women/children/elders for each brave. It is no small group, a cluster of families. In balance to the noncombatants counted skeptically above, here we see little reason to doubt that this group totals at least 300 "actual" Pequot people, and we enter that number below as Assimilated: blending in where they can. It doesn't seem extremely difficult to "disappear" that way.

The records reflect English confusion, or rather "Indian" intelligence, as Captains Stoughton and others pursue Winthrop's justice. The Williams letter just cited (117) complains also that Eastern Niantic Wequashcook "is the man" who "shelters Audsah, the murderer of [trader John] Oldham," and "keeps his head so long upon his shoulders" (Chronology 1636, 1639). The same Native protection of "murderers" goes on at Narragansett. Though Williams learns the names of six of them there (WCL1: 184), Stoughton and others report that a total of 10, connected with that earlier group of 72 "surrenders" at Narragansett (last chapter), are surely "departed" from there for Mohegan country or "Pequot" itself. Another 10 fugitives become Miantonomo's; and 5 of those "run off" farther, to join family ahead of them with Uncas (WCL1: 127, 187n12). We add a total of 20 to the Assimilated below.[88]

---

[88] Stoughton seems handy at driving them off (July 6, WPF3: 443): "We cannot declare all the means that we [use]...yet this for a taste. For the Narragansetts, we leave the Pequots [as] gifts (and booty, etc.), to sleep with them for the present; because we will make no disturbance. Only we take notice of what we can learn out because we conceive that, for gifts intended for peace especially, they may and ought to [be] led to account about [the Pequots] in convenient time; and [we ought to] animate them to the work of bringing under the open enemy." The "common" enemy is everybody else at Narragansett: perhaps they don't like gifts from men who mass-murdered and took "servants" from their families six days ago on June 28.

And so we come to the Hartford Treaty's dispensations (September 21, 1638, text in Vaughan 340). Mason records 20 Pequots "given" to Eastern Niantic Sachem Ninigret, and so does Williams (M40; WCL1: 187n10). We enter 20 thus below.

What is the fate of that "almost 100" noncombatants shipped from Quinnipiac? Mason, perhaps flush with his year, somehow reports two groups of 80 Pequots each "at" Hartford; and "his" 160 he sees divided equally and declared henceforth Narragansetts and Mohegans (M40). But the Treaty's text counts differently. It says only that "there be or is reported...to be by the said [Natives], 200 Pequots living [with them] that are men, besides squaws and papooses" (341).

Do those women and children include the "almost 100" from Quinnipiac? Rather than allow a double-count, we think it must; because the "Quinnipiac Pequots" are the biggest and hardest-to-manage group of all, disposed of nowhere else. The Treaty's "reported" 200 men likely include "about 60 men"---not to mention their families---whom Mason and Uncas force just this month (Sept. 1638) to join the Mohegans, after they try to relocate on the Pawcatuck with plenty of coveted corn (M40-43; G138-9).

We cannot explain how or why these groups of prisoners (Quinnipiac's women and children, Pawcatuck's "men" plus families) seem to end up in Native "custody" before Treaty-day. Boston has "prisons." What we do know is that, to the English, the Hartford Treaty deals with the "mother-lode" of all known or reported Pequots taken in the war. Its Native report, then, of 200 "men, besides" their people, is an underestimate. James Mooney's much-regarded population studies conclude that this Hartford dispensation concerns no less than 700 Native souls. (See his 1907 "Pequot" 230; reappraised, like most of Mooney's work, as under-estimation: Salisbury 23).

With so many sub-groups converging here, we want to resist temptations to assume. So, we'll grant only 2.5 dependents to each of the 200 men reported by Natives and accepted by Hartford. This brings us a total of 500 Pequot men, women and children to enter below.[89]

Meanwhile, of course, even more people are finding new lives outside and around official records. Williams reports 7 Pequot women and one man "come in" (WPF3: 446), for which we total 8 below (as a number easy to get right). He has intelligence of bigger groups he can number. 200 Pequots are on the verge of a bit more revenge against the Narragansetts (June 21, WPF3: 434), but a coastal "mist" deters them and they vanish. We, striving for conservatism, add 100 for this group.[90]

---

[89] This 500-total is smaller than McBride's: "Approximately 200 to 300 Pequot warriors (and presumably their families) were probably" given, he writes (105), to the Mohegans. We address below the "second group" of "120 males" that McBride sees given here to Wequash. Though McBride follows the same Treaty-text we use, and includes Williams' letters (*Complete* 6: 60-69 and 84-89), we cannot agree with his Hartford calculations and show why by chapter's end. Also part of our estimate: the Treaty, in dividing all reported prisoners, carefully notes that the Narragansetts "already" have "11" Pequots, and so it gives 11 more Pequots (rather than Mason's memory of equal halves) to Uncas. The award of the would-be Pawcatuck Pequots to Uncas' Mohegans enrages the Narragansetts, who (via Niantic brethren) claim that these Pequots "belong to them." It is one part of the Uncas-and-Miantonomo struggle over southern New England's future after Mystic.

[90] Simmons' *Spirit of the New England Tribes* offers examples of braves affected by "mist." Leland and others point to links between sea-mists off these coasts and smoke from the pipes of Maushop, Gluskap, Chepi, Granny Squant, and other powerful figures of Northeastern Native religions and traditions.

Williams speaks fair Eastern Algonquian too, and has more Native friends than almost any Englishman these days (it's part of Roger's "problem"). He hears of "other companies" also roving the region, "four-score in one surviving" (WPF3: 436). Counting one such company below, we add 80.

Add one for Mamoho, Sachem of Mystic.[91]

Finally in this Escaped/Assimilated part of calculations, we depend on historian McBride's expertise for three last number-specific estimates of Pequots in these dispersions. (See his "Archaeology" in Hauptmann/ Wherry 104-5 and notes). Bear with us for these answers and you will have what you need to judge for yourself (our purpose). We disagree with McBride at several points of this journey, but do respect his Pequot community-based knowledge. And his research gives us ways to bring precision to the number we seek, of post-war Pequots.

First of three: McBride estimates 120 Pequot "males" after the war "with Wequash" on Niantic lands. You recall Wequash "a disaffected Pequot living in Niantic territories" (McBride), who helps the English little against Mystic. The number itself comes with Williams' description of Wequash's success after the war, through marriage to Sassacus' mother (*Complete* 6: 67). Like Uncas and Miantonomo, Wequash sees the future in human numbers.

---

[91] On June 2 Mamoho is reported at Nipmuc Showatuck (WCL1: 77n16; WPF3: 427), and then Stoughton goes after him (and "Samm") back at Pequot River (June 28, WPF3: 435). On July 6 Mamoho "is" at Quinnipiac (WPF3: 441), just "lately" at the Mohawks; on July 28 his wife Wincumbone and children are taken at Quinnipiac (noted). If there himself, Mamoho is separated from them, rejoins Sassacus toward the Mohawks, and escapes again although wounded at his Sachem's supposed death. His wife and children are "Winthrop's" now. We wish him all good things whatever happened (in what we thought history *used* to call "oblivion," WCL1: 77n16), and count him as Escaped.

Who knows better than the Pequots the actual post-war families of the Eastern or Pawcatuck Pequots; families who in spite of Mason after all, are there in 1650 to receive a 500-acre reservation "on the east side of Long Pond in North Stonington." If they were "120" later returning to Pawcatuck, they likely included many of the same would-be "60" first prevented by Mason from living there (just above). If we half this first of McBride's three estimates, and "add" only 2 family for each of them, we come after all to his 120, and enter that number having tried it.

Second, McBride reports 72 Pequot men and 8 boys known living at Nameag, in 1646 only eight years after the war (he cites Williams *Complete* 6: 67 and an unpublished "List").[92] We count this as only 40 below---not as "doubt" but to answer the possibility that, over 10 years' time, a smaller original group of Pequots increases to McBride's total there. (A decade's doubled population is known.)

At last, for the same reason plus those noted below,[93] we derive from McBride's third estimate 150 Pequots in his report of "350-400

---

[92] The "List of the Pequot Indians at Pequot Plantation about the Time of the Settlement 1646" he calls the "Eva Butler MSS" at the Indians and Colonial Research Center of Mystic, CT.

[93] According to Haines/Stekel's *Population History of North America*, the maximum birth-rate (and net population increase) for "white" people in the 17th century was 3.01% to 3.03%. If this third estimated group did "begin" with 150 at Mashantucket rather than McBride's 350-400, what do we find? Apply a conservative 2.0% birth rate (equal to 3 babies per year amid 150 people). Multiply that by 12 years after Hartford/1638. The result is "only" 36 Pequots born at Mashantucket by 1650, totaling perhaps 186. To reach McBride's figure of 350-400 Mashantuckets by 1650, their "original" band would almost have to be at least 300 persons. We want our final numbers to reflect the most conservative judgment we can make: you can see here the "other" indications, higher than our own.

individuals" spread among one Niantic Bay village and four more on the west banks of the Thames/Pequot River. These are ancestors of the Mashantucket Pequots living "in the mid-17th century." That is, circa 1650, or 12 years after Hartford.

We begin to arrive at Mystic, and more. According to all sources we can find, the Pequot Nation before The Pequot War numbers about 3,000 persons. This is the preferred number for Mooney (230), Starna (46), and McBride (104, with 4,000 his maximum).

By those same sources, the Pequots number about 1,000 persons after the war. So we have about 2,000 Pequots for whom to account.

You recall the total of Pequots Killed or Enslaved: 346. That number should increase slightly, because there are vague but accepted claims of Pequot "heads" being delivered "daily" to the English (for ex. DYW 127). Further, hints from tradition say that Mr. John Gallop, a boat-captain at Quinnipiac, enjoys tying up "Indians" and throwing them into the sea---at Quinnipiac perhaps as many as 30 (Drinnon 44). For these reasons we increase the Killed/Enslaved total (by 40) to 386.

Our total of 1,595 Escaped/Assimilated Pequots must gather in 7 "stragglers": the 6 Pequot males (at least) reported escaped from Sassacus' "death" among the Mohawks; and the young boy first-found at Quinnipiac but never "rounded up" on record. We reach a final total of 1,602 Escaped Pequots.

With 2,000 Pequots to account for, subtract first the 1,602 Escapees. For all our conservative skepticisms toward both sides of these calculations, what we are left with (as Sherlock Holmes remarked) "must be the truth." This final subtraction leaves a total of 398 Pequots who "must" have been Killed or Enslaved from Mystic to the end of The Pequot War: all of twelve more than we arrived at (386) in hard numbers.

The Mystic Massacre dissolves like somebody's very bad dream.[94]

The captains wanted to believe, and "martialist" tradition wants everyone to believe, that they did what they said at Mystic. Time to worry again; because surrounding the hardest possible numbers are echoes of yet more Pequot "survivals," and we cannot dismiss that some become frightening distant thunder over victorious New England.

Recall the young man now "christened" to play the role of a "Pequot servant" named *Reprieve* in Governor Winthrop's life. His real name is Jaguante Tunkawatten, and he is not a Pequot but a Manissean, of Block Island (WCL1: 129n14). Roger Williams, blending together calls for general mercy and his own purchase of Prudence Island from the spoils, tells this young man's journey.

---

[94] Compare the number-specific estimates from both sides in Cave's *Pequot War*: 72 Killed or Enslaved, and 217 "given to the Indians" (here, Escaped/ Assimilated). We realize that Cave does not propose to count or show every single "soul" on record. On that basis, what supports his quite traditional generalizations? He notes (177) that "It is now clear that [the English] portrayals of the Pequots bear little resemblance to reality." Shouldn't that be on the *first* page of what the publisher (University of Massachusetts Press) calls this "first full-scale analysis" of the war? How much more qualified were the book's 1990s "outside readers" than those who nodded to DeForest in 1850? They were at least more qualified than *The Boston Sunday Globe* ("a masterful analysis"); than *Choice* ("well-researched...a solid narrative...challenges many existing interpretations"); and few were as qualified as Amherst College historian Barry O'Connell ("Cave's scholarship is impeccable"). All these are on the back of Cave's book. Yes, "That's marketing." We reply, That's history too, as produced under business and tenure "time and circumstances": our guide to the future, as sure as the past got us here.

[October 1637: 127] Sir, your servant Reprieve
lodged here [at Providence] two nights, and Miantonomo tells me that five days [before] he lay a night
with him, and is gone [now] to Block Island.

He is very hopefully improved since I first saw him;
and [I] am bold to wish that he might now take his last
farewell of his friends; to whom you would rather be
pleased to give leave to visit him at Boston. For you
cannot believe how hard it is for him to escape much
evil, and especially uncleanness while he is with them.
The good Lord be pleased to bless him to you, and to make
you a blessing to him and many others....(WPF3: 508-9)

Amid the region-wide hunt for Pequots after Mystic, Jaguante
Tunkawatten travels the countryside (until November we presume:
he's not much to Winthrop's records). Williams the evangelist is
"glad to see this poor fellow" and that he is "careful to please" his
new master(s): Williams praises Tunkawatten's attention to Mr.
Governor's "leave for 28 days": "Though he could stay but 6 days
where he desired to stay longest, yet he will not lie." It seems that
Tunkawatten's "brother goes along with him to stay some while,
till the spring." Obvious question: In war-time Boston, how and
why does an "Indian" enslaved as "a Pequot" arrange to go visiting
across the theatre of war, and with a free-ranging "brother"? Where
does this "brother" live?

Tunkawatten and Williams between them reveal loose seams in
the colonies, busy at their prayer-vigils and starved for "Indian"
intelligence:

[November 1637] Your native Reprieve requests
me to write a word for himself, and another for the
Sachem of Block Island. For [Reprieve] himself, he tells
Me [that] when he departed hence, being alone, he wan-
Dered toward Nipmuc. At Niantic, [Sachem] Juanemo
said he was a spy from Mr. Governor, and threatened to

> kill him. [Juanemo] denied that there were [any]
> Pequots, saying---though Reprieve saw many himself---
> that they were all gone to Monahiganick [likely Mohegan
> country]. So, he came back in fear of his life to Wepiteam-
> mock, Miantonomo's brother in law; who lent him a canoe
> to Block Island, where he stayed but six days. (WPF3: 508)

Tunkawatten's personal patrol brings in four Native communities and the Mohegan refuge beyond. Is he a spy, "wandering" for his own relief, or both? He can have any kind of reason to wander north to Nipmuc villages "near the headwaters of the Blackstone and Quinebaug Rivers" (WCL1: 95); but Native "traffic" headed that way these days means Pequots, coastal peoples the young Block Islander may know. Why does he not go free with them? He fears Winthrop's reach to bring him back (the colonies are good at retrieving runaway-indentures). He knows he is not to pursue or make new Native bonds, or allow sexual "uncleanness" in his life. But if Tunkawatten sees his own life as Winthrop's, he knows that others do not. He reports no Pequots to the north: Tunkawatten goes out as Winthrop's eyes and finds Native eyes on him.

Tunkawatten is not Pequot: he turns around. He has "pretty passage" on the war's frontiers with Winthrop's "paper." Soon he arrives at Juanemo's Niantic village, and there he strikes a quick nerve. Juanemo is scared enough of spies (guilty, that is) to blurt out the "Indian party line" ("All Pequots gone Mohegan!"), as he sees Tunkawatten noting many Pequots there---and the host threatens to kill Mr. Governor's man. Tunkawatten flees to Mason's old promised guide, Wepiteammock, and he doesn't keep this guest around. He too knows the youth's real desire and hands him a boat out into the cold. Tunkawatten disappears; but both Sachems see the spy coming and behave against their norms, as if they have company to conceal.

A brother of Miantonomo's, Yotaash, tells Williams that co-Sachem Canonicus has "some Pequot women" around: Canonicus denies it (WCL1: 187n11). After the Hartford Treaty too, the Wangungks near Wethersfield deny their way out of a charge of hiding "Pequot warriors" and families (WJH2: 614-5; WPF6: 258-9).

With these quasi-specifics, we have other hints deserving consideration. Stoughton reports "a great number" with the Nipmucs (WPF3: 431). Williams mentions "other companies" of Pequots, some as large as 80 men (436 as above). Miantonomo tells Williams of "diverse more...in woods" (447). The English hear of "scattered" Pequots fighting Nipmucs (445). Williams insists that "Those Inlanders [of the Pequots] are fled up toward the Mohawks" (452), and Davenport seems to sum up: "the body of Pequots...yet live." Two years later (July 1640), Williams points Niantic Sachems "still refusing to yield up any of those Pequots to death, to whom they promise life" (WCL1: 203). Vaughan notes "some" in future Pennsylvania and Virginia (376n63). If we see no substance in these, we can hardly see any in equally-general reports of Pequots killed.

We need to know one further historical clue on where many of the Pequots go. From at least 1640 to 1644 (three to seven years after Mystic), the colonies are troubled again with many-sided rumors of Native American "conglutination" (Williams, WPF3: 436; WCL1: 204n5). The 1640 warning from Plimoth's Bradford (WPF4: 258-9) of "a great present" of wampum sent from the Narragansetts to the Mohawks is hardly the first link among them and the Pequots we have seen. By 1644, Plimoth's Winslow is sure: "The Narragansetts prepare for war...[The] Mohawks have promised to aid them with a thousand men in the spring" (WPF4: 427).

Maybe the Mohawks hear Miantonomo's visionary words of 1641 (Ch. 5). Maybe they now regret killing Sassacus and other Pequots, or they are listening to him and them as veteran victors. The Mohawks seem ready by all accounts to send 1,000 braves far from home for a "Narragansett" cause. The adolescent Pequot boys sheltered by the Mohawks in 1637 are now prime-age warriors.

"Maybe." The word has disserved us for a long time. Once in awhile, earned, it serves as a referent for things that cannot be dismissed.

We return you to the question. Which is more likely: that Mason's, Underhill's and tradition's claims about Mystic are accurate; or that the "massacred" hundreds find more than enough room among the records, relatives, numbers, options, and clues to be, at the very least, survivors?

Eric S. Johnson's careful study of Uncas relates that by 1643-- only six years after The Pequot War---the "Mohegan" population is 2,000 to 2,500 persons strong. No early, pre-war source counts the Mohegans as more than a few hundred. Where do the thousands come from? Johnson refers us to James Mooney's "1500": Mooney works back from the count on two Pequot reservations in 1674 ("Pequot" 230, "Mohegan" 926). Johnson's other source is Williams, on Uncas' many ways of gathering Pequots to himself (WCL1: 117-121).

We do not forget the hundreds certainly killed, lives ruined in slavery, generations displaced and forever changed. Nothing will excuse that. This is not a book of miracles. It is a book of "brave Pequots"---whatever group of braves in which we find them.

7

Mystical Massacre

> Military enterprises are the most effective means
> of keeping a people occupied, for nothing arouses
> their interest so much as an important war....Every-
> one who is able is ready to play his part either in
> council or in action, and all discontent is vented on
> the common enemy. The rest of the people either
> follow the camp to bring supplies and to perform
> other necessary services, or remain at home to offer
> prayers and vows to God for ultimate victory; or at
> least are so stirred by expectation and by news of the
> progress of the war that there is no place for thoughts
> of revolt in their minds. Either in thought or in deed,
> everyone is preoccupied by the war.
>
> ---Botero, "Discourse Upon the Means
> of Well-Governing" (1577/1608), in Hale 21

> Not one person for a stone in Jerusalem.
>
> ---An Israeli grandmother
> during a televised political protest

The traditions of The Pequot War are not histories, or military
histories: if they scarcely describe what happened, they cannot
guide anyone to victory. They are instead a sacred tantrum of
frustrated wishes for imperial domination: sacred because crucial
to the colonizers' fantasies of themselves, and because they are not

to be questioned, so convenient are they to self-gratification at the expense of other peoples.

This did not prevent the captains' chronicles and writings after them from becoming important blueprint for United States colonial expansion westward, a new integument of "progress" confined within a human history now called Before and After Jesus. This war's paradigms---ignorance of the land, childish "savages," innocent and all-conquering white men with guns, The Bible to hold it together and bless each windfall of others' wealth--- appeared to "work" wherever the violence of total war could make them seem to. The short-term rewards of murder outlive the men who commit it, but their children inherit wealth that blinds conscience to the facts (the only hope of healing) and makes them sick with its injustice.

None of it proves the heroes' methods, however convenient and compelling. It condemns their children to keep running away from "daemons" (mistakes with consequences) unrecognized, until now and then, the speaking world and the presence of "others" demand they face facts. Conditioned (socialized, educated and rewarded) for looking anywhere but within themselves for causes, the builders of empire follow our captains at Mystic. Inevitably faced with the "empty" truth, they burn and kill their way out and swear that, by God, they're in control. God, of course, never shows up with confirmation; but wealth and silence will serve until He does.

There is no honorable point in history kept separate from how the living live. This tradition stems from a root before Mystic: a fantasy of Plimoth Plantation's Captain Myles Standish as American frontier-expert, qualified to train new generations of colonizers to conquer another fantasy: "empty land." The short-tempered "little chimney's" results and his "trainband's" more-oblivious ones prove him an intercultural hazard. Standish got the job and glory because his mercenary methods matched the real desires of Puritan and later colonizers. The Pequots, paradigms too, traded space for time against their invaders' needless savagery and, as we see in Connecticut today, their alliances with the larger "real world" have brought them through to new thresholds of hope. They literally danced in the flames of oppression, and were not forgotten by other peoples outside the books who later confronted holy progress and holocaust.

The colony goes about its business of globalization, its wishes and methods the same from Wounded Knee and Vietnam to Middle Eastern oilfields. Very little seems likely to change such profitable convenience except a catastrophe so severe that denial is no longer an option. As Mather intended with his Biblical warning on Mason's first page, "This shall be written for the generations to come, and the people...shall praise The Lord." This indeed means Us. "These issues are not merely about people who died long ago or about things disconnected from the present. Rather, they are about past-present relations" (Rubertone xv).

The traditions not vindicated in Cave's *The Pequot War* alert us to other value in his work: a chance to wake up and break out. Cave shows us afresh the Puritans' literal belief in The Bible as an American political guide, a fit precedent and a practical plan for intercultural behavior. Thanks to educational traditions born of the same theology, Old Testament instructions on how to profitably subdue the "unbelieving outsiders" of cosmopolitan Canaan scarcely changed as Puritan colonies became the "exceptionalist" United States:

> The ancient inhabitants of your holy land you
> [Yahweh] hated for their loathsome practices,
> their deeds of sorcery and unholy rites....You deter-
> mined to destroy them at our fathers' hands, so that

this land might receive a colony of God's children
worthy of it. Even so, since these were men, you treated
them leniently...to destroy them bit by bit....although you
knew very well they were inherently evil...and fixed in
their cast of mind; for they were a race accursed
from the beginning. (*The Book of Wisdom* 12: 3-11)

This was the faith of Myles Standish's Pilgrim leaders, and it suited his own war-centered worldview. It gave Mason and Underhill "sufficient light" to "declare, with Scripture," that "sometimes" whole populations of the "other" side (never their own) "must perish" (U81). "Sometimes the case alters," he adds on his own exiled way out of town. "We will not dispute it now"; and we have rarely done so to the root. "Business" goes on---"savages" with targeted wealth, pulpit, temper, blank check, guns and all.

How? The magisterial, myopic 2-volume edition of Bradford's *History* edited by Adams, Ford, Deane and others appeared in 1912 as part of a wave of American effort to save and establish its literatures. It guided generations of well-meaning teachers in bringing "tradition" into our schools (tradition, as Charvat details, already as Christian-evangelical as can be), and its editors list these "grave disadvantages" born of The Pequot War. "Sudden plunder" and the profits of slavery inspiring new greed and theological license; "Indian cruelties" born of colonists' "wholesale killing"; "mistrust" near and far as solemn promises proved worthless beside convenience. Unless education helps citizens truly learn from so much, they arrive at new nightmares born of that supreme fiction "necessity." As those editors put it, "only time was needed to make another war of extermination inevitable" (FBH2: 259n3).

But if the Puritans taught transatlantic early America to change, we also can teach ourselves. If this book gave you worthwhile pleasure through a sharper idea of its subjects, it is only one of many such works "out there" dismissed by schools, publishers and media with other serviceable preoccupations. "Progress" will be a murderous myth until the goal for measuring it can bear to be stated in plain language.[95]

People worldwide would like to hear it. On November 8, 2002, National Public Radio's *All Things Considered* detailed an international study conducted over several years by Toronto consulting-firm Environics International. It found that 66% of people surveyed in 47 proclaimed democracies do not believe that their governments' ways express "the will of the people": they rather perceive that an elite, unelected, and hidden few enforce their own will from a narrow top down and around the world, through economics as well as war. The myth of a "free marketplace" that spontaneously "fills needs" by the miraculously-rational "choices" of its members seems a fable that only the "top" believes. "People know what's going on, they always do," the Environics spokesperson said; "and they're looking in other places for other kinds of leaders for the future."

Wars end, nations and churches perish (Native tribes too) when people walk out on leaders and visions that do not truly sustain the sustainable. Would-be Power confines people until they somehow

---

[95] Reviewing Curtis White's *The Middle Mind: Why Americans Don't Think For Themselves* (HarperSanFrancisco 2004), DeMott (7) writes: "We live in a crusted-over world...a place that's stale, overfamiliar, oblivious of 'the world-making capacities of the imagination.' Instead of questioning and resisting 'daily reality,' instead of recognizing it as a 'work of the human imagination'...we bow down to it as 'the only God-given, natural and inevitable world'"..."[O]ur 'lifestyle' has for the last half-century been the equivalent of a state of war between ourselves and those folks who will provide us cheap, cheap natural resources, and more recently cheap, cheap consumer goods or pay the price....What the hell is the ...world supposed to make of the fact that we were instructed by our com-mander-in-chief to help in the 'war effort' against terrorism by shopping?'"

regain more accurate existential bearings. The world's manifold realities---what some Native people call the "Multiverse"---penetrate a bubble of "belief" in artificial, arbitrary limits that confine people from the world, that distort it to a monster "for" them. Walls confine rather than protect. Some people cling hungrily to the fort, conditioned to fear a world without scripted certainties: others cannot resist its potentials and legitimate common feast. They tame the monster by talking with it, against the rules, and leave behind that life in the fort with its "means of well-governing" us. Preventing that escape is the "cultural work" of the traditional Pequot War.

Let us confront the patterns and "training" detailed here and which this war left as instructions for living in the hard-wire of American ways.

Vain and stubborn monologic in the face of others clearly our human equals; ineptitude masked with arrogance; morality as a pardon-tale for greed, convenient conformity to both; violent narcissism despite invitations to a more realistic (many-sided) world; the choice of war and massacre rather than negotiation offered by others; the oddly-proud negligence of history, and the use of it in education to fog and foil fact, intercultural justice, and peace. These are the patterns in this book's specifics---born of dumping European social problems into "empty wilderness" and then, by way of new "nonconformist" colonies on each frontier, stumbling onto short-term plunders of wealth. The "victors" read each disastrous debauch as a reward for virtue, but each soaks the nervous system in hunger for more at any price.

For example, Plimoth's Edward Winslow stands poor and culturally doomed beneath his colony's bloodsoaked flag, demanding more of what got him there (Ch. 4, end). He owes his life and "home" to other (Native) peoples who in fact owe him and his specious evangelism nothing: he finds himself in a hole and keeps digging. But that way leads only down. The colonies hurt other peoples for "advantage" (the root-word of "profit"), rather than cooperate as mere equals; and when the fathers hear from the peoples hurt, they want to hurt them again, for by God, *they're* not adapting. "This works---at least insofar as all Others fall silent, one way or another." A mighty fortress is this deity, a "rock" to cling to in a sea of relativity he denies and refuses to learn.

What we *do have*, then, is history rich with spiritual growth--- "How The Puritans Doomed Themselves." What we get from education is "How To Keep Trying to Believe Yourselves God's Only Children." It didn't work centuries ago, and it certainly won't in the graveyard of empires. Time to worry; for "Mystic-ism" is only a formula for fiasco.[96]

---

[96] "Capital enemy" Sassacus never was confirmed dead. Today The United States has more weapons than the next fifteen countries combined. Consider "Hunt for Osama: Why Can't We Find Him?" by Johanna McGeary and Douglas Waller, *Time Magazine*, Nov. 25, 2002: p. 30-35; and "Losing Control?" by Tim McGirk and Michael Ware, *Time*, Nov. 18, 2002, 56-59. "Remember 'Osama, Dead Or Alive'? The President's indelible declaration of U.S. intention to get him, back in the first days of the war on terrorism...made the capture or demise of the al-Qaeda leader essential to victory. In the months since...the Administration has downplayed the importance of the man...." "Of course, pursuing enemy elements more aggressively carries the risk of further alienating innocent Afghans who invariably get hassled during security sweeps. 'No one ever forgets that American soldiers came into their house and trawled through their women's clothing. Nor do they forgive,' says Mullah Mohammed Khaksar.... 'Doesn't the U.S. realize that with every one of these operations, their enemy is not decreasing but increasing with fresh, embittered new recruits?'" (59). "The U.S. concedes it has lost momentum in Afghanistan, while its enemies grow bolder." "If the U.S. has won the war...maybe somebody should tell the enemy it's time to surrender ....These days American bases are coming under rocket or mortar fire three times a week on average" (56). "Catching the perpetrators of such assaults after the fact

We and the world do not have to reach the limits of suffering to learn: that's only the way we are headed half-awake now. Is there a way out of this addiction, "living" by wresting self-destructive "advantage" from all that is? "There is something appalling in the consciousness of utter isolation," hinted Adams (*Three Episodes* 75). Colonists who flattered themselves as "isolated" and taught their children to do so could not fail "to exaggerate rather than diminish the danger" around them. Thus they acted in appalling ways that made their problems worse. No way out; except getting to know other peoples and their views.[97]

---

is usually all but impossible. After enduring a barrage of wildly aimed rockets on their base last month, commanders of the 82nd Airborne Division decided to mount a helicopter- and artillery-backed assault of 520 infantrymen on a high mountain valley rumored...as an al-Qaeda staging post. Up in the valley, this massive invasion force encountered only a lone man, who popped off a few rifle shots and then fled. He was never caught" (58). "Laments Afghan Interior Ministry Intelligence Chief Niamatullah Jalili: 'Al-Qaeda is using this town [Angurada] and there's nothing we can do.' U.S. forces are frustrated at their inability to strike at al-Qaeda operatives they know are inside. Says Col. Roger King, spokesman for the U.S. military: 'It's not like they're wearing uniforms and staying at a base that we can watch'"(35). Nor is Iraq's Saddam Hussein.

[97] Andrew Bacevich's *American Empire* (Cambridge: Harvard University Press 2002) is set forth for your inspiration by *The Boston Globe*'s Alan Wolfe (Nov. 17, 2002: pp. D1-D4). Wolfe's review, "The Phantom Empire," begins that "The Left and Right agree: The United States---once a republic that minded its own business---has become an empire that looks after everyone else's. They're wrong." Wolfe's conclusion: "Bacevich is right to say that there is a fundamental continuity to American foreign policy, but it isn't the continuity he thinks [*sic*]. For many years, Americans have resisted any expensive and long-lasting involvement with countries whose ways of life are thoroughly unfamiliar. We resist an imperial role for America not because we are humanitarians and internationalists, but because we are stingy with [tax-money for exporting our form of] government, and lack genuine interest in the rest of the world. Our best defenses

Which, then, do we want: a rigorously accurate, sophisticated past that really can take everybody toward more freedom? Or narcissistic fables of master and victim that limit, weaken and do harm? We can build what Aime Cesaire called a humanity big as the world, or build forts.[98]

---

against empire, as it turns out, lie not in our virtues but in our vices." Depend on this grinning turpitude to oil wars for conspicuous consumption. It already has. See Seymour Hersh's 2003 reportage in *The New Yorker* and Thomas Friedman's *The Lexus and the Olive Tree*: both correlate America's long "deep penetration" of Saudi Arabia as a prime "exploitation target" with the fact that 11 of the 15 airline-hijackers of 9/11/01 came from that country.

[98] Cesaire, sometimes called "the father of Negritude" and a leader of postcolonial analysis, taxed colleagues who, "while claiming to be dedicated to rigorous logic, sacrifice so willingly to prejudice and wallow so voluptuously in cliches." He found this "significant" of "thousands of Europeans or...of the Western petty bourgeoisie"; who "have never been further from being able to live a true humanism---a humanism made to the measure of the world" (56-7). Prisons cost more in every way than new Harvards, yet America builds more prisons. But staying inside the fort weakens you in every way. Untangle this sickly logic from Increase Mather's 1676 *Brief History*: "It is evident that we may truly say of [Wampanoag] Philip, and the Indians who have fought to dispossess us of the land which The Lord our God hath given to us...'I have not sinned against thee, but thou dost me wrong to war against me'....Yea, they kept [Philip's] land not from him, but for him; who otherwise would have sold himself out of all. And The Gospel was freely offered to him and to his subjects, but they despised it. And now behold how they reward us! Will not our God judge them? Yea, he hath and will do so" (Slotkin ed. 152).

This is a *widely-influential* mind using symbols (language) to "detach" and hide itself from "reality" by *any* definition. Consider that "back then" as well as now, for example in contemporary war-torn Palestine/Israel, the *alternative*---to this fear-choked "religious" neurosis that denies plain-sight theft of land with words, walls and "settlements"---is the refusal of violence; is negotiated coexistence leading to inevitable intermarriages of peoples and cultures; and hence, to "decay" of each side's elite's symbolic fantasy-world of racial/cultural

You need a fort---or do you?---when "others" can enter your truly-secret places. A fort is a choice for self-confinement against vulnerability. To uncover what "Mystic" and The Pequot War teach us of how to respond to the world, compare David Wagner's ethnologically-precise images of Native Americans in this book against those by an unknown artist in DeForest. The "Indian Family" comes from a time when more, not less, Native-cultural information was available. Yet these figures are not "Indians," but serviceable objects; figments of imperial desire.

The pensive, stoic father-and-warrior is a sketch-class Apollo, sad because of his "doom," and yet threatening from the quiver of his arrows to his muscles and scarcely-adequate loincloth. His son is a Dionysian fawn who looks down, a promising trait, on the daughter; but his bow reveals that he is not to be trusted as he grows. A mother, of course, cannot share the shameless garb, nor trifle to show us her face as she watches her husband's back. She is half-angel, by virtue of wings that are actually a papoose; and half-seductress, with her tasteful cleavage, trade-bangle and wild hair. They are all creatures of a romantic, twilight world connected by the great moon-crescent of their boat: "threateningly beautiful," the two semi-gendered youths most "savage" and sexy. This is as sensual as it gets within Connecticut statutes of 1852.

"purity." How can coexistence *be* such a terrifying prospect except as the end of a one-sided ego? "The sociopath sees other people as objects to be manipulated and used, much as the rest of us would use a screwdriver or a kleenex. The sociopath feels no empathy for others, although he can fake empathy, and he feels no shame or remorse about abusing people. In his universe, he is the center, and everyone else exists only to serve him" (Post by one "Glenn Campbell" at http://Counterpunch.org Sept. 16, 2003). Take it a step further, for the colonies did to make "our" world: Narcissism that forces itself by "preemptive war" on other peoples is psychosis.

AN INDIAN FAMILY

Objects of Desire: An "Indian Family" from DeForest page 8 (1852)

It's alright though, this semi-nude tableau: after all, they're not white people, but "specimens." It's educational. In private with this you can stretch your confines with curiosity, or even illicit desire; but this is nobody you'd prudently marry. Anyway, they're gone (or at least, they're fading from the 1850s Western Hemisphere, now that they seem invisible back East). It's very sad, God's progress. Hence the loving detail of this tribute to the "vanished."

In case you don't understand that as intended, the other image from DeForest ("Battle at Fairfield") shows what "happens" to creatures like that and to any traitor mixing with them. We find the "savages" in a wilderness-nowhere, and they outnumber us. At top left, note yon fading, ineffective archer in his sylvan glade (complete with authentic New England Great Plains headdress), facing the entry of white men with guns, at far right. The archer's arrows are child's play. The hero at center needs no armor, or even boots: his armor is the upper-class status in his clothes. Of course his Old World "inferiors" (like the soldier with armor and helmet) are more than a match for the "Indian" swooning backward; but the new American hero disdains The Middle Ages. His wonderful natural courage (it's that bracing American air) puts him at even more heroic risk, as another brave calls for help behind his back. Guerrilla-treachery is the only thing that ever brings him down.

But too late! For at left arrives proper planter-soldiery, the "minute men" with almighty guns, to turn the tide---if our hero needs help at all. One "savage" lies already at his feet, in the sexy spread-eagle of noble doom, dismanned of his club in fair fight. His Indian clone-brother (they all look alike) begs the hero's mercy; but it's well-deserved justice in the neck for them and for all "savages" who disturb the peaceful war. From here, our hero dashes off to fetch back Snow Bosom (his ice-queen), the colonies' blonde/blue-eyed mascot. In America's more-private collection of books for

BATTLE AT FAIRFIELD SWAMP

Objects of Violence: from DeForest 149

"adults" (bottom shelf, behind the Cooper), he finds her tied to a tree for savage imaginings. Ain't it awful! It's a scene from Nowhere: Utopia.[99]

Inside the fort we learn to turn to mystical massacre when, really, it's just not working. Such books and images relieve the stresses of desire and of empty victory against it. It gets worse---grows more bloody and more "popular"---all the way to high-tech Hollywood as we keep indulging this circle of desire and rage. We become wired for one of many possible responses, because it makes us feel even briefly in control of a relative universe we're too afraid and impatient to know. Evangelism has un-taught us how to learn from it. If we want to survive we had better start remembering.

"Mystic-ism" prevents having to stop, observe, face what we're doing wrong, and change. The cruel irony is what we forfeit in our sleepy obedience: a solid basis for more freedom, wonder, and joy in creative self-evolution. For a delusion that is not control at all.

---

[99] These images represent *wishes*---psychological remakes of complex realities into pseudo-gratifications not being obtained in real life. There is no lack of first-rate scholarship showing the programmatic diligence of American education in passing on these necessarily sadomasochistic, short-term-serviceable substitutes for multicultural history, literature and social policy. The increasingly commercialized erotic valence of "captivity narratives," featuring titillating frontier temptations of body and culture, was the core of "redemption literature" from Mary Rowlandson's (massive editions from 1682) through the 1790s' "Panther Captivity" (a "bestseller") and on through Cooper. Such were the texts by which colonial Americans bonded themselves (around their fears) into a nation-state. The most remarkable equally-read exception was *The Life of Mary Jemison* (1824), whose teller loved her Native life and paid dearly for it ("I did not tell…half of what it was," qtd. in Walsh 49). See Anderson, Armstrong/Tennenhouse, Barrett, Boose, Davidson, Drinnon, Elson, Fiedler, Kaplan/Pease, Kolodny, Pearce, Reynolds, Rogin, Slotkin, Spengemann, Strong and Walsh.

The Pequots win their war because they face the need for changed tactics. Their victory is not so much because there was American space in which to scatter, for really they never left their home. More important was their Ice Age sense of time, in which they framed their plan for surviving a self-involved Progress. We too have choices that correspond to our vision and courage, from Mason's Dr. Pell to those who refused Vietnam. You cannot *give away* your power---only believe that you have none.

> From the earliest days at Wessagusset [scene of the
> "Weymouth Massacre"] and in The Pequot War, down
> to the very last election held in North Carolina [include-
> ing lynchings of Afro-Americans]---from 1623 to 1898---
> the knife and the shotgun have been far more potent and
> active instruments in our dealings with inferior races than
> the code of liberty or the output of The Bible Society.

These, in the words of Charles Francis Adams, Jr., were the hard facts that America needed to confront 267 years after "Mystic" (delivered in a patriotic address at Lexington, Mass.; qtd. in Drinnon 309). Yes, Adams continued, colonists' dealings with "inferior races" had been "a process of extermination"; "but for that very reason," genocide had been "the salvation of [the white] race. It has saved the Anglo-Saxon stock from being a nation of half-breeds---miscegenates, to coin a word expressive of an idea."

Violence, always "in defense"---defense of an "innocent" narcissism that "just happens" to steal others' lives and wealth. "Defense" against knowing there are other options: a fort against feelings that may lead beyond its own scripted preoccupations. Desire. Wall out or annihilate those who draw us beyond ourselves (the meaning of *ecstacy*), because if we don't, we marry them. Marry them and we lose our identity as beings chosen by (our) God from all Nature, for a mystic purpose nobody wants to articulate. We'd be merely human, only equal.

As it is, imperial culture turns for comfort to ideas and, soon, actions in which vulnerable, mortal flesh becomes soothing omnipotent word.

> The report of the horrid and unprovoked cruelties of the Pequots, practiced upon the defenseless inhabitants of Connecticut colony, roused the other colonies to harmonious and spirited exertions against them...[by] which means the whole fort [at Mystic] was very soon enwrapt in flames!....The enemy were now in a deplorable situation. Death inevitable was their portion. Sallying forth from their burning cells, they were shot or cut to pieces by the English. Many of them, perceiving it impossible to escape the vigilance of the troops, threw themselves voluntarily into the flames!
>
> The violence of the flames, the reflection of the light, the clashing and roar of arms...exhibited a grand and awful scene! In less than two hours from the commencement of the bloody action...eighty wigwams were burnt, and upwards of eight hundred Indians destroyed! Parents and children, the sannup and squaw, the aged and the young, perished in promiscuous ruin! The loss of...English was comparatively trifling, not exceeding 25....
>
> Few enterprises were ever perhaps achieved with more personal bravery....Even the great armaments and battles of Europe are comparatively of little importance....The most warlike and terrible tribe of Indians in New England [was] completely exterminated.
> (Henry Trumbull, *History* 1836: 29, 33-35)

Feel better? Trumbull built this wishful fiction from Mason's, Underhill's, Bradford's and others', and DeForest (Ch. 4) based his upon them and Trumbull. It tells much about the writers, nothing about the subjects. What "culture" produces people who write this for truth, for pleasure? Is it the work of a childish savage? A savage child?[100]

What different human lives permeate the same original pages! Meet again Wincumbone, wife of Mystic's Sachem Mamoho. Lion Gardener tells of her in his early attempts to establish trade near Saybrook (G125). At a Pequot river-camp, Wincumbone sees anger building and "makes signs" that a man of Gardener's should "be gone." It saves the man's life, and Gardener does not forget. He testifies for Wincumbone's and her children's "better" treatment in Mr. Governor's hands.

More, because of bonds like that across official lines, Gardener has a basis for true bravery, true justice. Years later, he's among

---

[100] Editor Orr prepares you to read Mason and company (xviii), citing John "Manifest Destiny" Fiske's *Beginnings of New England* on "the overthrow of the Pequots." "As a matter of practical policy, the annihilation of the Pequots can be condemned only by those who read history so incorrectly as to suppose that savages, whose business it is to torture and slay, can always be dealt with according to the methods in use between civilized peoples. A mighty nation like The United States is in honor bound to treat the red man with scrupulous justice and refrain from cruelty in punishing his delinquencies. But if the founders of Connecticut, in confronting a danger which threatened their very existence, struck with savage fierceness, we cannot blame them. The world is so made that it is only in that way that the higher races have been able to preserve themselves and carry on their progressive work." With this education, how would you handle "next time"? "There is a remnant of the Pequots still existing," Orr adds via sub-editor Williams (118). "They live in the town of Groton [on] eleven acres of poor land....They are more mixed than the Mohegans with negro and white blood....A short time since, I [saw] most of the tribe together. They are more vicious, and not so decent or so goodlooking a people as the Mohegans. This however may be owing to their being more mixed with other blood."

Long Island Shinnecocks who are in trouble and fear a massacre (G144-5). Their Sachem is accused of a woman's murder, but Gardener knows him innocent. "Then I said...I will stay here [as a hostage] till you all know it is well with your Sachem. If they bind him [at the English court of law], bind me; and if they kill him, kill me." The Shinnecocks answer "with a great cry," and in short order help bring the real murderers to what they all consider justice. This can just ruin a classroom devoted to "Mystic-ism," an empire bent upon hiding from itself. Perhaps America's one "vice" that *can* function as a virtue is its deep wide disregard for anything but a "serviceable" past. For when it wakes to the facts of how *un*serviceable "tradition" has actually been, its maundering monologic can begin to change, to the good of everybody's world.

The frontier happens in a universe of relativity. Cultures are equal because they have equally-unique origins and views of the universe. But all "beliefs" are not equally-accurate descriptions of this world in our midst. Indians, for example, are not children or *savages* as some people want to believe. In the last analysis, "Mystic" presents us with what writer Susan Griffin calls a crisis in delusion.

You may learn and/or want to believe one thing, but you live in a world always larger and more complicated. The crisis is the choice this presents. Discover and face the place where you are and its "other" peoples, and with them create new realities and ways that (like the early transatlantic between Natives and Europeans) smooth a humanly-imperfect coexistence. Or, blind yourself to those things and, as your masters demand, try to force the world to resemble your wishes, with crusades according to a fantasy of yesterday. But the world, naturally, resists, and it won't be "only" others who get hurt. What, after all, has modern Israel gained for its fundamental refusal of a "mixed blood" future? Certainly not security for its "pure" culture.

Notice rough tough Captain Underhill: he almost faints like a blushing nun when two young English girls of Wethersfield come back from Pequot captivity and the older one reveals that only "God" saved her from intimate contact with a Pequot (U70-77). "The eldest of them was about sixteen." "Demanding of her how they used her, she told us they did solicit her to uncleanness." Oh, she prayed and prayed, Captain-sir.

The girl is not raped. She is invited, in a context where rape is possible as part of war, if not approved by Native custom (Axtell, *Essays*). The girl declines because she is not alone (that little sister with her), and her treatment tells her they are going home. Reverend Underhill, mortified at the girl's narrow escape from his own fears, gushes a seven-page sermon---that you, the grumbling colonist, must also say No. That only "God," who knows your "illicit desires," prevents you from "suffering" as she did. The girl, like you, is already "so ungrateful" *before* abduction that she needs discipline against temptation. "God's hand is upon" her, for "remissness in all...ways" (U71). This, again, means You. No talking. The Fort is "not to be questioned" (Ch. 1).[101]

---

[101] The Pequot-produced film *The Witness*, shown at the Mashantucket Pequot Museum in Ledyard, CT, also reproduces the Mason/Underhill story. The 30-minute film's tremendous impact registers afresh the generations of belief in the reports of what happened there. Though it retains many clichés of its genre (grunting vs. talking, an Uncas who even *looks* "evil," etc.), its educational effect is still radically opposite that of tradition: we never lose sight of who causes the whole catastrophe. The same is true of the new film *Mystic Voices*, produced by Guy Perrotta and Charles Clemmons, premiered in Spring 2003. Maybe someday the Pequot War exhibit will consist of what is also at Mashantucket now: a huge dugout boat in the Museum's entrance-hall, full of Pequot family moving out of harm's way.

Underhill means to prevent uncleanness, any mixture of his "pure" culture; to make her and us reproduce his values, though he can't say what they are. He aims to prevent the undisciplined on any side from betraying the values that will live on as America in his image---if his English can just plant it right, and forget they are policing it. "God" plugs up the leaks.

Not surprisingly, the colonists grow anxious. They rightly fear retribution for the violence generic to their self-centered way in the world. Imperialism will not teach them to handle feeling and desire, only to stifle them, unless a proper matrimony that subordinates/erases the "other" can extend the fortress further. And still they find the world endlessly full of beautiful peoples. With time and repeatedly worse crises, colonists "must" inflict even harsher discipline: soon, "savage" and "girl" alike must perish. In Underhill's mind they come together and die as one being, as in the crowning moments of progress-literature by Trumbulls and DeForests.

These uncontrolled, unpredictable beings must perish, or "not understanding," they'll not choose the Fort. Insiders will not be able to keep from outsiders. The latter must die or the former will come to give in. "Go Native." It's that ungovernable, ravishing beauty. Like a real Eve in a real Garden, proffering an apple whose "threat" is supreme: "They must not become as gods." Never awaken and learn to make their world.

> Benefiting and hurting others are ways of exercising one's power upon others: that is all one desires in such cases. One hurts those whom one wants to feel one's power, for pain is a much more efficient means to that end....[But] certainly the state in which we hurt others is

> rarely as agreeable, in an unadulterated way, as that in
> which we benefit others. It is a sign that we are still
> lacking power; or it shows a sense of frustration in the
> face of this poverty.... (Nietzsche, *The Gay Science* 86)

"Hurting others is a sign that one lacks power!" exclaimed Nietzsche's editor Kaufmann. James Joyce (on reading that) said it too: "Cruelty is weakness." Real and imagined, that is what "Mystic" is about. We can refuse this part of our inheritance, open our eyes beyond the captains, and embrace a new past; one that can end our still-colonial Western "time to worry." We hope this journey brings you sightings of rewards for change, beyond old horizons.

Finally, a challenge: "Mystic" may also be a "massacre" near you. Here is one with all the sacred signs. You recall Captain Underhill thrown out of Massachusetts. He took his skills along. DeForest describes his career as a mercenary soldier hired on by the Dutch of New Amsterdam, for their "Indian wars" of 1643-44 (206-8). The Dutch were building Wall Street, and feared resentful "savages" outside the wall. Underhill needed "a job."[102]

---

[102] Steve Wick and Bill Bleyer, Staff Writers for a Website called *Long Island History.com*. "A Man Hated and Hailed: Englishman John Underhill led the slaughter of Indians in defense of European settlers." Undated: viewed Feb. 2002, *http://www.lihistory.com/3/hs306a.htm*. The writers say that "by his own accounts [*sic*], he and his men killed more than 1,000 Pequots" at Mystic. They got the second part sort of right: "As a people, the Pequots all but disappeared from the landscape after Underhill was through with them." "It was unfortunate," adds descendant Gloria Baylis Tucker of The Underhill Society, "but he wasn't the only one....He was just doing a job." The job got him an Oyster Bay estate he called Killingworth. Ms. Tucker is shown here at the Underhill Monument in Mill Neck (built 1907). It "features four plaques on its base showing Underhill reading to a group of Indians, who are kneeling worshipfully at his feet. On the cover of the book are the words, 'Love One Another.'"

Paid by Governor Kieft and his planters, Underhill set to work on numerous killings and a "small" massacre of Massapequa people at Fort Neck. Then, returning in February 1644 to the Stamford area, he "followed Mason's example at Fort Mystic" (208), and set fire to a surrounded but "on their guard" palisaded village. "The same result followed," DeForest reports.

Strictly in context here---We hope so! "This terrific slaughter put an end to the war." We challenge you to prove/disprove this to the world. First clues (208): "The Dutch chroniclers expressed their gratitude for the victory in the same devout strain....They remarked it, for instance, as a particular providence that, when the attack was made on the village, 'the Lord had collected most of their enemies there, to celebrate some peculiar festival.'"

The Lord, or the chronicles? The difference makes all the difference in the world.

CODA:
'We Do Not Know How'
by
Little Owl/Ruth Duncan, Duda/Elderwoman of the Quinnipiac

The Dawnlanders are spread
round about, like seed
cast to the wind!
Many of us
are dead now, but some
find salvation
in a cave or marsh.

Upon the mountain, for a time
we may stand
in prayer,
but the strangers
may capture us, even there,
with some falling trap
and forever we must
work without
rest.

It's because they
crave
the riches that cannot
satisfy and so,
to gain their own
liberty,
they take away ours!
Alas! We do not know how
to improve such hearts
as these of the strangers.
They will not even hear
what their own
stories teach.

An Annotated Chronology
of The Pequot War
(Note: Table of Source-Abbreviations with Works Cited)

1500?-1600   Sachem Tamaquashad and "Mahican" people migrate into Connecticut country from regions south of "Albany" on the Hudson. Tamaquashad is *aka* Pekoath, or Pequot (Caulkins 1895: 221: 1), and these "Mahicans" become known as Mohegans and Pequots. Also, c.1600 their Sachem is one Wopigwooit (*Woppequoit*), poss. known to the Dutch as Tatobem (Caulkins 1895: 21; DeForest 73; Cave 298n34). Salwen reports evidence (65; and 1969) for "long...in situ development" on Connecticut lands; Salisbury agrees (263n82). Good differing analysis of Uncas' "Genealogy" in WCL1: 115-16n11.

Some Algonquian-speakers use "Pequot" or *Paquatauog* (Peale) to signify "Destroyer"; for the Mohegans/Pequots rapidly establish home territory of appr. 30 sq. mi. between the Niantic and Pawcatuck Rivers, from the Atlantic coast to inland headwaters of the Pequot/Thames River abutting Nipmuc lands. With as many as 13,000 persons just before "Contact" (Starna 46; Snow *Archaeology* 34, 39), the Mohegans/Pequots impose wider "tributary" status on neighboring peoples by intermarriage, control of trade and force of arms.

Affected peoples include the Niantics, split into Eastern poss. under Sequeen (Salisbury 277n14), and Western under Sassious (Swanton 1952: 1, Brasser 1971: 68); as well as southern Nipmucs of "Quinabaag" (Drake 104, Gookin 7); the small "River Tribes," from the Weekapaug River (eastern RI) south to "New Haven" Bay, and the Long Island Shinnecock (Gardener 138). Only the more numerous Narragansetts can "successfully stand up to" the Pequots (Soulsby 2). Trade, marriage and feud continue into "Contact" times.

1590? Pequot Sachem Wopigwooit/Tatobem's main village stands on Pequot Hill (in "Groton") near the Mystic River, site of the 1637 assault. His braves fight three "battles" (DeForest 54-61) with those of Sequeen/Sequassen: the latter takes refuge among Narragansetts, with many Niantics.

Tatobem's son, Sassacus, lives 5 mi. west at Noank (Fort Hill, *aka* Pequot/New London), on the Thames/Pequot River. Drake (1833 [2001]: 104) calls it Weinshauks. Sassacus' "tributaries" include as many as 26 villages (McBride, Peale, DYW 126).

1614 Dutch adventurer Adriaen Block explores Connecticutt coasts and records "Pequatoos...enemies of the Wapanoos [Wappingers?]" (DeLaet in Jameson 1909: 42-3). His map locates "Pequats" west of Mystic River, "Morhicans" west of Pequot/Thames.

NOTE: For more evidences on origins of the Mohegans under Sachem Uncas (at Shantok/Uncasville) see 1627 and 1634 below. Cave 66 cites Weinstein 1991, Means 26-33 on clues that Mohegans were a "distinct separate" people, whose Sachems disputed Pequot hunting-rights north of main Pequot villages (Salisbury 206). Gardener (G136) and Mason (M20) say they "had but that year [1637] come from the Pequots."

1616-1618 Amid increasing transatlantic contacts, European diseases ravage Native New England, killing up to 90% of

Massachusetts and other groups. The Narragansetts reportedly suffer "less" than most (FBH1: 223), but by 1637, Mohegan/Pequot numbers fall by 77% (Starna 46; Orr viii). Their powerful reputation persists (Wood 80, "a stately warlike people...just and equal in their dealings") though reduced to about 3000 persons.

1620   England's Puritan "Pilgrims" arrive at Patuxet/Plimoth, Massachusetts. Promising 1621 tribal treaties give way to rancor, fort-construction, mutual suspicions of attack-conspiracies.

1622-1623   Wessagussett/ first Weymouth Colony (MA) begins and disperses on Mass. Bay: English misunderstandings of/ disregard for Native and transatlantic practices, plus rivalries with Plimoth bring about a "massacre" of up to 12 Massachusetts.

1624   Ma-Re Mount (Merrymount) on Mass. Bay thrives by transatlantic methods incl. gun-trade, cohabitation and "revels," (suppressed 1630). Morton's *Canaan* (1637) notes "trade and traffic" with Pequots.

1627   Mohegan/Pequot Sachem Uncas marries daughter of Sachem Tatobem (M7; Johnson 31), giving him "royal" affiliation as brother-in-law of Sassacus. The Dutch bring wampum-trade to Plimoth (Robinson 19). The trade's gradual expansion greatly enriches both Narragansetts and Pequots.

1629   Mass. Bay Company "advance men" under Capt. Endecott settle Salem.

1630 Massachusetts Bay Colony founded under Governor John Winthrop Sr.

1631 Plimoth's Edward Winslow travels Connecticut River regions. Several Sachems (Podunk, Wagincut and other Pequot "tributaries") visit Boston to invite English traders, are refused (WJH1: 61). Sassacus struggles to hold his 26 villages together incl. those of Wequash and Soso on banks of Pawcatuck River (Salisbury 210, Cave 56). Narragansetts under Canonicus and Miantonomo reportedly hope to ally with the English against Pequots.

1632 Miantonomo visits Gov. Winthrop's house at Boston (July 13). June: Pequot Sachem Tatobem allows Dutch West Indian Co. to establish Fort New Hope at Dutch Point (near future Hartford: Jennings 188; *NY Coll. Docs.* II: 139-140). Plimothers too obtain rights from Sachem Natawanute (Bradford 1908: 301, Salwen 173); but smallpox kills most Natives of the area within 2 years.

1633 Another epidemic decimates Native New England through 1634, incl. 700 Narragansetts (Salisbury 191; WJH1: 118). English/Dutch rivalries over Connecticut land and Pequot trade increase as colonist John Oldham and others explore and plan to establish Wethersfield and Windsor "above" the Dutch river-post, to intercept rich fur-trade from the north. By next year, they secure permission from local Wangunk Sachem Sowheag (Peale 23).

The Pequots kill several (Narragansett?) Native people poss. trying to trade at Dutch Point. The Dutch close down the post: the Narragansetts prepare for war (DeForest 72-3; Salisbury 82, 210; Jennings 189; Cave 58-9).

1634   The Dutch take Pequot Tatobem hostage: when they receive ransom, they murder him (DeForest 72-3; Salisbury 263, 289). Mamoho (FBH2: 257) becomes Sachem of Mystic Village/Fort: Sassacus becomes Pequot Great Sachem at Weinshauks/Noank, and pursues justice.

Mohegan Uncas conflicts with Sassacus over Pequot Sachemship, for which Uncas has made five attempts. Councils confirm Sassacus. Uncas is exiled to the Narragansetts, returns forgiven, is driven out again (DeForest, Johnson).

The Mohegans' numbers? Roger Williams (WCL1: 117) claims "not above 40 or 50," others say 70 braves, 400-500 people (U67); poss. 1700 persons (more citations end of Ch. 6). They settle not far up the Pequot/Thames River near Montville. As Soulsby (3) summarizes records, the Mohegans bitterly resent Sassacus, but lack adequate allies to "overwhelm" his Pequots.

The Narragansetts invite John Oldham to live/trade on Dutch Island: he declines (WJH1: 146; WPF3: 502). Western Niantics, Pequots strike on the Connecticut River (U56-8), killing Virginia interloper Capt. Stone (banished by Mass. Bay), Capt. Norton and crew in revenge for Tatobem (WPF3: 177, WJH1: 138-40; Jennings 189, 195).

Oct.-Nov.: Trade halted, the Pequots invite Mass. Bay to establish relations, ask help ending Narragansett conflict (WJH1: 138-9, 148-9, Cave 124-7). Boston demands Stone's killers: Pequots try to explain their justice. Narragansetts watch closely, accept English mediation (Cave 70). This Mass. Bay/Pequot "treaty" maintains peace till 1636, but parties' different understandings of it become manifest (WJH1: 199, DeForest 104).

1635   As English with Samuel Stone/Wm. Goodwin establish Hartford (Peale 23), English under John Winthrop Jr. and Lion Gardener (for Lords Say/Brook) erect Saybrook Fort on the Connecticut River, against further Dutch access (Drake 188). Summer-Oct.: Religious/social issues within Mass. Bay Colony result in migrations to "river towns" Wethersfield, Hartford, Windsor. Plimoth's claims and colonists there are effectively forced out (Soulsby "Pequot" 4; Jennings 196-7, 203; Cave 99).

1636   March: Henry Vane (younger) defeats Winthrop for Boston governorship, latter becomes "deputy." May: Rev. Hooker and more Mass. Bay colonists migrate to Connecticut river-towns, secure permission from Suckiaug Sachem Sequassen/Sequin to plant "six large miles into the wilderness" (Peale 23). June: Plimoth's Jon. Brewster (WPF3: 271) reports statements by Uncas that Sassacus killed Stone's men and planned to attack a Plimoth boat. Uncas also says the Pequots are "certain of an English attack," as river-town colonists hold "training days" and make "indiscreet speeches" (V101; Jennings 202).

Mohegan numbers-estimates now range from "too few for a deer hunt" to "less than 400" (Johnson 31), from "not fifty adult men" to 600 persons (WCL1: 117, 119; Mooney 1928: 4).

Sassacus' Pequots, at war with Dutch and uneasy with English newcomers, repeat efforts to make peace with Canonicus'/ Miantonomo's Narragansetts (Bradford 1962: 182). Summer: Roger Williams banished from Mass. Bay amid Antinomian and other controversies: Narragansetts permit his "Providence" homestead (Salisbury 212).

July: Mass. Bay's Gov. Vane informs Winthrop Jr. at Saybrook of Boston's ultimatum: Pequots must either fulfill 1634 treaty (as construed by Mass. Bay), or consider it void and English "revenge" imminent (Salisbury 212). At Saybrook Fort, Pequot negotiators and W. Niantic Sachem Sassious meet with Gardener, Winthrop Jr. and others. The English demand surrender of Stone[1]s killers and 1634[1]s massive "treaty tributes." As Pequots hold to their views, Sassious places his people under Winthrop Jr.'s "protection," but they realign with Pequots as hostilities begin (WPF3: 285; M34; WCL1: 69; Jennings 204).

Amid July stalemate, trader John Oldham is killed near Block Island, most likely "at random" by E. Niantic sagamore Audsah (WJH1: 189-92, WPF3: 412, 500; and see 1639). By Aug. 8, Miantonomo[1]s Narragansetts have "good success" avenging Oldham (WPF3: 192). But on Aug. 25, Mass. Bay sends John Endecott, Underhill and soldiers to kill "the men of Block Island" and "from thence," hopefully to the Pequots "to draw them to a parley, and so to some quiet end" Vane/Winthrop in FBH2: 243; WPF3: 193).

After costly failures at Block Island, Endecott lands at Saybrook, is scolded by Gardener for "raising wasps" with hostile actions. Delayed by Pequot diplomatic feints, Endecott attacks villages/ crops along Connecticut River (DeForest 96-99). Pequots harrass Saybrook, seek negotiations, safety for noncombatants. "Rebuffed" by Gardener (Jennings 213), Pequots again seek alliance with Narragansetts (Cave 124-7).

Since May, Mass. Bay has outcast Williams monitor/discourage any Pequot-Narragansett alliance (4 MHSC6: 189); Williams Letters 6: 231-2). For 3 days, Williams does his "utmost" to foil their plans (WCL2: 611). With his help, Gov. Vane makes a treaty with Narragansetts (WJH1: 198, FBH2: 243); but the Antinomian Vane departs for England by next August.

Williams, poss. via Miantonomo, sends Boston a sketch-map of Pequot home territory (MHSC3: 1: 161; rpt. FBH2: 250), and urges a stealth-attack led by alienated Pequots Wequash and Wuttack-quiackkommin, "valiant men" living 3-4 years with Narragansetts and who "know every pass and passage" (Drake 105). Later, Williams notes that Wequash "was suspected to deal falsely when he went to hunt for the Pequots" (WPF3: 450). Neither individual plays any recorded role in the war.

Oct.: At Boston, Miantonomo pledges mostly neutrality against Pequots (Williams Correspondence 1: 72-3; WJH1: 199, 3: 237-8; DeForest 104). Nov.: As-yet unmolested river-towns "mock" Gardener's plea for help at Saybrook (Jennings 215; Cave 128-33). Acc. to Salisbury (214-5), Mass. Bay Sachem Cutshamekin (brother of Neponset's Chikatawbak) is "most effective" arguing that Narragansetts should abandon the Pequots. Miantonomo offers a Narragansett attack on Pequots with Mass. Bay assent but is refused (WPF3: 411-14; WCL1: 78-9).

1637　　April: Boston General Court authorizes levy of men and taxes for war. Miantonomo visits Williams, agrees to help Boston if they "spare women and children" (Robinson 23; WPF3: 414). Mass. Bay plans 200-man assault by June (Jennings 215), but divisions among colonial parties persist (Cave 136-8). Wethersfield's English evict (and later reinstate) local Native people. They appeal to the Pequots, who attack Wethersfield April 23 (WJH1: 213; WPF3: 407-8). May: The river-towns commission Capt. John Mason and 90 men to make "offensive war" on the Pequots (FBH2: 249). He and Capt. Underhill (Saybrook Company with 20 men) arrive at Saybrook (WJH1: 217), as Rev. Hooker urges Winthrop/Boston to "execution" and "not to do this work of The Lord's revenge slackly" (WPF3: 408).

Mason's/Underhill's commission calls for attack on Sassacus' Weinshauks (WPF3: 407-8). At Saybrook, Gardener doubts the adequacy of Mason's forces, and Uncas'/Mohegans' loyalty: Uncas kills several nearby Natives assumed to be Pequots (WJH1: 223-4).

For reasons much debated (see Cave 209n47 vs. Jennings 218-221; Ch. 1 here), the English captains decide to attack not Weinshauks but Pequot Sachem Mamoho's Mystic "from the rear." They sail to Miantonomo's village, join with their and E. Niantic "auxiliaries." Boston's Capt. Patrick (via runner) urges Mason to wait for his 40 soldiers (WPF3: 421). Mason arranges Pequot River rendezvous with him instead.

c.May 23: Mason's/Underhill's force marches overland, arrives at E. Niantic Ninigret's fort and briefly surrounds it to deprive Pequots of warning. Complaints are rife at "desertions" of Native allies through the action (WPF3: 411, FBH2: 252; Orr xvi-xvii). Williams later works "to perswade" the English they are gone "for provision" or to attack other Pequot forts (WPF3: 426).

May 26: At dawn the English surround Mystic Village/Fort and attack. Native allies waver between weak participation and withdrawal (WPF3: 427). As this book argues, Mystic by now is likely an empty decoy. Acc. To Winthrop (WJH1: 225), slain Pequots include "two chief sachems," 150 braves and 150 women/children. Accounts in Orr disagree.

At Weinshauks, Sassacus' main force learns of the attack (Jennings 225). Pequot braves assault Narragansetts/Mohegans and the English, who retreat with many wounded ("opprest with multitudes...wanting powder and...arrows" (Williams in WPF3: 426). They manage rendezvous with Capt. Patrick sailing their boats, who sees their state, hesitates to land (WJH1: 223-4). Patrick and Underhill collide.

With Underhill embarked for Saybrook, Mason and Patrick march there too, attack W. Niantic allies of Pequots (M34). More Pequots flee to Ninigret's E. Niantic villages (Drake 106; Ch. 5 here). Some take refuge in Mystic's Owl's Nest Swamp (FBH2: 249). Through summer, others flee to Long Island, to Quinnipiac and Nipmuc villages and, beyond, to the Mohawks. "At least 300" Natives (likely W. Niantics, M42-3) defend Pequots as "good men," skirmish with Uncas' Mohegans.

English captains, supplied with many towns" levies of men (Orr x, xii, xiv) pursue Pequots and Sassacus (M36-9; WPF3: 427-31, 451-53; Cave overview 157-162). Orr: records show "determination...to exterminate and to follow up the advantage gained" (x). Underhill records 1500 "souls" killed in 2 months (U49). At last, rumors report Sassacus, Mystic's Mamoho and many others "fled up toward the [Mohawks]" (WPF3: 451, 456: Mamoho's wife/children captured, 457). Williams (452) reports that "The body of the [Pequot] men yet live, and are only removed from their dens"---and adds "suspicions" of "new" Pequot/Mohawk alliance. Winthrop tells Wm. Bradford of estimates that Pequots "slain and taken [are] in all about 700," that "the Indians in all quarters [are] so terrified, as all their friends are afraid to receive them" (457). By August Winthrop estimates 800-900 Pequot casualties (DYW 127).

Acc. to Williams via Miantonomo (WPF3: 448), Sassacus must "beg" allies for help. August: Acc. to Winthrop (WJH1: 229, DYW 127), Messrs. Ludlow and Pynchon deliver to Boston "part of the skin and lock of hair" of Sassacus. Bradford (2: 258) suggests Narragansetts "hired" Mohawks to kill him, but Mamoho/others are spared.

E. Niantic Sachem Ninigret refuses to surrender "his" Pequots (DYW 131); is later "delinquent" paying English tributes and "inveigling with the Mohawks" (Vaughan 172, 378n39). By 1645 amid new tensions, Ninigret says that "No Englishman should step out of his door to piss, but he...be killed." Mason (M40) and Uncas' braves drive Pequots from Pawcatuck River village, and they become Mohegans. Miantonomo complains of many English lies/injustices to "friends" (Robinson 24).

1638   March: Antinomian exiles incl. Anne Hutchinson remove to "Portsmouth" RI. June: Mohegan Sachem Uncas, refuting Narragansett accusations, promises to "submit" to English rule "touching the Pequots he had" (WJH1: 271; Williams in WPF3: 496). Acc. to Johnson's citations (35), Mohegan numbers jump from "400 to 600" pre-war to 2,500 "six years later."

Sept. 21: Treaty of Hartford (rpt. in Vaughan 340) divides "200 Pequot...men besides squaws and papooses" among Narragansetts/ Mohegans: the conquered "shall no more be called Pequots but" members of the latter nations. Underhill's *Newes from America* and Vincent's *True Relation* published. Masons composition uncertain (see Chs. 4-5 here, Mather/Drake ed.). Gardener's chronicle in mss. till 1833 (3 MHSC 3: 131-160).

Acc. to Burgess (42-3), McBride (97, 105) and Salisbury ("Indians" 83), Pequots gather at Stonington (Eastern) and Mashantucket (Groton). They are forbidden their tribal and home-river's name (G120), language; cannot trade or provide own subsistence; "whites" also forbidden to live with them. By 1675 their religion is also "illegal," but no Christian conversions are recorded.

1639 May: Miantonomo denied Boston's permission to take in more Pequots (Williams 1988: 1: 196). June: Acc. to Dutch David de Vries (*Voyages* 86), the "real" killer of Capt. Stone (poss. Audsah) boasts of the act on the Connecticut River (Jennings 227). Earlier (Aug. 1637, DYW 128; WJH1: 237), Narragansetts had "sent us the hands of three Pequots...one the chief of those who murdered ...Stone."

1640 Sept.: Winthrop (WJH2: 6-7) and Bradford begin to worry rumors of Narragansett-Mohawk alliance against New England.

1641 August: Miantonomo visits Montauk, Long Island, to appeal for pan-Native alliance (G142; Robinson 22, 27-8). Sachem Waiandance/Wyandot reports it to Boston, thence to Uncas (Sainsbury 1971: 118-19).

1643 New England's Articles of Confederation (WJH2: 100-105) link Mass. Bay, Plimoth, Connecticut, New Haven and exclude Providence. Miantonomo and Narragansetts allow Mass. Bay dissident Samuel Gorton to settle at Warwick RI (RIC1: 130). Gardener (G119) numbers Mohegans at "about 70 or perhaps a few more" on 3000 acres at Montville.

May: As United Colonies of New England form (WJH2: 131-2), Uncas attacks a kinsman of Miantonomo's (Sequassen). Mass. Bay sanctions Miantonomo's revenge, loans body-armor; but Uncas captures Miantonomo at Shantok fight (Drake 64-5). Sept.: Miantonomo held at Hartford. The United Colonies' commissioners' first official act orders him killed (Cave 167), and 5 of 50 Native "elders" assent to his murder by "friend to the English"

Uncas (FBH2: 364-66; Drake 65, 90; Jennings 268-9). Narragansett-Mohegan bitterness increases (WPF3: 444).

That same year, the Narragansetts appeal to beleaguered King Charles I "not to be forced from their religion" or "invaded by war" for refusing (in Pulsifer ed., *Acts of the United Colonies* 2: 43-9).

1644 Plimoth's Winslow (WPF4: 427-8) informs Winthrop that "the Narragansetts prepare for war [and] the Mohawks have promised [them]...a thousand men" (also in Gardener G140-142). Winslow reports also the Dutch killing of Capt. Patrick in Underhill's presence.

1650 After assisting United Colonies war against Ninigret's Niantics (Johnson 43), Pequots receive 500 acres at Noank. McBride, Burgess detail the Pequots' subtle forms of cultural syncretism and long-term maneuvering (via leaders such as Robin Cassacinamon and many later others) to preserve tribal identity through the 20th century's and today's "renaissance."

1675-76 Captain Benjamin Church, the most successful tactical officer of "King Philip's War," describes his own struggles with fellow colonists' persistently unsuccessful tactics in his *Entertaining Passages* (Slotkin ed.). For example (403-4, 412):

> ...Mr. Church now begins (no succor coming to
> him) to think it time to retreat, saying The Lord have
> mercy on us, if such a handful of Indians shall thus dare
> such an Army!
>
> Upon this it is immediately resolved, and orders are
> given, to march down into [Mount Hope] Neck....There
> Philip [Metacomet, the Wampanoag leader] has staved

all his drums, and conveyed all his canoes to the east side
of Mattapoysett River. Hence it is concluded, by those that
were acquainted with the motions of those people, that
they have quitted the Neck...which they soon find to be true.
The enemy are not really beaten out of Mount Hope Neck,
though it is true they fled from thence; yet it was before
any pursued them. It was but to strengthen themselves, and
to gain a more advantageous post. However, some and
not a few [Englishmen] please themselves with the
fancy of a mighty conquest.

A grand council is held, and a resolve passes, to build
a Fort there....And to speak the truth, it must be said that
as they gain not that field by their sword, nor their bow, so
it is rather their fear than their courage that obliges them
to set up the marks of their conquest.

Mr. Church looks upon it, and talks of it with contempt....
[He] had rather do anything in the world than stay there to
build the fort....[While] these things are [happening], Philip makes his escape, leaving his country, flees over Taun-
ton River, and Rehoboth Plain, and Patuxet River....And
now another Fort is built at Pocasset, that proves as
troublesome and chargeable as that at Mount Hope...while
our enemies are fled some hundreds of miles into the
country, near as far as Albany. And now strong suspicions
begin to arise of the Narragansett Indians, that they are
ill affected, and design mischief....

1983   The United States Federal Government "recognizes" the
Pequots.

2003   August 4th: Internet daily journal *Salon.com* publishes
"The War According to David Hackworth: The retired colonel
[career-officer, decorated Vietnam veteran] calls Donald Rumsfeld
an 'asshole' whose bad planning mires U.S. troops in an ugly
guerrilla conflict in Iraq. His sources? Defiant soldiers sending

dispatches from the front." *Salon.com Archives* interview by Jonathan Franklin:

> ...*Franklin:* How do you see the combat situation evolving in Iraq?
>
> *Hackworth:* There is no way the Guerrilla is going to win. He knows that, but his object is to make us bleed....
>
> The Americans have their head up their ass all the time. All the advantages are with the Guerrilla: he will be watching. He is like an audience in a darkened theater, and the U.S. troops are the actors on the stage, all lit up, so the Guerrilla can see everything on stage, when they are asleep or when his weapons are dirty. The actor can't see shit in the audience....
>
> ...The American Army is trained to break things and kill people, not the kind of selective work that is needed. You don't use a tank brigade to surround a village: instead, you set up ambushes along the route. It is all so similar to what I saw in Vietnam, this tendency to be mesmerized by big-unit operations. But if you fight like a Guerrilla, everything is under the table, in the dark, done by stealth and surprise. There is no great glory--- except the end result.
>
> America has never been capable of fighting the Guerrilla. From General Custer, who fucked it up, you can fast-forward to today. [In Afghanistan and Iraq] they are proving it again. The U.S. military never, never learns from the past. They make the same mistakes over and over again....

WORKS CITED & SELECTED

Abbreviations Used Throughout

FBH   *Of Plimoth Plantation*, by William Bradford (C.F. Adams Jr. *et als'* 2-volume edition of 1912)

WPF   *The Winthrop Papers* edited by Forbes

WJH   *Winthrop's Journal* edited by Hosmer

DYW   *The Journal of John Winthrop* edited by Dunn/Yeandle

WCL   Roger Williams' *Correspondence* edited by LaFantasie

MHSC/P Massachusetts Historical Society *Collections*, *Proceedings*

H15   Vol. 15 (*The Northeast*) of *The Handbook of North American Indians* (Trigger ed.)

Adams, Charles Francis, Jr., ed., *Prince Society Edition of New English Canaan* (by Thomas Morton, 1637). New York: Burt Franklin 1883

---, *Three Episodes of Massachusetts History: The Settlement of Boston Bay*. 2 Vols, 1892. Rpt. New York: Russell & Russell 1965

Anderson, Benedict, *Imagined Communities: Reflections on the Origin and Spread of Nationalism*. London: Verso 1991

Armstrong, Nancy, and Leonard Tennenhouse, *The Imaginary Puritan: Literature, Intellectual Labor and the Origins of Personal Life*. Berkeley: University of California Press 1992

Axtell, James, *The European and the Indian: Essays in the Ethnohistory of Colonial North America*. New York: Oxford University Press 1981

Barrett, Louise K., *The Ignoble Savage: American Literary Racism 1790-1890*. Westport CT: Greenwood Press 1975

Boose, Lynda, "Techno-Muscularity and the 'Boy Eternal': From the Quagmire to the Gulf." In Kaplan/Pease eds., *Cultures of United States Imperialism*, 581-616

Bradford, William, *History of Plimoth Plantation 1620-1647*. Edited by Charles Francis Adams, Jr., Gamaliel Bradford, Jr., Morton Dexter, Worthington C. Ford and Arthur Lord. 2 Vols. Boston: Houghton Mifflin 1912

---, *Of Plimoth Plantation 1620-1647*. Harvey Wish, ed. New York: Capricorn Books 1962

---, *Bradford's History "Of Plimoth Plantation" from the Original Manuscript 1623-46*. Boston: Wright & Potter 1901

---, *History of Plimoth Plantation, 1606-1646*. William T. Davis, ed. New York: Charles Scribner's Sons 1908

---, *Of Plymouth Plantation 1620-1647*. Francis Murphy, ed. New York: Random House 1981

Bradley, James W., "Native Exchange and European Trade: Cross Cultural Dynamics in the Sixteenth Century." In *Man In The Northeast*, 33 (Spring 1987): 31-46

Bragdon, Kathleen J., "'Emphaticall Speech and Great Action': An Analysis of 17th-Century Speech Events Described in Early Sources." In *Man In The Northeast*, 33 (1987), 101-111

---, *Native People of Southern New England 1500-1650*. Norman: Oklahoma University Press 1996

Brasser, Theodore J., "The Coastal Algonkians: People of the First Frontier." In *North American Indians in Historical Perspective*. Eleanor G. Leacock and Nancy O. Lurie, eds. Pp. 64-91. New York: Random House 1971

---, "Early Indian-European Contacts." In Trigger, ed., H15, 78-88

Brown, Alexander, ed., *The Genesis of the United States...A Series of Historical Manuscripts Now First Printed.* 2 Vols. including large foldout of "The Velasco Map" of American East Coast c. 1610 (1: 456-7). Virginia Historical Society 1890. Rpt. New York: Russell & Russell 1964

Burgess, Kim, "The Pequots' Conversion to Christianity." In Niezen, *Spirit Wars* 42-45

Burke, Charles T., *Puritans at Bay: The War Against King Philip and the Squaw Sachems.* New York: Exposition Press 1967

Burton, William J. and Richard Lowenthal, "The First of the Mohegans." In *American Enthnologist* 1 (4: 1974), 589-599

Calloway, Colin G., *The American Revolution in Indian Country: Crisis and Diversity in Native American Communities.* New York: Cambridge University Press 1995

Caulkins, Frances Manwaring, *History of New London, Connecticut. From the First Survey of the Coast in 1612, to 1852.* Hartford CT: Press of Case, Tiffany & Co. 1852

Cave, Alfred A., *The Pequot War.* Amherst: University of Massachusetts Press 1996

Cesaire, Aime, *Discourse on Colonialism.* Trans. Joan Pinkham, 1955. Rpt. New York: Monthly Review Press 1972

Charvat, William, *The Origins of American Critical Thought 1810-1835.* Philadelphia: University of Pennsylvania Press 1936

Church, Benjamin, *Entertaining Passages Relating to Philip's War.* Boston 1716. Rpt. in Slotkin, ed., Judgment

Cronon, William, *Changes in the Land: Indians, Colonists, and the Ecology of New England.* New York: Farrar, Straus & Giroux 1983

Davidson, Cathy N., *Revolution and The Word: The Rise of the Novel in America.* New York: Oxford University Press 1986

DeForest, John W., *History of the Indians of Connecticut: From the Earliest Known Period to 1850.* Hartford: W.J. Hamersley 1851

DeLaet, Johan, *Extracts from the "New World"* [1625, 1630, 1633, 1640]. In *Narratives of New Netherland 1609-64.* J. Franklin Jameson, ed., 29-60. New York: Charles Scribner's Sons 1909

DeMott, Benjamin, "One Nation, Two Paths To Change: Social Critics Call for Reflection and Cooperation." *The Boston Sunday Globe*, Oct. 26, 2003, pp. D7-8

Dempsey, Jack, ed., *New English Canaan by Thomas Morton of 'Merrymount': Text, Notes, Biography & Criticism.* Scituate MA: Digital Scanning Inc. 2000

---, *Thomas Morton: The Life & Renaissance of an Early American Poet.* Scituate MA: Digital Scanning 2000

---, ed., *Good News from New England and Other Writings on the Killings at Weymouth Colony.* Scituate MA: Digital Scanning Inc. 2001

---, producer, *Thomas Morton & the Maypole of Merrymount: Disorder in the American Wilderness 1624-1647.* 2-hr. video-documentary (1992) distributed by producer: 45 Broadway, Stoneham MA 02180/USA; 781-438-3042; jd37@mindspring.com

---, producer, *NANI: A Native New England Story.* 1-hr. video-documentary (1998) distributed by producer (previous entry); and by V-Tape (Toronto) and Shenandoah Films (Arcata CA)

DeVries, David Petersen, *Voyages from Holland to America, A.D. 1632 to 1644.* Henry C. Murphy, trans./ed. New York: Billine & Brothers 1853

Drinnon, Richard, *Facing West: The Metaphysics of Indian-Hating and Empire-Building.* New York: Schocken 1980

Dwight, Timothy, *The Conquest of Canaan*. 1785. Abridged in Paul Lauter et als, eds., *The Heath Anthology of American Literature*. Vol. 1 (1990). Second edition, Lexington MA: D.C. Heath 1994

Dyer, Gwynne, *War*. New York: Crown Press 1985

Elson, Ruth Miller, *Guardians of Tradition: American Schoolbooks in the 19th Century*. Lincoln: University of Nebraska 1964

Errington, Frederick, and Deborah Gewertz, "We Think, Therefore They Are? On Occidentalizing the World." In Kaplan/Pease eds., *Cultures*, 635-656

Fiedler, Leslie, *Love and Death in the American Novel*. [1960] Rpt. New York: Anchor Books 1992

Fitzhugh, William W., ed., *Cultures in Contact: The Impact of European Contacts on Native American Cultural Institutions A.D. 1000-1800*. Washington, D.C.: Smithsonian Institution Press 1985

Force, Peter, ed., *Tracts and Other Papers Relating Principally to the Origin, Settlement, and Progress of the Colonies in North America, From the Discovery of the Country to the Year 1776*. 3 Vols. Washington, D.C.: Peter Force, Printer 1836

Frazier, Patrick, *The Mohegans of Stockbridge*. Norfolk: University of Nebraska Press 1994

Gardener, Lion, *Leift Lion Gardener His Relation of the Pequot Warres*. (Composed c. 1660; rpt. 1833, 1859). Rpt. in Orr, History 116-149

Gookin, Daniel, ed., *Historical Collections of the Indians in New England, of Their Several Natures, Numbers, Customs, Manners, Religion and Government Before the English Planted There*. 1674. MHSC 1: 141-227

Griffin, Susan, *Pornography and Silence: Culture's Revenge Against Nature*. New York: Harper & Row 1981

Grumet, Robert S., ed., *Northeastern Indian Lives 1632-1816*. Amherst: University of Massachusetts Press 1996

Haines, Michael R. and Richard H. Steckel, eds., *A Population History of North America*. Cambridge UK: Cambridge University Press 2000

Hale, J.R., "16th-Century Explanations of War and Violence." *Past and Present* #51, May 1971, 3-26

Hauptmann, Laurence M. and James D. Wherry, *The Pequots in Southern New England: The Fall and Rise of an American Indian Nation*. Norman: University of Oklahoma Press 1990; Rpt. 1993

Herzog, Ze'ev, "Archaeology vs. The Bible." *The Chronicle of Higher Education*, January 1, 2000

Higginson, Francis, *New-England's Plantation*. 1630. Rpt. in Force Tracts Vol. 1

Hirsch, Adam J., "The Collision of Military Cultures in 17th-Century New England." *Journal of American History* 74 (1988): 1204-9

Hoadly, Charles J. and John Hammond Trumbull, eds., *The Public Records of the Colony and Plantation of Connecticut 1636-1776*. 15 Vols. Hartford: Case, Lockwood & Brainard 1850-1890

Hutchinson, Thomas, *A Collection of Original Papers Relative to the History of the Colony and Province of Massachusetts Bay*. Boston: Fleet 1769. Rpt. Cambridge: Harvard University Press 1936

Jemison, Mary, narrator to James E. Seaver ed., *The Life of Mary Jemison, Deh-He-Wa-Mis, The White Woman of the Genesee*. (1824: compilation rpt. 1877). Rpt. Scituate MA: Digital Scanning Inc. 2001

Jennings, Francis, *The Invasion of America: Indians, Colonialism, and the Cant of Conquest*. New York: Norton 1975

Johnson, Edward, *Wonder-Working Providence 1628-1651*. 1653. Rpt. J. Franklin Jameson, ed. New York: Scribner's 1910

Johnson, Eric S., "Uncas and the Politics of Contact." In Grumet, ed., *Lives* 29-47

Kaplan, Amy and Donald E. Pease, eds., *Cultures of United States Imperialism*. Durham NC: Duke University Press 1993

Kaplan, Amy, "'Left Alone With America': The Absence of Empire in the Study of American Culture." Introduction (3-21) to Kaplan/Pease, eds., *Cultures*

Kolodny, Annette, "Turning the Lens on 'The Panther Captivity': A Feminist Exercise in Practical Criticism." In *Critical Inquiry* Winter 1981; 8:2, 329-345

Krupat, Arnold, *Ethnocriticism: Ethnography, History, Literature*. Berkeley: University of California Press 1992

Kupperman, Karen Ordahl, "English Perceptions of Treachery 1583-1640: The Case of the American 'Savages.'" *Historical Journal* XX (1977), 263-287

---, "Thomas Morton, Historian." In *The New England Quarterly* Vol. 50, Dec. 1977: 660-664

---, ed., *Major Problems in American Colonial History: Documents and Essays*. Lexington MA: D.C. Heath 1993

Leach, Douglas E., *Flintlock and Tomahawk: New England in King Philip's War*. 1958. Rpt. New York: Norton 1966

Leland, Charles G., *Algonquian Legends*. 1884. Rpt. New York: Dover 1992

Lepore, Jill, *The Name of War: King Philip's War and the Origins of American Identity*. New York: Vintage 1998

Little Owl (Ruth Duncan), *Wah Quinnipiac Arkeis: Wunnonkou, Ea Kesuk, Quah Nompung---The Quinnipiac Nation: Yesterday, Today and Tomorrow: Poetry Written in Wampano, The Language of the Quinnipiac People, with English Translation by* [the Author]. Milltown, IN: The Author 2001. (201 Church St., Milltown IN 47145)

Malone, Patrick M., "Changing Military Technology Among the Indians of Southern New England 1600-1677." *American Quarterly* 25 (1973), 50-53

---, *The Skulking Way of War: Technology and Tactics Among the New England Indians*. New York: Madison 1991

Mandell, Daniel R., *Behind the Frontier: Indians in Eighteenth-Century Eastern Massachusetts*. Norfolk: University of Nebraska Press 1999

Mason, John, *A Brief History of the Pequot War*. See entry for Mather, *A Relation of the Troubles....* Rpt. in Orr, *History* 1-46

Mather, Increase, *A Brief History of the Warr with the Indians in New-England*. Boston: John Foster 1676. Rpt. in Slotkin, ed., *Judgment*

---, *A Relation of the Troubles Which Have Hapned in New England By Reason of the Indians There from the Year 1614 to the Year 1675*. Boston: John Foster 1677. Rpt. in Samuel G. Drake, ed., *Early History of New England*. Albany NY: J. Munsell 1864

McBride, Kevin A., "The Historical Archaeology of the Mashantucket Pequots, 1637-1900." In Hauptmann/Wherry, *Pequots* 96-116

Means, Carroll Alton, "Mohegan-Pequot Relationships." *Bulletin of the Archaeological Society of Connecticut* 21 (1947), 26-34

Mooney, James, "Mohegan." In Frederick W. Hodge, ed., (Vol. 1), *Handbook of American Indians North of Mexico*. 2 Vols. Washington, D.C.: Bureau of American Ethnology Bulletin 30, 1907. Pp. 926-7

---, "Pequot." In Hodge, ed. (Vol. 2) *Handbook*, 229-230

---, "The Aboriginal Population of America North of Mexico." In John R. Swanton, ed., *Smithsonian Miscellaneous Collections* 80 (7:4). Washington, D.C.: 1928

Mourt's Relation: A Journal of the Pilgrims at Plimoth. (Anonymous: London 1622) Rpt. Dwight B. Heath, ed. Chester CT: Globe Pequot 1963

Myers, Albert Cook, ed., *Narratives of Early Pennsylvania, West New Jersey and Delaware 1630-1707*. New York: Scribner's 1912

Nietzsche, Friedrich, *The Gay Science*. Tr. W. Kaufmann. 1882. Rpt. New York: Random House 1974

O'Brien, Francis J. Jr. (Moondancer) and Julianne Jennings (Strong Woman), *Understanding Algonquian Indian Words (New England)*. Newport RI: Aquidneck Indian Council, Inc. 1996. Revised ed. 2001. (12 Curry Avenue, Newport RI 02840-1412; email moondancer_Nuwc@hotmail.com)

Orr, Charles, ed., *History of the Pequot War: The Contemporary Accounts of Mason, Underhill, Vincent and Gardener*. Cleveland: Helman-Taylor 1897

"Panther Captivity, The," (attrib. Abraham Panther, 25 variant editions 1787-1814): "A Surprising Account of the Discovery of a Lady Who Was Taken by the Indians," rpts. in Wilcomb E. Washburn, comp., *The Garland Library of Narratives of North American Indian Captivities*, vol. 17 (New York 1978)

Parkhill, Thomas C., *Weaving Ourselves Into the Land: Charles Godfrey Leland, 'Indians' and the Study of Native American Religions*. Albany: State University of New York Press 1997

Peale, Arthur L., *Uncas and the Mohegan-Pequot*. Boston: Meador 1939

Pearce, Roy Harvey, *Savagism and Civilization: A Study of the Indian and the American Mind*. 1953. 2nd ed. Baltimore: Johns Hopkins University Press 1965

Peterson, Harold L., *Arms and Armor in Colonial America 1526-1783*. New York: Bramhall House 1956

---, *Arms and Armor of the Pilgrims 1620-1692*. Plymouth MA: Plimoth Plantation Inc. 1957

Pollard, H.B.C., *A History of Firearms*. Boston: Houghton Mifflin 1933

Pratt, Phinehas, *A Declaration of the Affairs of the English People that First Inhabited New England*. In Dempsey, ed., Good News

Pulsifer, David , ed., *Acts of the Commissioners of the United Colonies*. 2 Vols. *Records of the Colony of New Plimoth*, IX-X. Boston: W. White 1859

Reynolds, David S., *Beneath the American Renaissance: The Subversive Imagination in the Age of Emerson and Melville*. New York: Knopf 1988

Robbins, Maurice, *Wapanucket: An Archaeological Report*. Attleboro MA: Trustees of The Archaeological Society 1980

Robinson, Paul A., "Lost Opportunities: Miantonomi and the English in Seventeenth-Century Narragansett Country." In Grumet, ed., *Lives* 13-28

Rogin, Michael Paul, *Fathers and Children: Andrew Jackson and the Subjugation of the American Indian*. [1991] Rpt. London: Transaction Publishers 1995

Rogin, Michael, "'Make My Day!' Spectacle as Amnesia in Imperial Politics [and] The Sequel." In Kaplan/Pease eds., *Cultures*, 499-534

Rubertone, Patricia A., *Grave Undertakings: An Archaeology of Roger Williams and the Narragansett Indians*. Washington, D.C.: Smithsonian Institution 2001

Said, Edward W., *Culture and Imperialism*. New York: Alfred A. Knopf 1993

Sainsbury, John, "Miantonomo's Death and New England Politics 1630-1645." *Rhode Island History* 30 (4): 111-123

Salisbury, Neal, *Manitou and Providence: Indians, Europeans, and the Making of New England 1500-1643*. New York: Oxford University Press 1982

---, "Indians and Colonists After the Pequot War." In Hauptmann/Wherry, eds., *Pequots* 81-95

Salwen, Bert, "Indians of Southern New England and Long Island: Early Period." In H15, 160-176

---, "A Tentative 'in situ' Solution to the Mohegan-Pequot Problem." Pages 81-88 in William R. Young, ed., *The Connecticut Valley Indians: An Introduction to Their Archaeology and History*. Springfield MA: Springfield Museum of Science Publication n.s. 1 (1), 1969

Schlieff, Karle, ed., *1602: Gosnold*. Published/Distributed (2001) by the editor: 6 Pento Road, Woburn, MA 01801

Simmons, William S., "Southern New England Shamanism: An Ethnographic Reconstruction." In Wm. Cowan, ed., *Papers of the Seventh Algonquian Conference*. Ottawa: Carleton University Press 1976

---, *Spirit of the New England Tribes: Indian History and Folklore 1620-1984*. Hanover NH: University Press of New England 1986

Slotkin, Richard, *Regeneration Through Violence: The Mythology of the American Frontier 1600-1860*. Middletown CT: Wesleyan University Press 1973

--- and James K. Folsom, eds., *So Dreadful A Judgment: Puritan Responses to King Philip's War 1676-1677*. Middletown CT: Wesleyan University Press 1978

---, "Buffalo Bill's 'Wild West' and the Mythologization of the American Empire." In Kaplan/Pease, eds., *Cultures*, 164-184

Snow, Dean R., "Late Prehistory of the East Coast." In H15, 58-69

---, *The Archaeology of New England*. New York: Academic Press 1980

Soulsby, Mary Guillette, "Paucatuck (Eastern) Pequots." A Report Prepared for the Connecticutt Indian Affairs Council. Pages EP1-10 in *American Indians In Connecticut: Past to Present*. Hartford CT: State Library, State of Connecticut 1979

---, "The Mohegans." Pages M1-M15, previous entry

Spengemann, William C., *A Mirror for Americanists: Reflections on the Idea of American Literature*. Hanover NH: University Press of New England 1989

Starna, William A., "Pequots in the Early 17th Century." In Hauptmann/Wherry, eds., *Pequots* 33-47

Strong, Pauline Turner, "Captivity in White and Red: Convergent Practice and Colonial Representation on the British-Amerindian Frontier 1606-1736." In Daniel Segal, ed., *Crossing Cultures: Essays in the Displacement of Western Civilization*. Tucson: University of Arizona Press 1992

Swanton, John R., "The Indian Tribes of North America." *Bureau of American Ethnology Bulletin 145*. Washington, D.C.: 1952

Thomas, Peter A., "Cultural Change on the Southern New England Frontier 1630-1645." In Fitzhugh, ed., *Cultures in Contact*

Thornton, Russell, *American Indian Holocaust and Survival: A Population History Since 1492*. Norman: University of Oklahoma Press 1987

Trigger, Bruce G., ed., *Volume 15: The Northeast. The Handbook of North American Indians*. William C. Sturtevant, General Editor. Washington, D.C.: 1978

Trumbull, Henry, *History of the Discovery of America, of the Landing of Our Forefathers at Plymouth, and of Their Most Remarkable Engagements with the Indians in New-England, from Their First Landing in 1620 Until the Final Subjugation of the Natives in 1679*. Boston: George Clark 1836

Uncas [Mohegan Sachem c.1600-1683; from his spoken words], "The Genealogy of Uncas." Rpt. in *The Trumbull Papers*: MHSC Vol. 9, 5th Series: Boston 1885

Underhill, John, *Newes from America*. 1638. In Orr, ed., History 47-86

Vaughan, Alden True, *New England Frontier: Puritans and Indians 1620-1675*. Norman: University of Oklahoma Press. 1965. Third Edition 1995

Viincent, Philip, *A True Relation of the Late Battell Fought in New England, Between the English and the Pequet Salvages*. 1638. In Orr, ed., History 93-111

Wallace, Anthony F.C., *The Death and Rebirth of The Seneca*. 1969. New York: Random House 1972

Walsh, Susan, "'With Them Was My Home': Native American Autobiography and *A Narrative of the Life of Mrs. Mary Jemison*." In *American Literature* Vol. 64 #1, March 1992: 49-70.

Weinstein, Laurie, "Land, Politics and Power: The Mohegan Indians in the Seventeenth and Eighteenth Centuries." In *Man In The Northeast* 42: 9-16

Williams, Roger, *The Correspondence of Roger Williams*. 2 Vols. Glenn W. LaFantasie, ed. Hanover NH: University Press of New England 1988

---, *Letters of Roger Williams 1632-1682*. John Russell Bartlett, ed. Providence RI: Narragansett Club and Providence Press Publications 1874

---, *Complete Writings of Roger Williams*. J. H. Trumbull, ed. 7 Vols. New York: Russell & Russell 1963

Winslow, Edward, *Good News from New England*. London 1624. Rpt. in Dempsey, ed., *Good News*

Winthrop, John, *Winthrop's Journal "History of New England" (1630-1649)*. James K. Hosmer, ed. 2 Vols. New York: Charles Scribner's Sons 1908

---, *The Winthrop Papers*. 3 Vols. Allyn B. Forbes, ed. Vol. 3 1630-1637. Boston: Massachusetts Historical Society (Merrymount Press) 1943

---, *The Journal of John Winthrop 1630-1649*. Edited by Richard S. Dunn and Laetitia Yeandle. Abridged Edition. Cambridge: Harvard University Press 1996

Wood, William, *New England's Prospect*. London 1634. Alden True Vaughan, ed. Amherst: University of Massachusetts Press 1977

INDEX